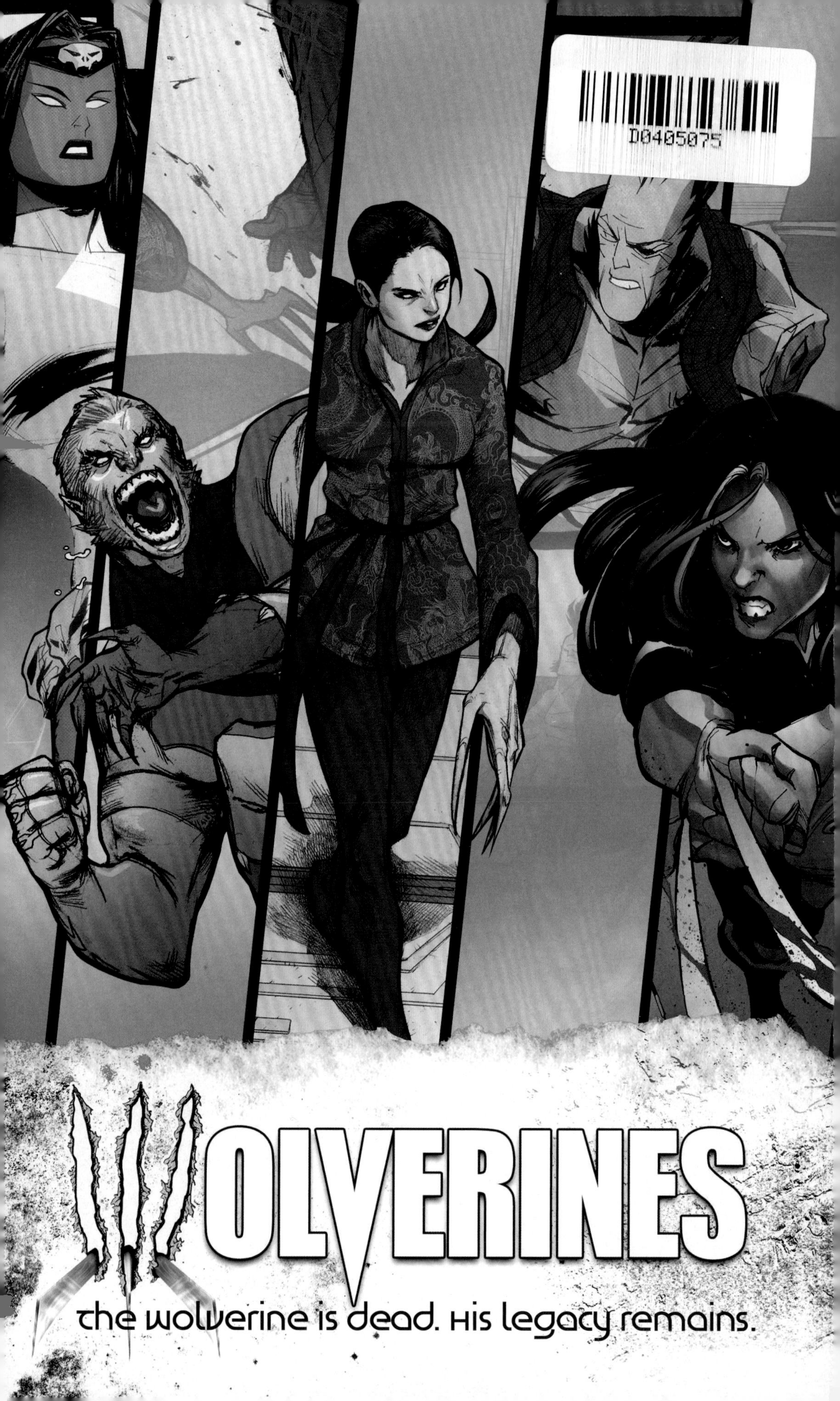

WOLVERINES

the wolverine is dead. His legacy remains.

PARADISE

SHOGUN

NEURO

ENDO

SKEL

JUNK

FANTOMELLE

THE WOLVERINES

MYSTIQUE

SABRETOOTH

LADY DEATHSTRIKE

DAKEN

X-23

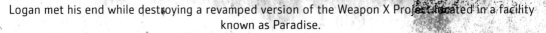

Logan met his end while destroying a revamped version of the Weapon X Project located in a facility known as Paradise.

Logan could not escape, but others did — five test subjects, all granted strange new powers. None were ever intended to survive outside the program, and all have been infused with a ticking clock in their DNA that will kill them unless it can be deactivated.

These lost weapons kidnapped a group of five of Wolverine's deadliest associates in the hope that their healing factors might hold the answer to saving the test subjects' lives. The refugees from paradise hold significant leverage over the five killers — secret "control words" that can manipulate, sedate or even kill each of them.

Meanwhile, Wolverine's old buddy Fang is back in town, beer in hand, and determined to have the weekend with Logan he was robbed of by his friend's murder. So far, Sabretooth and Daken have gone on their own journeys with Fang, each one revealing something about the two men that they would otherwise not want to see. These trips have also revealed that Fang is seeking Logan's murderer — and he's convinced it's one of the Wolverines. Annoyed by Fang's torture of her teammates, X-23 demands to be taken next, and Fang willingly complies.

Meanwhile Mystique, Junk, Daken and Sabretooth plot a way to escape from Fang and the rest of the Paradise survivors.

COLLECTION EDITOR: **JENNIFER GRÜNWALD**
ASSISTANT EDITOR: **SARAH BRUNSTAD**
ASSOCIATE MANAGING EDITOR: **ALEX STARBUCK**
EDITOR, SPECIAL PROJECTS: **MARK D. BEAZLEY**
SENIOR EDITOR, SPECIAL PROJECTS: **JEFF YOUNGQUIST**
SVP PRINT, SALES & MARKETING: **DAVID GABRIEL**
BOOK DESIGNER: **JAY BOWEN**

EDITOR IN CHIEF: **AXEL ALONSO**
CHIEF CREATIVE OFFICER: **JOE QUESADA**
PUBLISHER: **DAN BUCKLEY**
EXECUTIVE PRODUCER: **ALAN FINE**

WOLVERINES VOL. 3: THE LIVING AND THE DEAD. Contains material originally published in magazine form as WOLVERINES #11-15. First printing 2015. ISBN# 978-0-7851-9735-5. Published by MARVEL WORLDWIDE, INC., a subsidiary of MARVEL ENTERTAINMENT, LLC. OFFICE OF PUBLICATION: 135 West 50th Street, New York, NY 10020. Copyright © 2015 MARVEL No similarity between any of the names, characters, persons, and/or institutions in this magazine with those of any living or dead person or institution is intended, and any such similarity which may exist is purely coincidental. **Printed in Canada.** ALAN FINE, President, Marvel Entertainment; DAN BUCKLEY, President, TV, Publishing and Brand Management; JOE QUESADA, Chief Creative Officer; TOM BREVOORT, SVP of Publishing; DAVID BOGART, SVP of Operations & Procurement, Publishing; C.B. CEBULSKI, VP of International Development & Brand Management; DAVID GABRIEL, SVP Print, Sales & Marketing; JIM O'KEEFE, VP of Operations & Logistics; DAN CARR, Executive Director of Publishing Technology; SUSAN CRESPI, Editorial Operations Manager; ALEX MORALES, Publishing Operations Manager; STAN LEE, Chairman Emeritus. For information regarding advertising in Marvel Comics or on Marvel.com, please contact Jonathan Rheingold, VP of Custom Solutions & Ad Sales, at jrheingold@marvel.com. For Marvel subscription inquiries, please call 800-217-9158. **Manufactured between 5/22/2015 and 6/29/2015 by SOLISCO PRINTERS, SCOTT, QC, CANADA.**

10 9 8 7 6 5 4 3 2 1

WRITERS

CHARLES SOULE (#11 & #13) & RAY FAWKES (#12 & #14-15)

ARTISTS

ARIELA KRISTANTINA (#11), ARIO ANINDITO (#12),
JASON MASTERS (#13), SALVADOR LARROCA (#14)
& JUAN DOE (#15)

COLOR ARTISTS

SONIA OBACK (#11 & #14), MATTHEW WILSON (#12),
GUY MAJOR (#13) & JUAN DOE (#15)

the wolverine is dead. His legacy remains.

WOLVERINES

THE LIVING AND THE DEAD

COVER ART

KRIS ANKA (#11-12) & GUILLEM MARCH (#13-15)

LETTERER
VC'S
CORY PETIT

ASSISTANT EDITOR
CHRISTINA
HARRINGTON

EDITORS
KATIE KUBERT
& MIKE MARTS

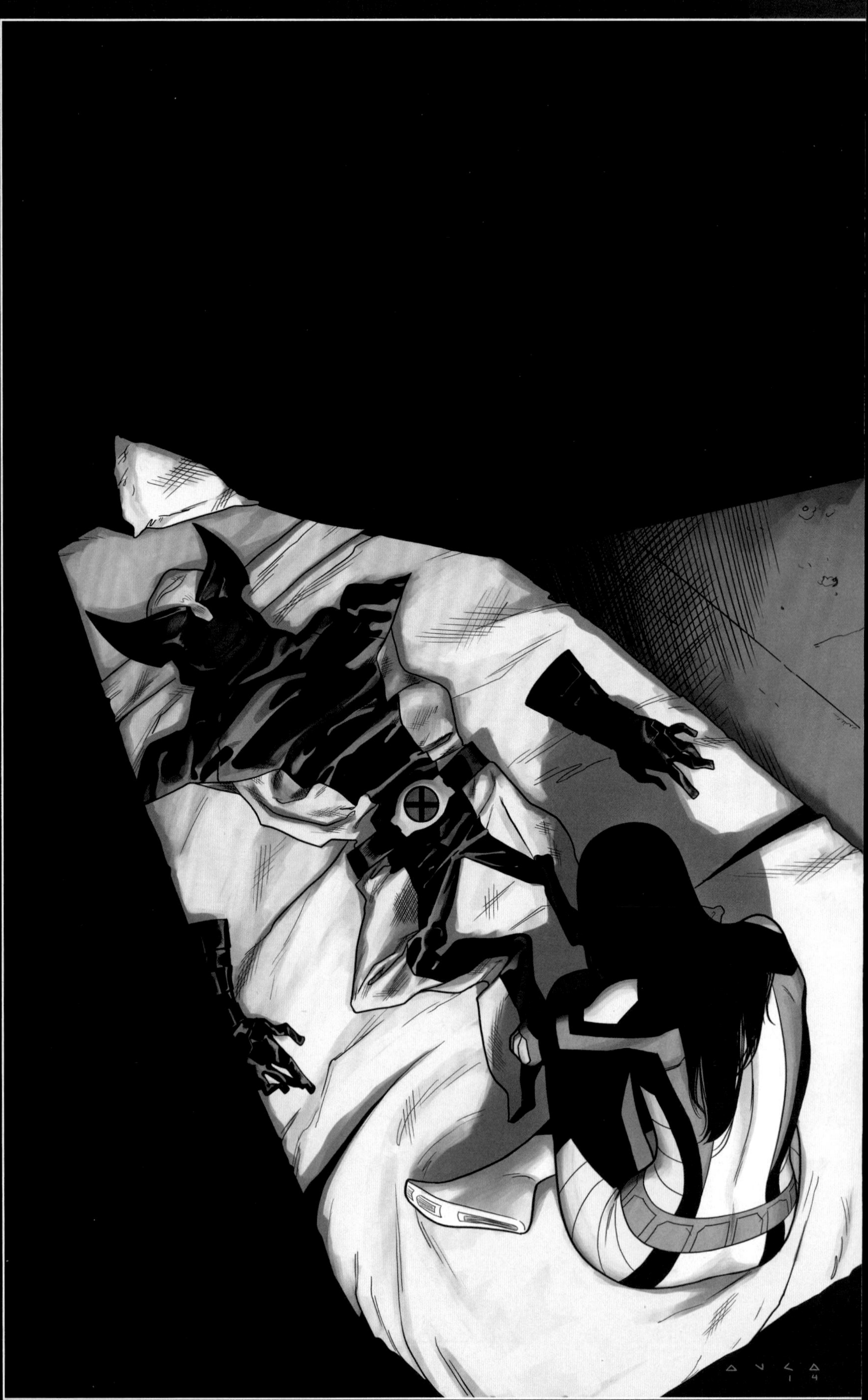

#11

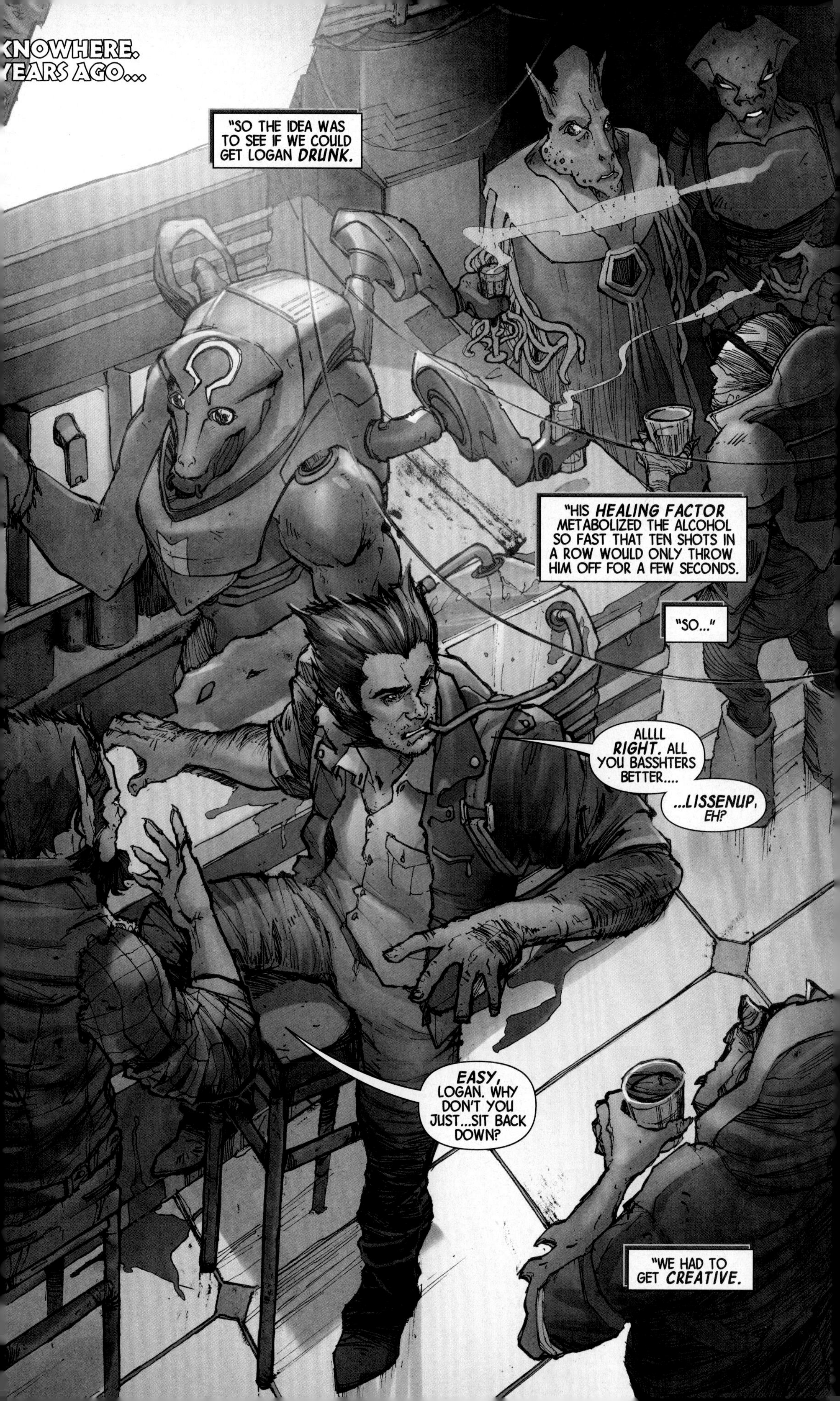
KNOWHERE. YEARS AGO...
"SO THE IDEA WAS TO SEE IF WE COULD GET LOGAN DRUNK.
"HIS HEALING FACTOR METABOLIZED THE ALCOHOL SO FAST THAT TEN SHOTS IN A ROW WOULD ONLY THROW HIM OFF FOR A FEW SECONDS.
"SO..."
ALLLL RIGHT. ALL YOU BASSHTERS BETTER....
...LISSENUP, EH?
EASY, LOGAN. WHY DON'T YOU JUST...SIT BACK DOWN?
"WE HAD TO GET CREATIVE.

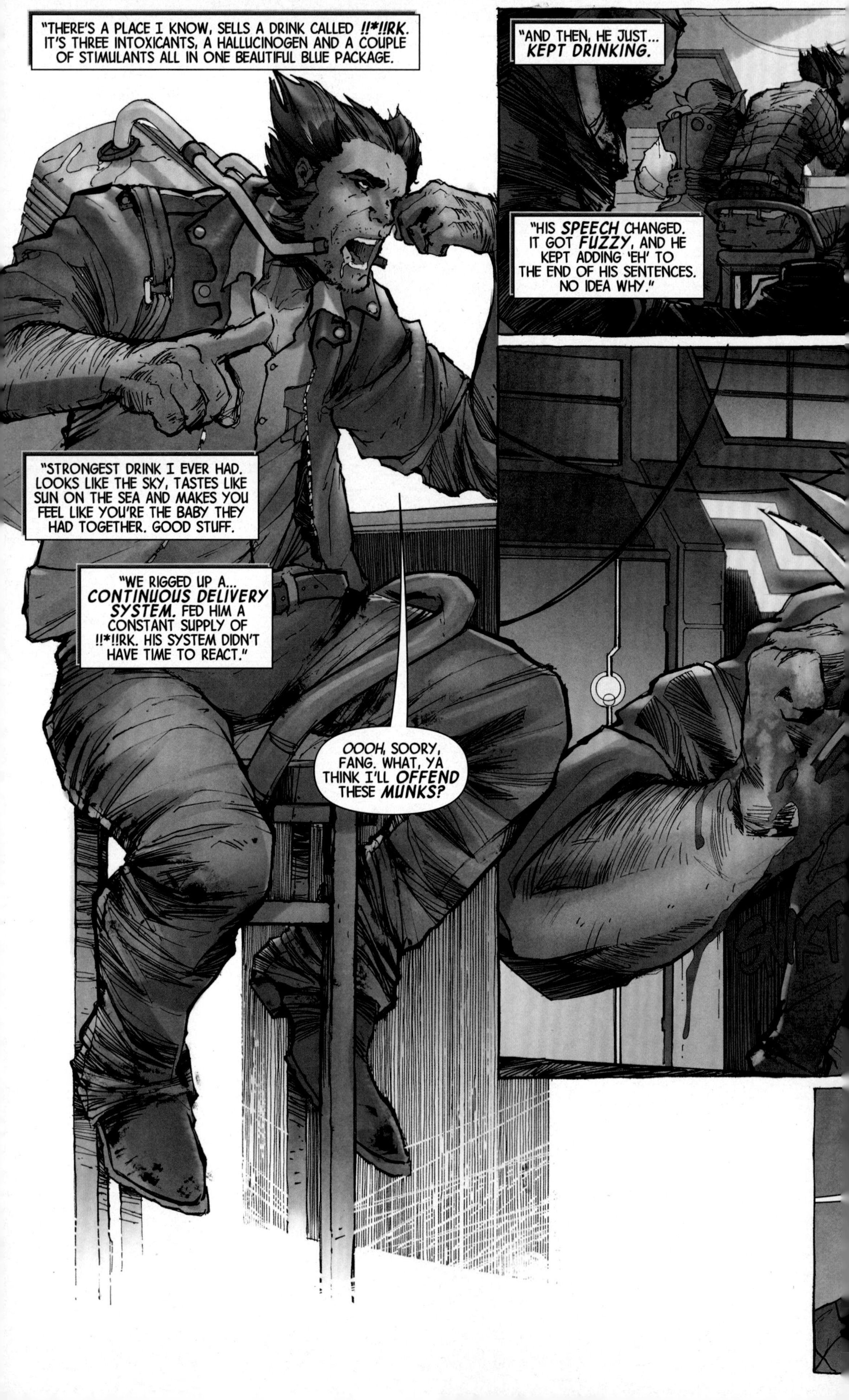
"THERE'S A PLACE I KNOW, SELLS A DRINK CALLED !!*!!RK. IT'S THREE INTOXICANTS, A HALLUCINOGEN AND A COUPLE OF STIMULANTS ALL IN ONE BEAUTIFUL BLUE PACKAGE.
"STRONGEST DRINK I EVER HAD. LOOKS LIKE THE SKY, TASTES LIKE SUN ON THE SEA AND MAKES YOU FEEL LIKE YOU'RE THE BABY THEY HAD TOGETHER. GOOD STUFF.
"WE RIGGED UP A... CONTINUOUS DELIVERY SYSTEM. FED HIM A CONSTANT SUPPLY OF !!*!!RK. HIS SYSTEM DIDN'T HAVE TIME TO REACT."
"AND THEN, HE JUST... KEPT DRINKING.
"HIS SPEECH CHANGED. IT GOT FUZZY, AND HE KEPT ADDING 'EH' TO THE END OF HIS SENTENCES. NO IDEA WHY."
OOOH, SOORY, FANG. WHAT, YA THINK I'LL OFFEND THESE MUNKS?

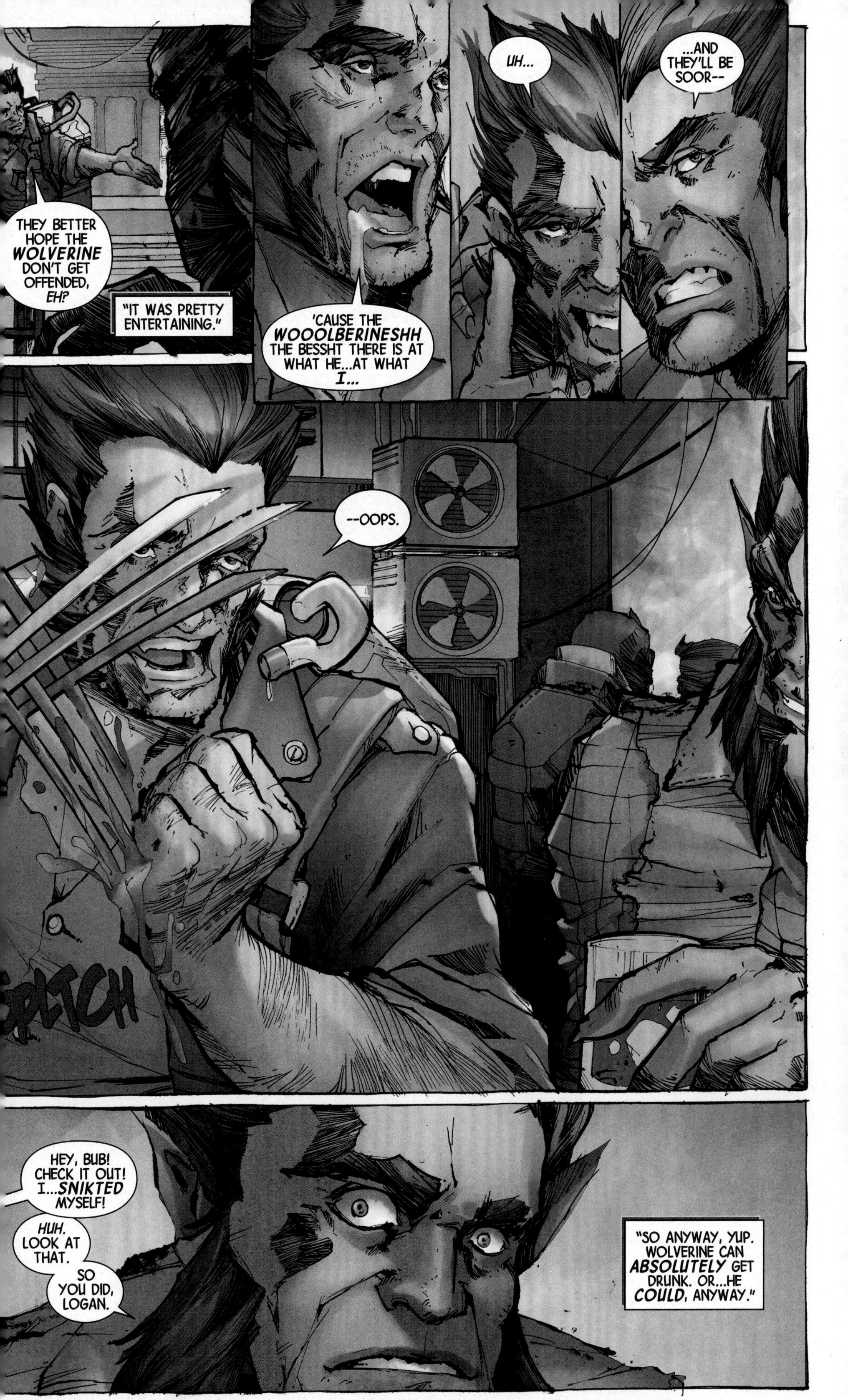
THEY BETTER HOPE THE WOLVERINE DON'T GET OFFENDED, EH?
"IT WAS PRETTY ENTERTAINING."
'CAUSE THE WOOOLBERINESHH THE BESSHT THERE IS AT WHAT HE...AT WHAT I...
UH...
...AND THEY'LL BE SOOR--
--OOPS.
SPLTCH
HEY, BUB! CHECK IT OUT! I...SNIKTED MYSELF!
HUH. LOOK AT THAT.
SO YOU DID, LOGAN.
"SO ANYWAY, YUP. WOLVERINE CAN ABSOLUTELY GET DRUNK. OR...HE COULD, ANYWAY."

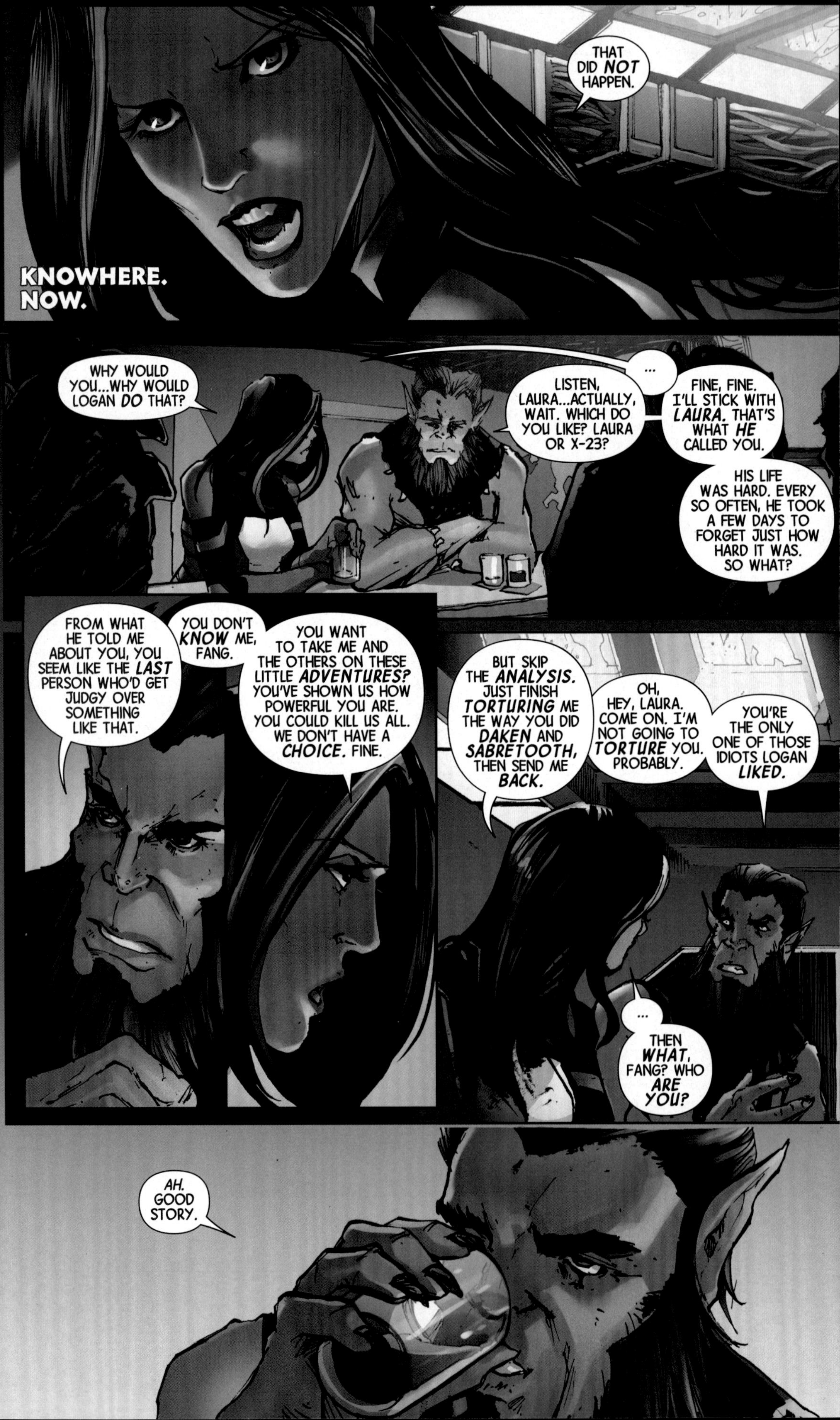
THAT DID NOT HAPPEN.
KNOWHERE. NOW.
WHY WOULD YOU...WHY WOULD LOGAN DO THAT?
LISTEN, LAURA...ACTUALLY, WAIT. WHICH DO YOU LIKE? LAURA OR X-23?
...
FINE, FINE. I'LL STICK WITH LAURA. THAT'S WHAT HE CALLED YOU.
HIS LIFE WAS HARD. EVERY SO OFTEN, HE TOOK A FEW DAYS TO FORGET JUST HOW HARD IT WAS. SO WHAT?
FROM WHAT HE TOLD ME ABOUT YOU, YOU SEEM LIKE THE LAST PERSON WHO'D GET JUDGY OVER SOMETHING LIKE THAT.
YOU DON'T KNOW ME, FANG.
YOU WANT TO TAKE ME AND THE OTHERS ON THESE LITTLE ADVENTURES? YOU'VE SHOWN US HOW POWERFUL YOU ARE. YOU COULD KILL US ALL. WE DON'T HAVE A CHOICE. FINE.
BUT SKIP THE ANALYSIS. JUST FINISH TORTURING ME THE WAY YOU DID DAKEN AND SABRETOOTH, THEN SEND ME BACK.
OH, HEY, LAURA. COME ON. I'M NOT GOING TO TORTURE YOU. PROBABLY.
YOU'RE THE ONLY ONE OF THOSE IDIOTS LOGAN LIKED.
...
THEN WHAT, FANG? WHO ARE YOU?
AH. GOOD STORY.

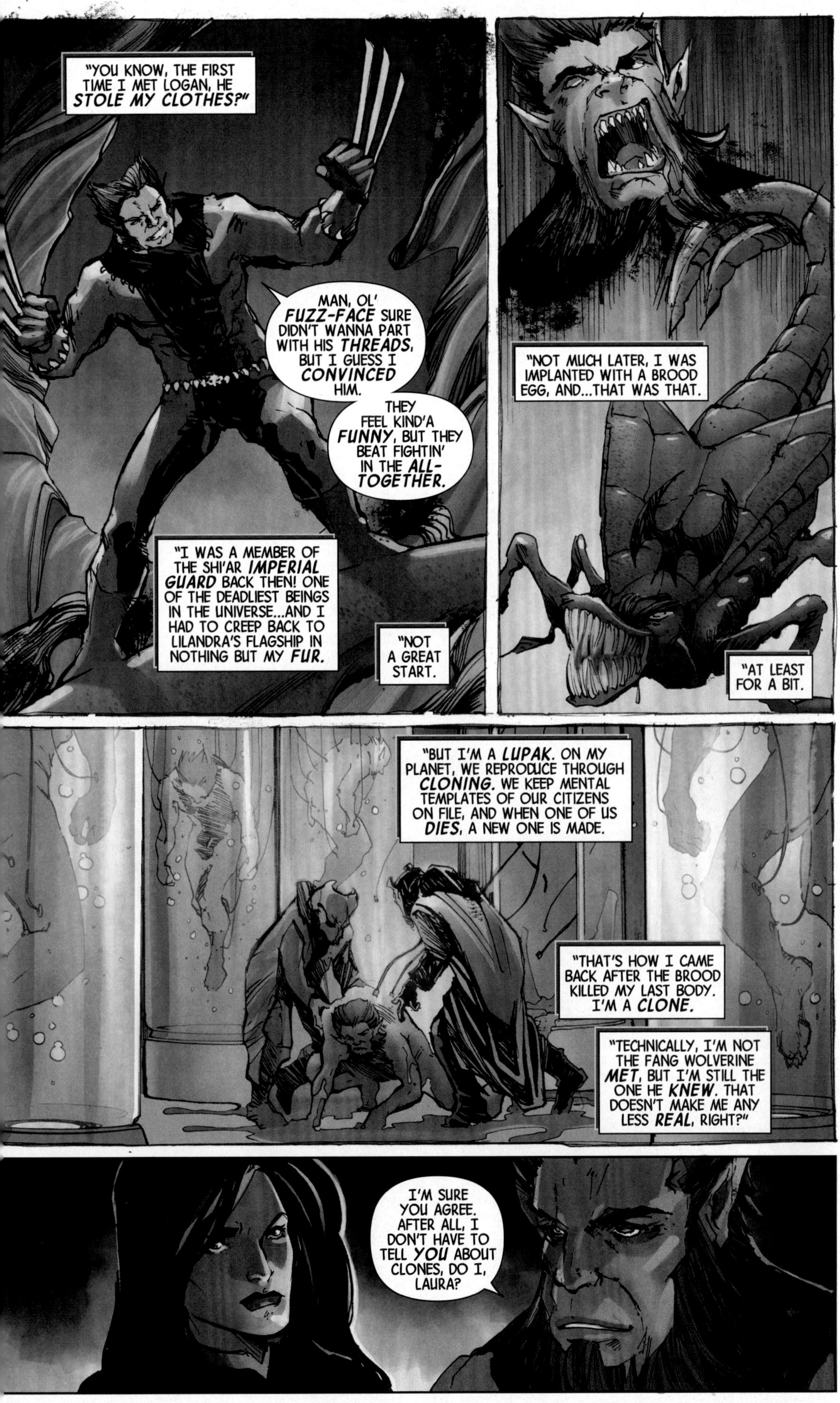
"YOU KNOW, THE FIRST TIME I MET LOGAN, HE STOLE MY CLOTHES?"
MAN, OL' FUZZ-FACE SURE DIDN'T WANNA PART WITH HIS THREADS, BUT I GUESS I CONVINCED HIM.
THEY FEEL KIND'A FUNNY, BUT THEY BEAT FIGHTIN' IN THE ALL-TOGETHER.
"I WAS A MEMBER OF THE SHI'AR IMPERIAL GUARD BACK THEN! ONE OF THE DEADLIEST BEINGS IN THE UNIVERSE...AND I HAD TO CREEP BACK TO LILANDRA'S FLAGSHIP IN NOTHING BUT MY FUR.
"NOT A GREAT START.
"NOT MUCH LATER, I WAS IMPLANTED WITH A BROOD EGG, AND...THAT WAS THAT.
"AT LEAST FOR A BIT.
"BUT I'M A LUPAK. ON MY PLANET, WE REPRODUCE THROUGH CLONING. WE KEEP MENTAL TEMPLATES OF OUR CITIZENS ON FILE, AND WHEN ONE OF US DIES, A NEW ONE IS MADE.
"THAT'S HOW I CAME BACK AFTER THE BROOD KILLED MY LAST BODY. I'M A CLONE.
"TECHNICALLY, I'M NOT THE FANG WOLVERINE MET, BUT I'M STILL THE ONE HE KNEW. THAT DOESN'T MAKE ME ANY LESS REAL, RIGHT?"
I'M SURE YOU AGREE. AFTER ALL, I DON'T HAVE TO TELL YOU ABOUT CLONES, DO I, LAURA?

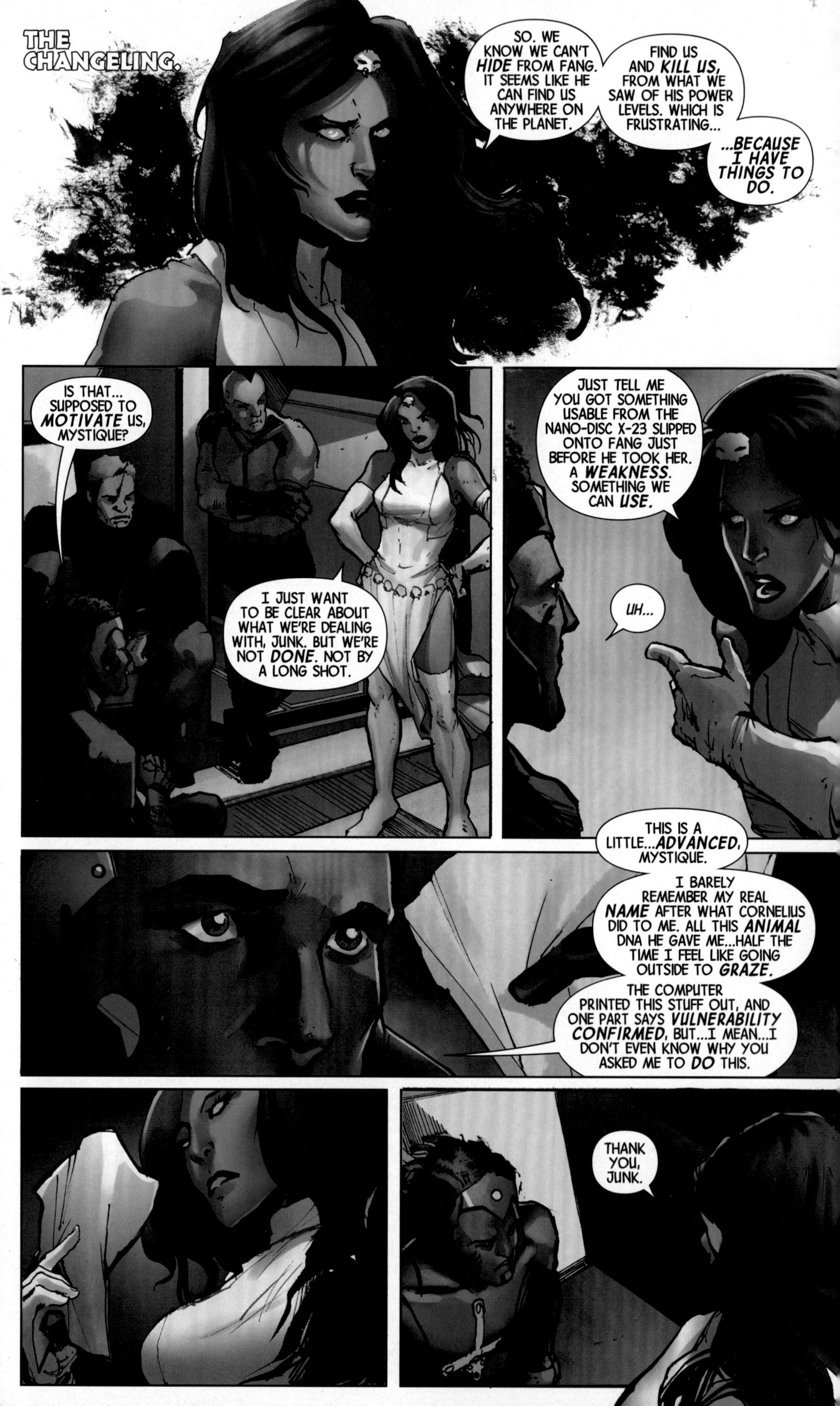
THE CHANGELING.
SO. WE KNOW WE CAN'T HIDE FROM FANG. IT SEEMS LIKE HE CAN FIND US ANYWHERE ON THE PLANET.
FIND US AND KILL US, FROM WHAT WE SAW OF HIS POWER LEVELS. WHICH IS FRUSTRATING...
...BECAUSE I HAVE THINGS TO DO.
IS THAT... SUPPOSED TO MOTIVATE US, MYSTIQUE?
I JUST WANT TO BE CLEAR ABOUT WHAT WE'RE DEALING WITH, JUNK. BUT WE'RE NOT DONE. NOT BY A LONG SHOT.
JUST TELL ME YOU GOT SOMETHING USABLE FROM THE NANO-DISC X-23 SLIPPED ONTO FANG JUST BEFORE HE TOOK HER. A WEAKNESS. SOMETHING WE CAN USE.
UH...
THIS IS A LITTLE...ADVANCED, MYSTIQUE.
I BARELY REMEMBER MY REAL NAME AFTER WHAT CORNELIUS DID TO ME. ALL THIS ANIMAL DNA HE GAVE ME...HALF THE TIME I FEEL LIKE GOING OUTSIDE TO GRAZE.
THE COMPUTER PRINTED THIS STUFF OUT, AND ONE PART SAYS VULNERABILITY CONFIRMED, BUT...I MEAN...I DON'T EVEN KNOW WHY YOU ASKED ME TO DO THIS.
THANK YOU, JUNK.

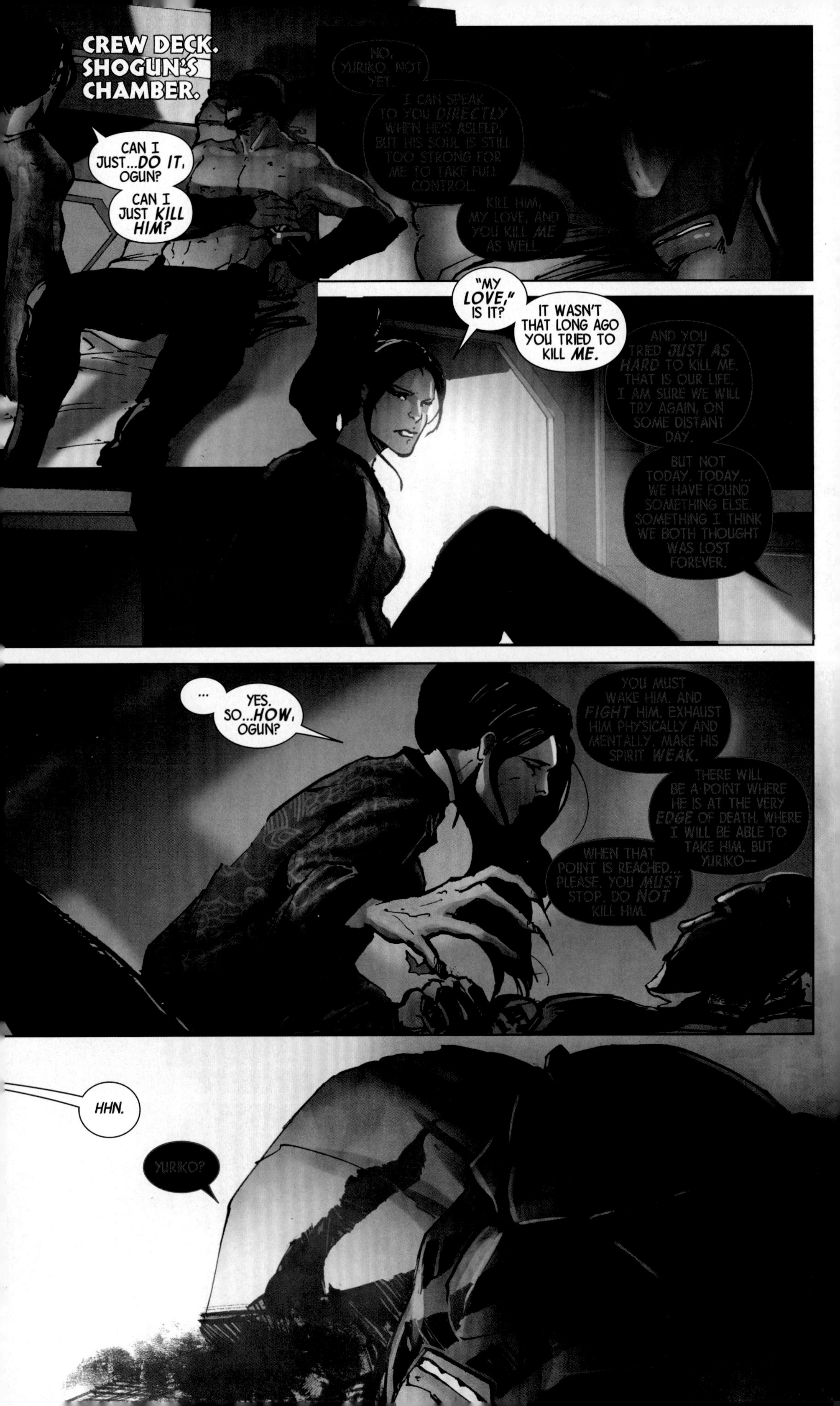
CREW DECK. SHOGUN'S CHAMBER.
CAN I JUST...DO IT, OGUN?
CAN I JUST KILL HIM?
NO, YURIKO. NOT YET.
I CAN SPEAK TO YOU DIRECTLY WHEN HE'S ASLEEP, BUT HIS SOUL IS STILL TOO STRONG FOR ME TO TAKE FULL CONTROL.
KILL HIM, MY LOVE, AND YOU KILL ME AS WELL.
"MY LOVE," IS IT?
IT WASN'T THAT LONG AGO YOU TRIED TO KILL ME.
AND YOU TRIED JUST AS HARD TO KILL ME. THAT IS OUR LIFE. I AM SURE WE WILL TRY AGAIN, ON SOME DISTANT DAY.
BUT NOT TODAY. TODAY... WE HAVE FOUND SOMETHING ELSE. SOMETHING I THINK WE BOTH THOUGHT WAS LOST FOREVER.
... YES. SO...HOW, OGUN?
YOU MUST WAKE HIM. AND FIGHT HIM. EXHAUST HIM PHYSICALLY AND MENTALLY. MAKE HIS SPIRIT WEAK.
THERE WILL BE A POINT WHERE HE IS AT THE VERY EDGE OF DEATH, WHERE I WILL BE ABLE TO TAKE HIM. BUT YURIKO--
WHEN THAT POINT IS REACHED... PLEASE. YOU MUST STOP. DO NOT KILL HIM.
HHN.
YURIKO?

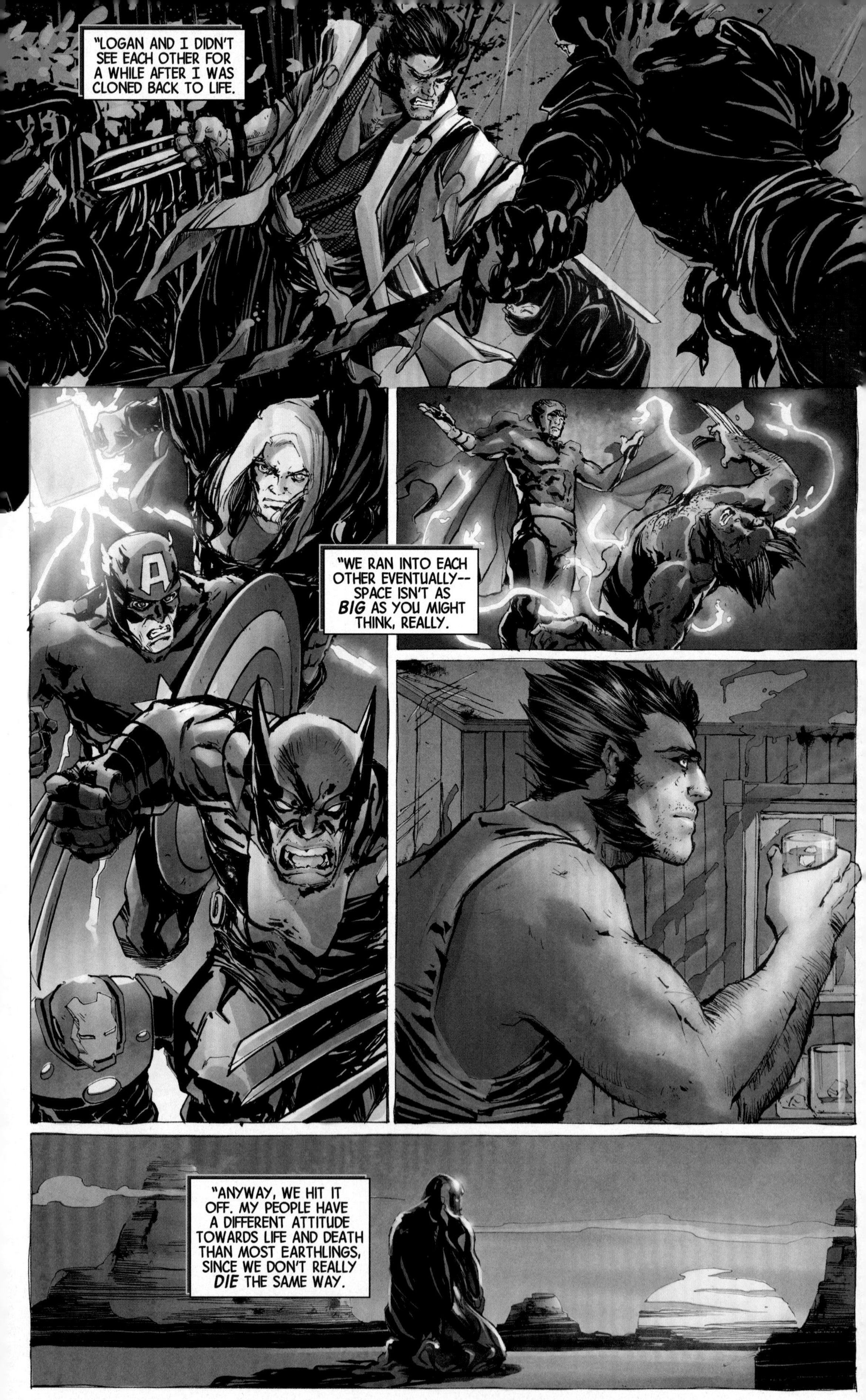
"LOGAN AND I DIDN'T SEE EACH OTHER FOR A WHILE AFTER I WAS CLONED BACK TO LIFE.
"WE RAN INTO EACH OTHER EVENTUALLY-- SPACE ISN'T AS *BIG* AS YOU MIGHT THINK, REALLY.
"ANYWAY, WE HIT IT OFF. MY PEOPLE HAVE A DIFFERENT ATTITUDE TOWARDS LIFE AND DEATH THAN MOST EARTHLINGS, SINCE WE DON'T REALLY *DIE* THE SAME WAY.

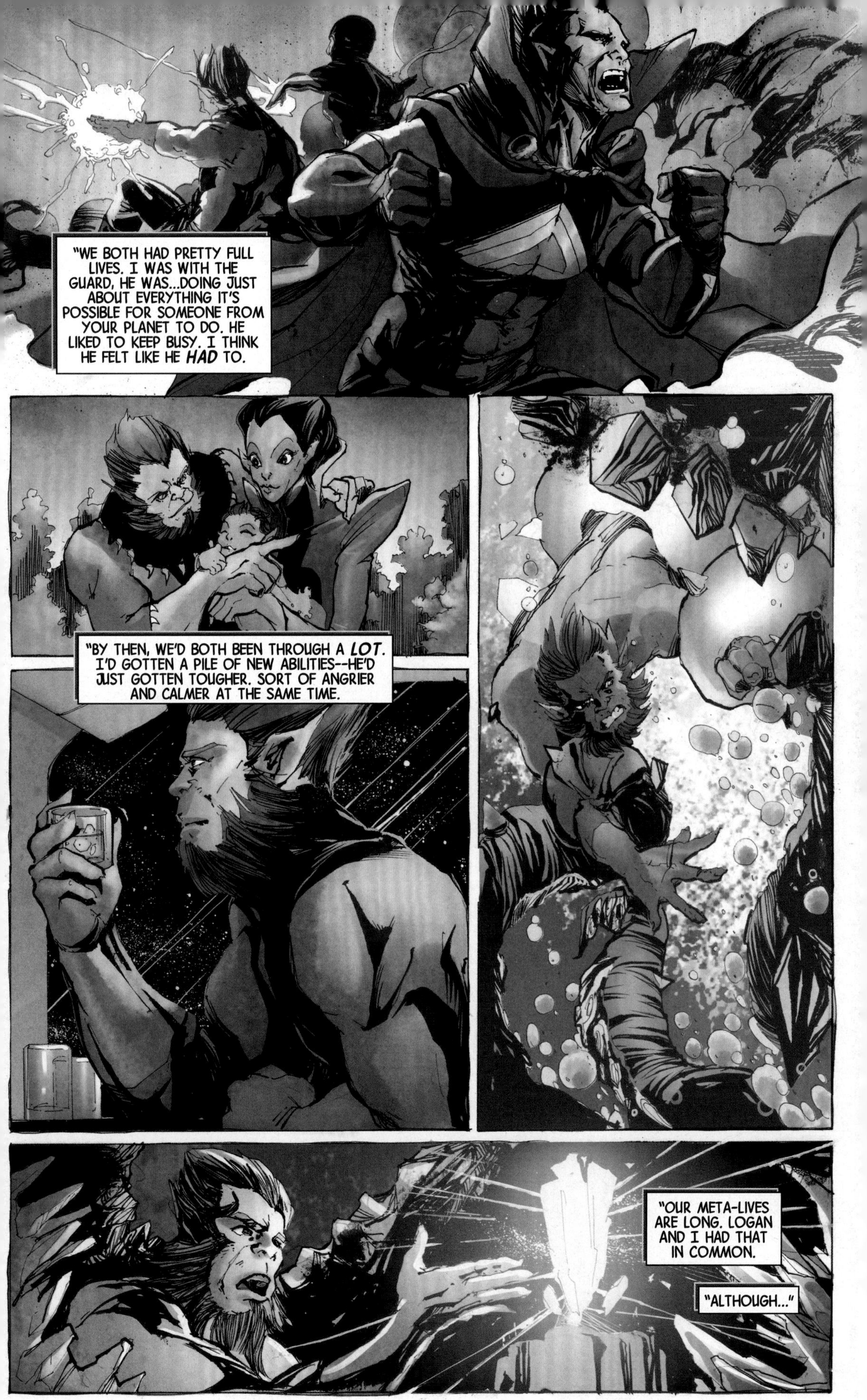
"WE BOTH HAD PRETTY FULL LIVES. I WAS WITH THE GUARD, HE WAS...DOING JUST ABOUT EVERYTHING IT'S POSSIBLE FOR SOMEONE FROM YOUR PLANET TO DO. HE LIKED TO KEEP BUSY. I THINK HE FELT LIKE HE *HAD* TO.
"BY THEN, WE'D BOTH BEEN THROUGH A *LOT*. I'D GOTTEN A PILE OF NEW ABILITIES--HE'D JUST GOTTEN TOUGHER. SORT OF ANGRIER AND CALMER AT THE SAME TIME.
"OUR META-LIVES ARE LONG. LOGAN AND I HAD THAT IN COMMON.
"ALTHOUGH..."

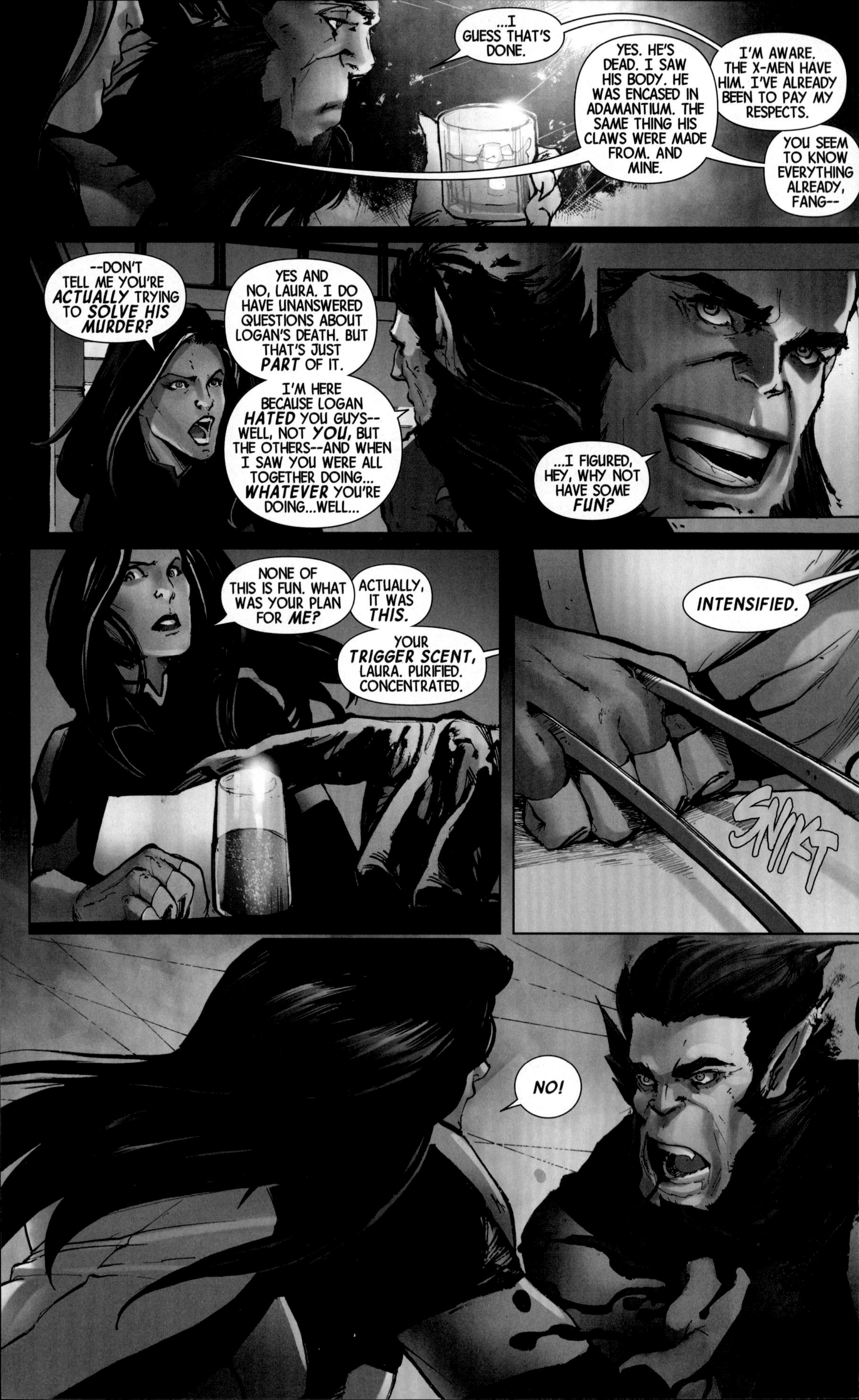
...I GUESS THAT'S DONE.
YES. HE'S DEAD. I SAW HIS BODY. HE WAS ENCASED IN ADAMANTIUM. THE SAME THING HIS CLAWS WERE MADE FROM. AND MINE.
I'M AWARE. THE X-MEN HAVE HIM. I'VE ALREADY BEEN TO PAY MY RESPECTS.
YOU SEEM TO KNOW EVERYTHING ALREADY, FANG--
--DON'T TELL ME YOU'RE ACTUALLY TRYING TO SOLVE HIS MURDER?
YES AND NO, LAURA. I DO HAVE UNANSWERED QUESTIONS ABOUT LOGAN'S DEATH. BUT THAT'S JUST PART OF IT.
I'M HERE BECAUSE LOGAN HATED YOU GUYS-- WELL, NOT YOU, BUT THE OTHERS--AND WHEN I SAW YOU WERE ALL TOGETHER DOING... WHATEVER YOU'RE DOING...WELL...
...I FIGURED, HEY, WHY NOT HAVE SOME FUN?
NONE OF THIS IS FUN. WHAT WAS YOUR PLAN FOR ME?
ACTUALLY, IT WAS THIS.
YOUR TRIGGER SCENT, LAURA. PURIFIED. CONCENTRATED.
INTENSIFIED.
SNIKT
NO!

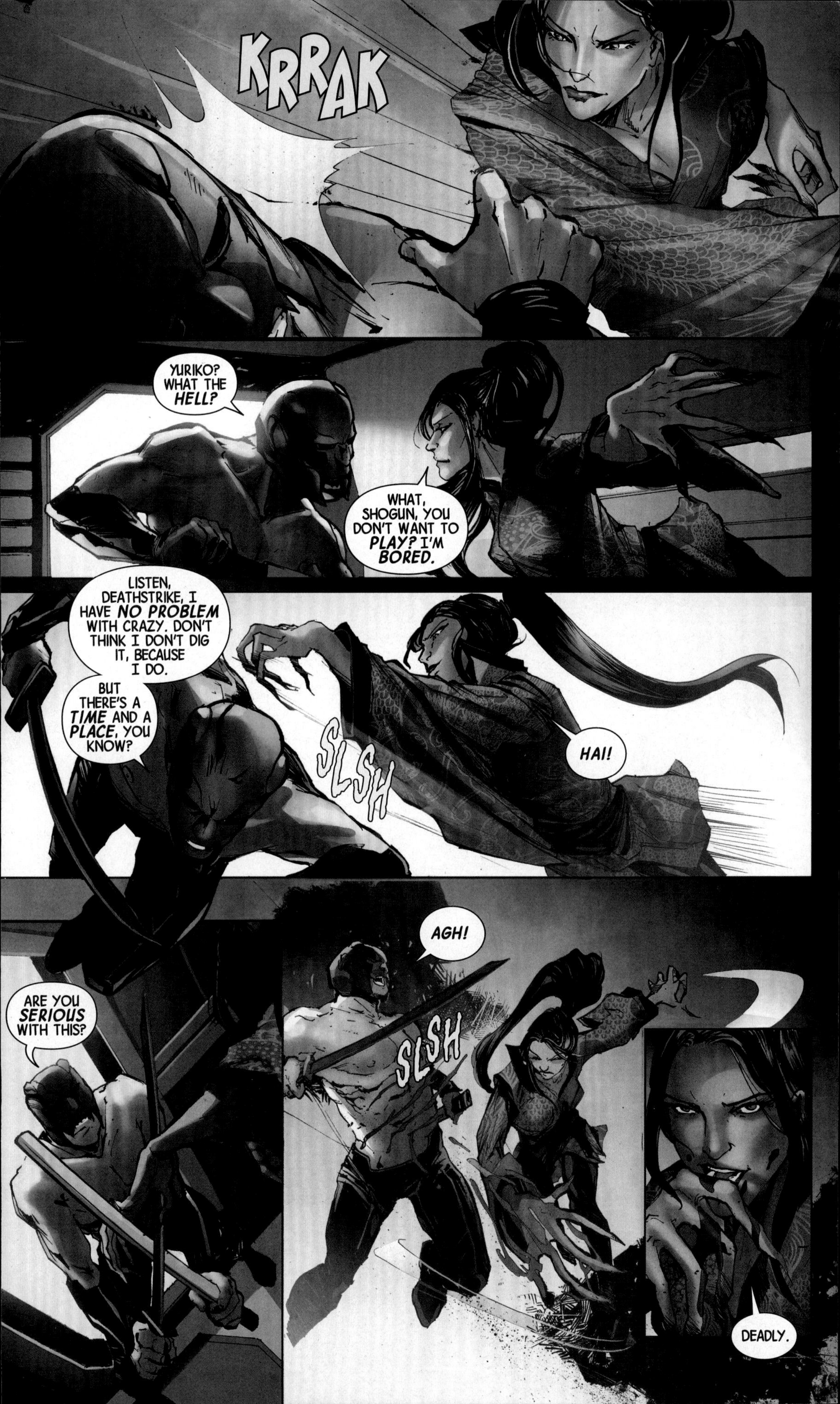
KRRAK
YURIKO? WHAT THE HELL?
WHAT, SHOGUN, YOU DON'T WANT TO PLAY? I'M BORED.
LISTEN, DEATHSTRIKE, I HAVE NO PROBLEM WITH CRAZY. DON'T THINK I DON'T DIG IT, BECAUSE I DO.
BUT THERE'S A TIME AND A PLACE, YOU KNOW?
SLSH
HAI!
ARE YOU SERIOUS WITH THIS?
AGH!
SLSH
DEADLY.

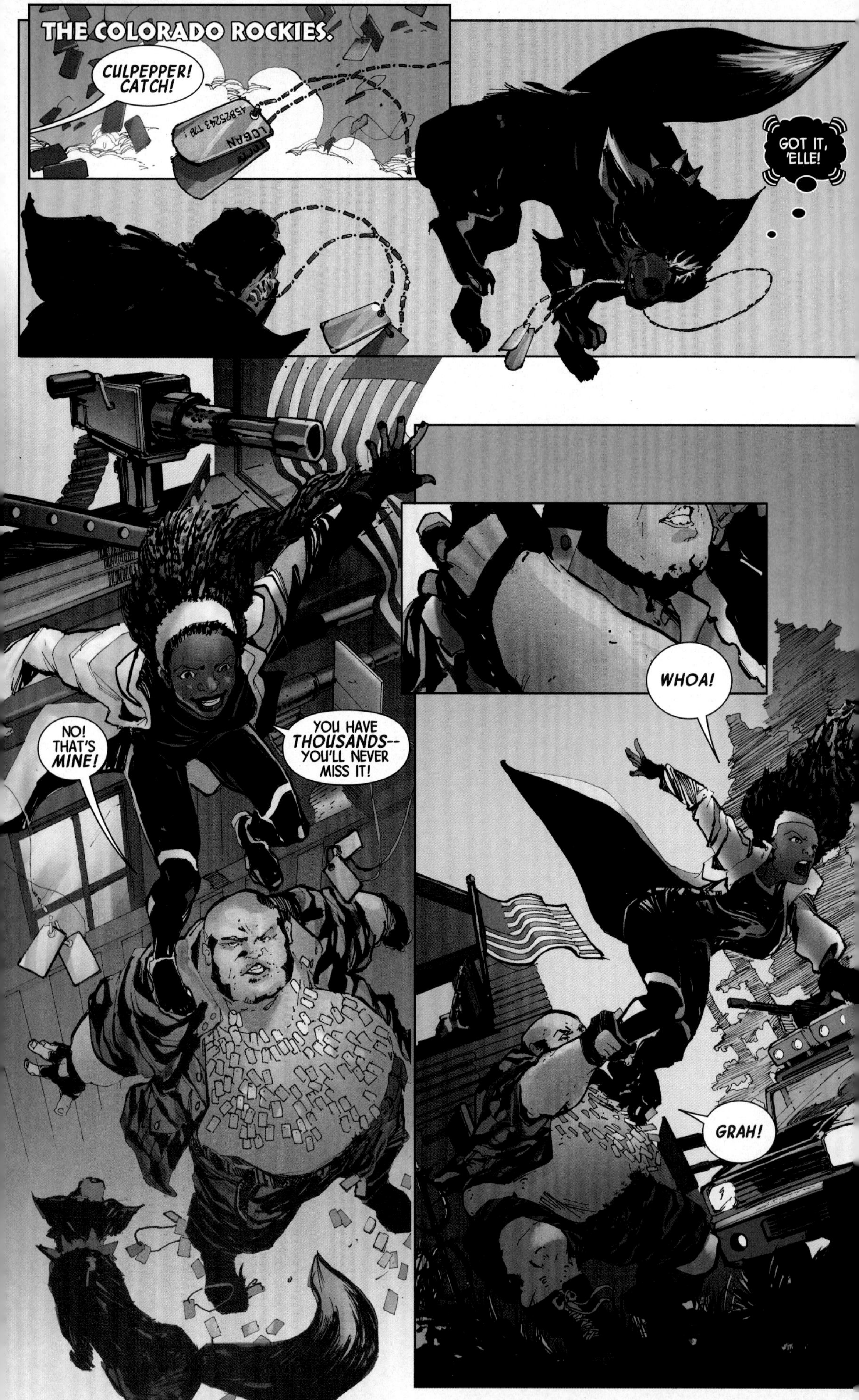
THE COLORADO ROCKIES.
CULPEPPER! CATCH!
LOGAN
458252431 78 I
GOT IT, 'ELLE!
NO! THAT'S MINE!
YOU HAVE THOUSANDS-- YOU'LL NEVER MISS IT!
WHOA!
GRAH!

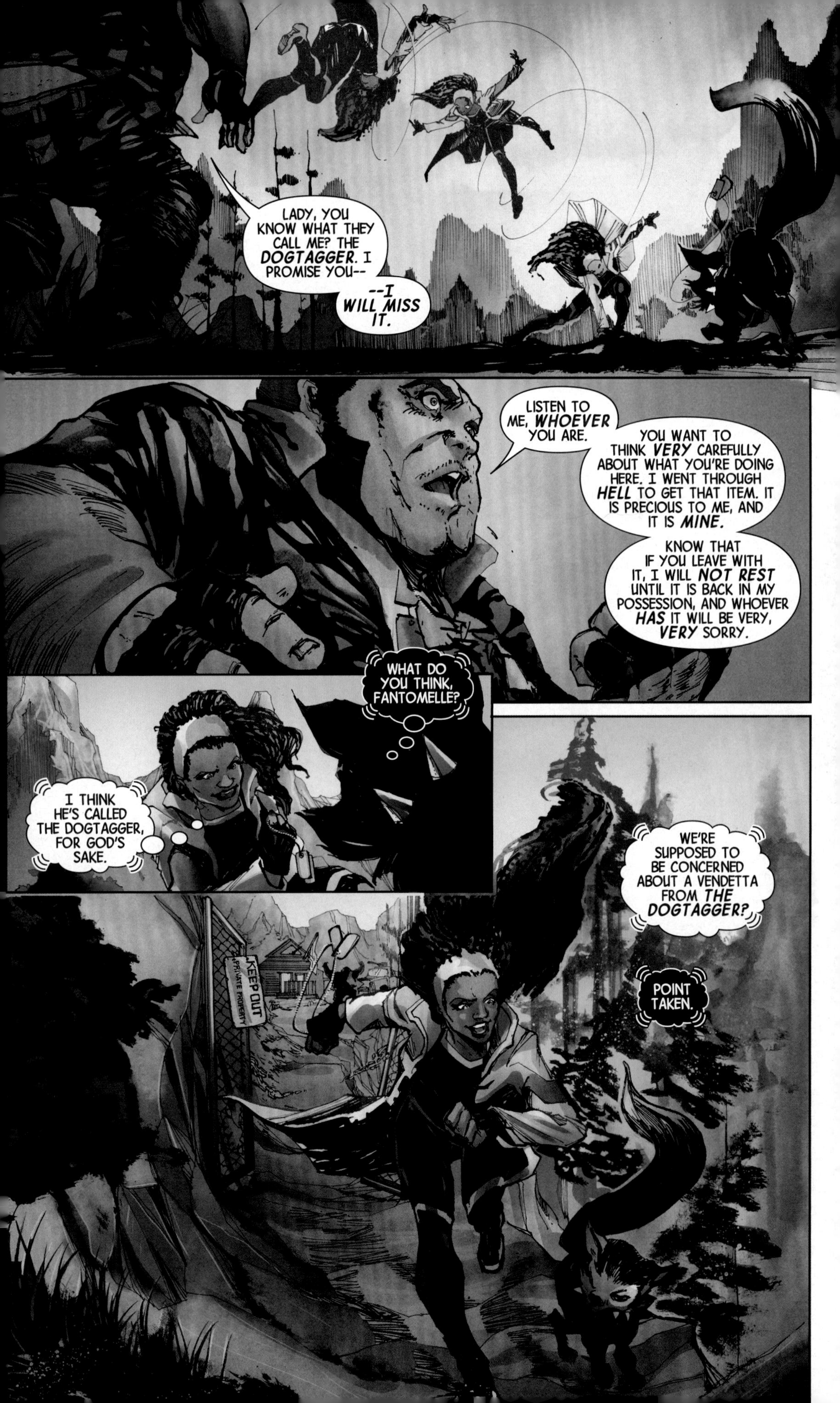

LADY, YOU KNOW WHAT THEY CALL ME? THE DOGTAGGER. I PROMISE YOU--
--I WILL MISS IT.
LISTEN TO ME, WHOEVER YOU ARE.
YOU WANT TO THINK VERY CAREFULLY ABOUT WHAT YOU'RE DOING HERE. I WENT THROUGH HELL TO GET THAT ITEM. IT IS PRECIOUS TO ME, AND IT IS MINE.
KNOW THAT IF YOU LEAVE WITH IT, I WILL NOT REST UNTIL IT IS BACK IN MY POSSESSION, AND WHOEVER HAS IT WILL BE VERY, VERY SORRY.
WHAT DO YOU THINK, FANTOMELLE?
I THINK HE'S CALLED THE DOGTAGGER, FOR GOD'S SAKE.
WE'RE SUPPOSED TO BE CONCERNED ABOUT A VENDETTA FROM THE DOGTAGGER?
KEEP OUT
PRIVATE PROPERTY
POINT TAKEN.

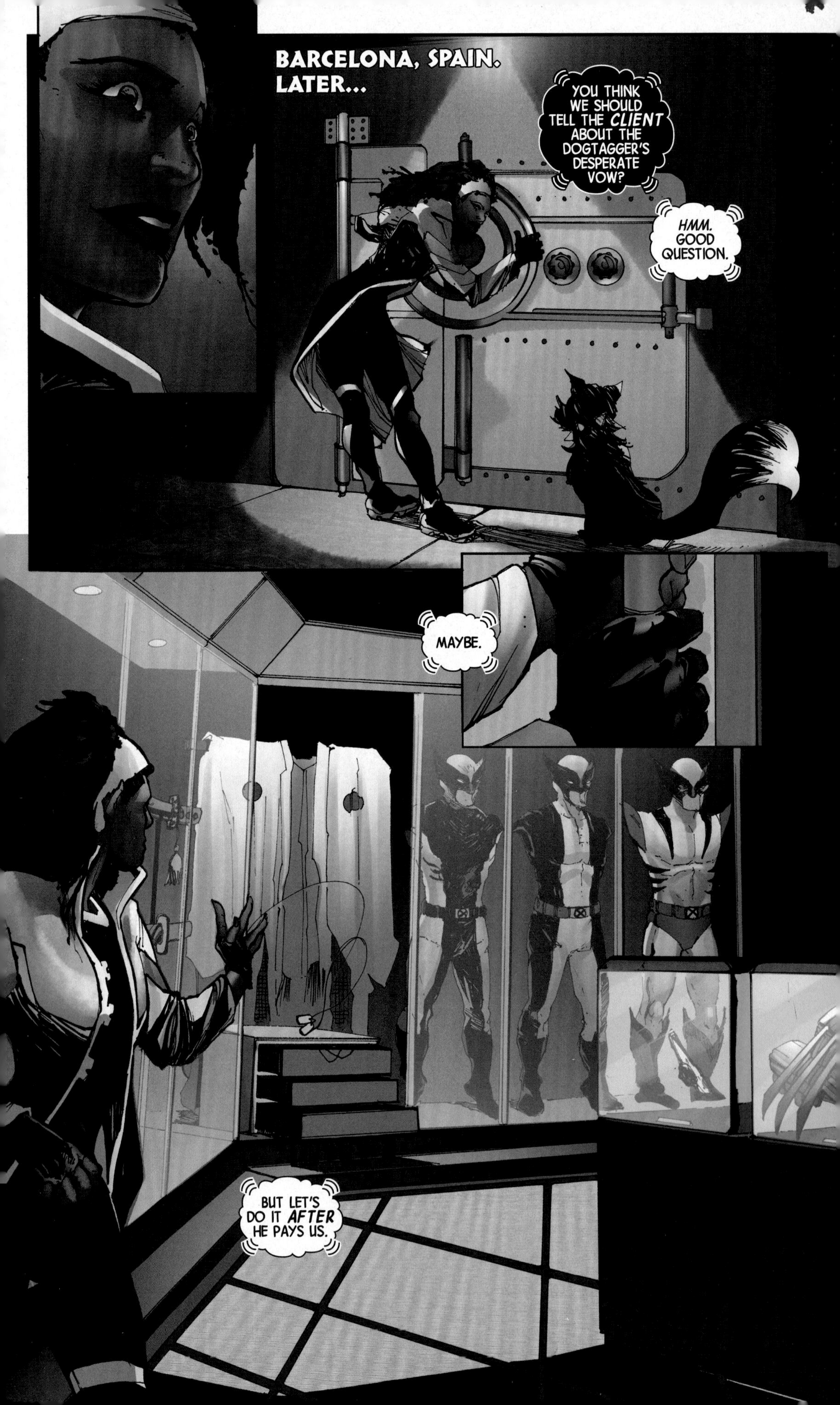

BARCELONA, SPAIN. LATER...
YOU THINK WE SHOULD TELL THE *CLIENT* ABOUT THE DOGTAGGER'S DESPERATE VOW?
HMM. GOOD QUESTION.
MAYBE.
BUT LET'S DO IT *AFTER* HE PAYS US.

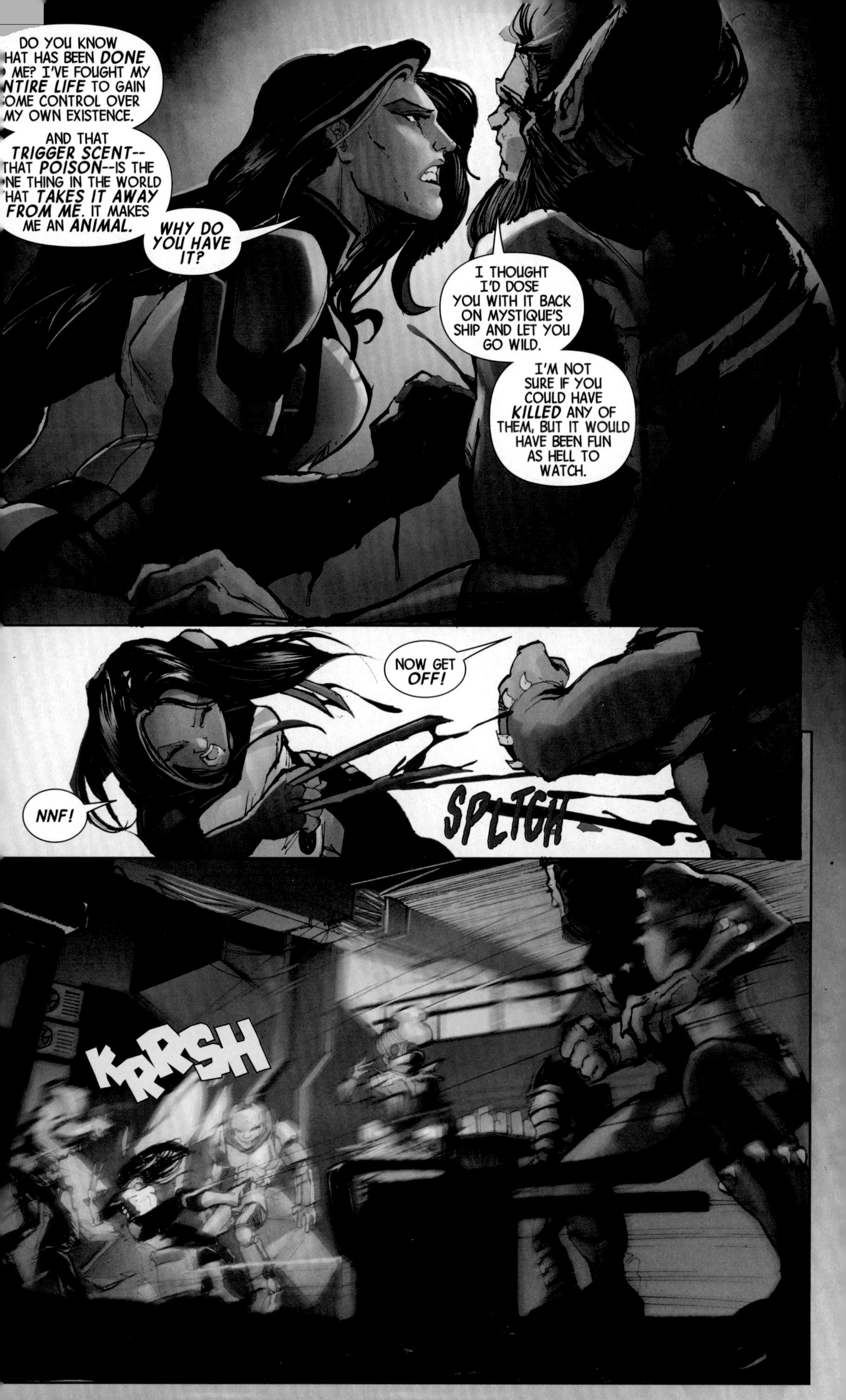

DO YOU KNOW HAT HAS BEEN DONE ME? I'VE FOUGHT MY NTIRE LIFE TO GAIN OME CONTROL OVER MY OWN EXISTENCE.
AND THAT TRIGGER SCENT-- THAT POISON--IS THE NE THING IN THE WORLD HAT TAKES IT AWAY FROM ME. IT MAKES ME AN ANIMAL.
WHY DO YOU HAVE IT?
I THOUGHT I'D DOSE YOU WITH IT BACK ON MYSTIQUE'S SHIP AND LET YOU GO WILD.
I'M NOT SURE IF YOU COULD HAVE KILLED ANY OF THEM, BUT IT WOULD HAVE BEEN FUN AS HELL TO WATCH.
NOW GET OFF!
NNF!
SPLTCH
KRRSH

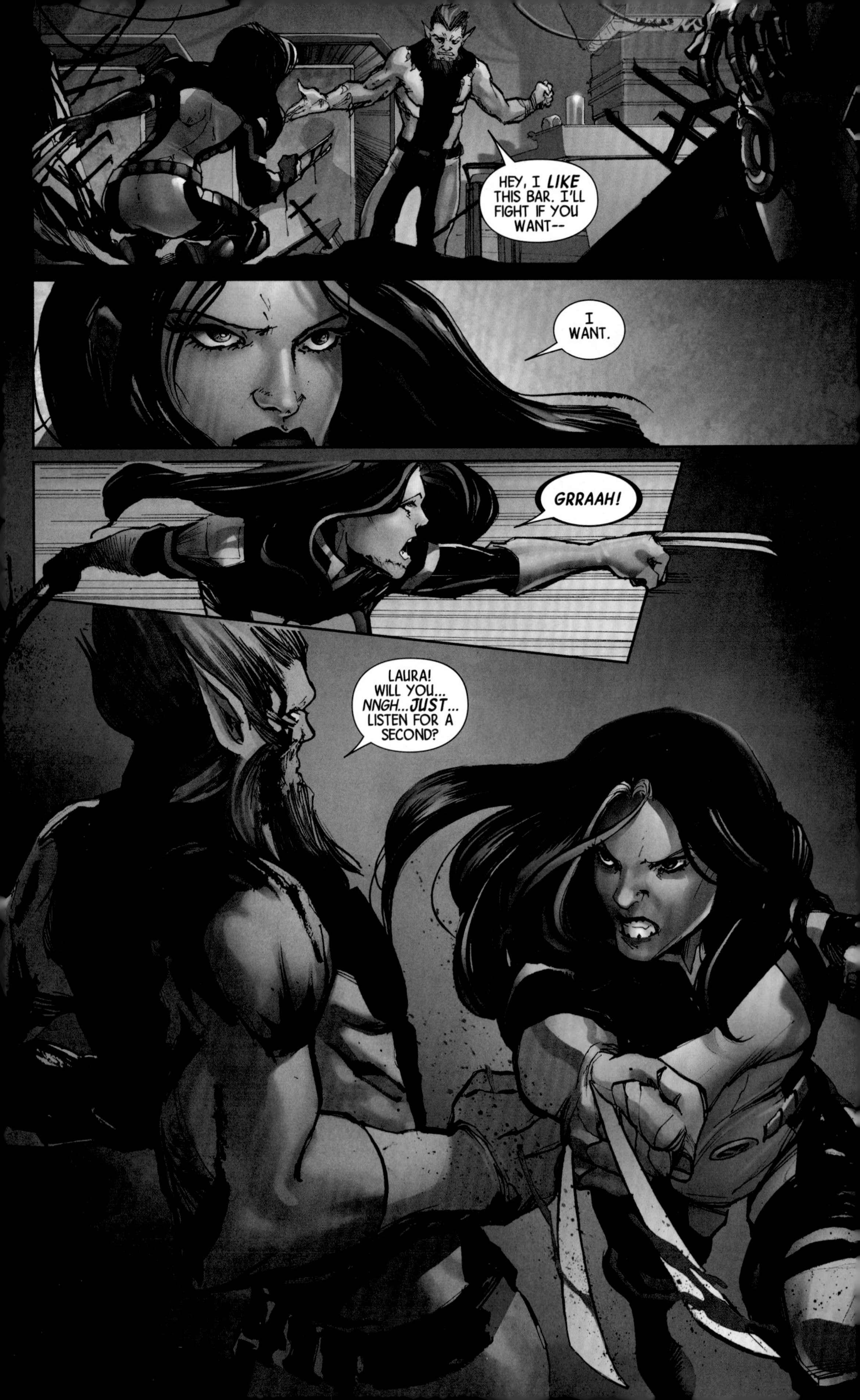
HEY, I LIKE THIS BAR. I'LL FIGHT IF YOU WANT--
I WANT.
GRRAAH!
LAURA! WILL YOU... NNGH...JUST... LISTEN FOR A SECOND?

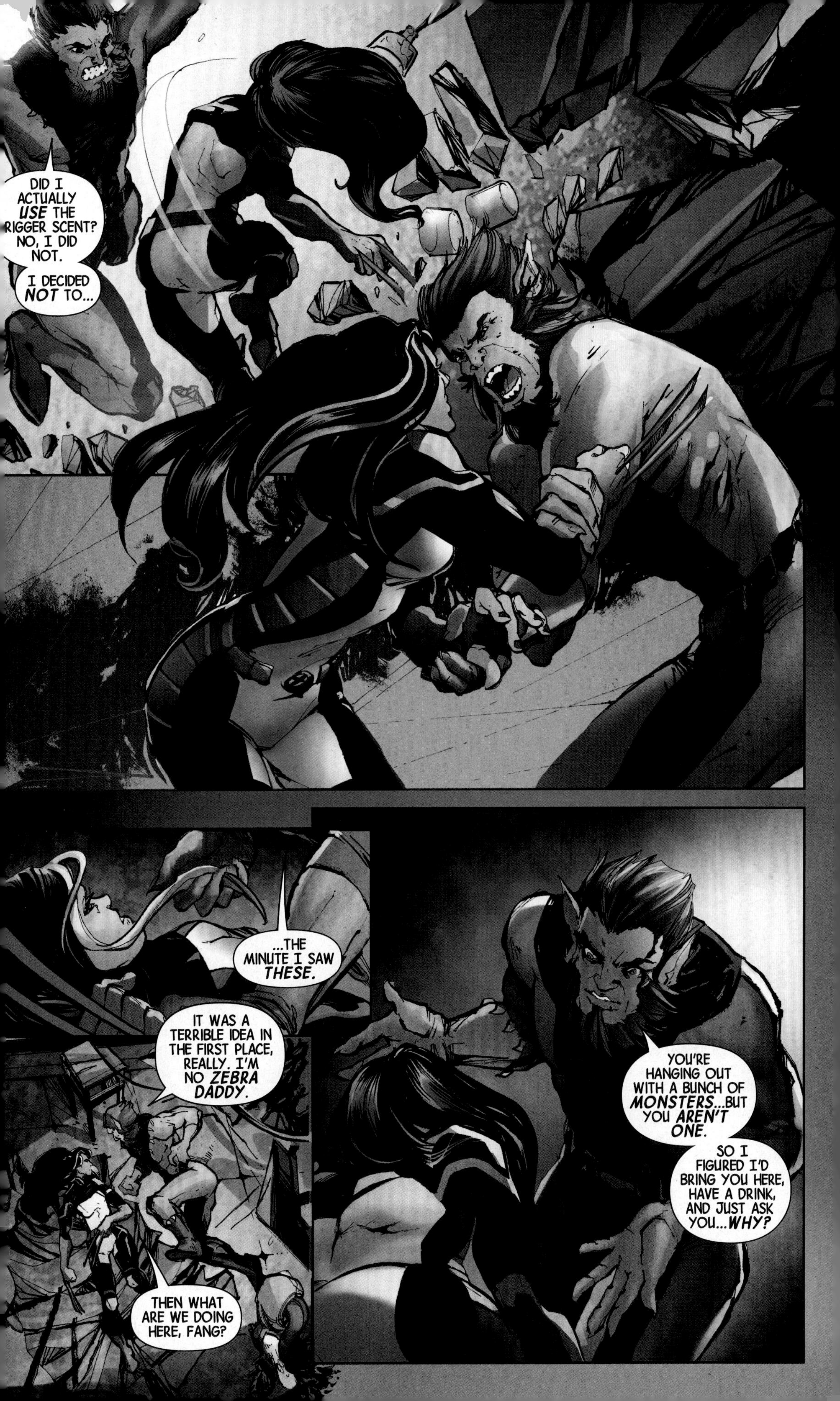

DID I ACTUALLY USE THE RIGGER SCENT? NO, I DID NOT.
I DECIDED NOT TO...
...THE MINUTE I SAW THESE.
IT WAS A TERRIBLE IDEA IN THE FIRST PLACE, REALLY. I'M NO ZEBRA DADDY.
THEN WHAT ARE WE DOING HERE, FANG?
YOU'RE HANGING OUT WITH A BUNCH OF MONSTERS...BUT YOU AREN'T ONE.
SO I FIGURED I'D BRING YOU HERE, HAVE A DRINK, AND JUST ASK YOU...WHY?

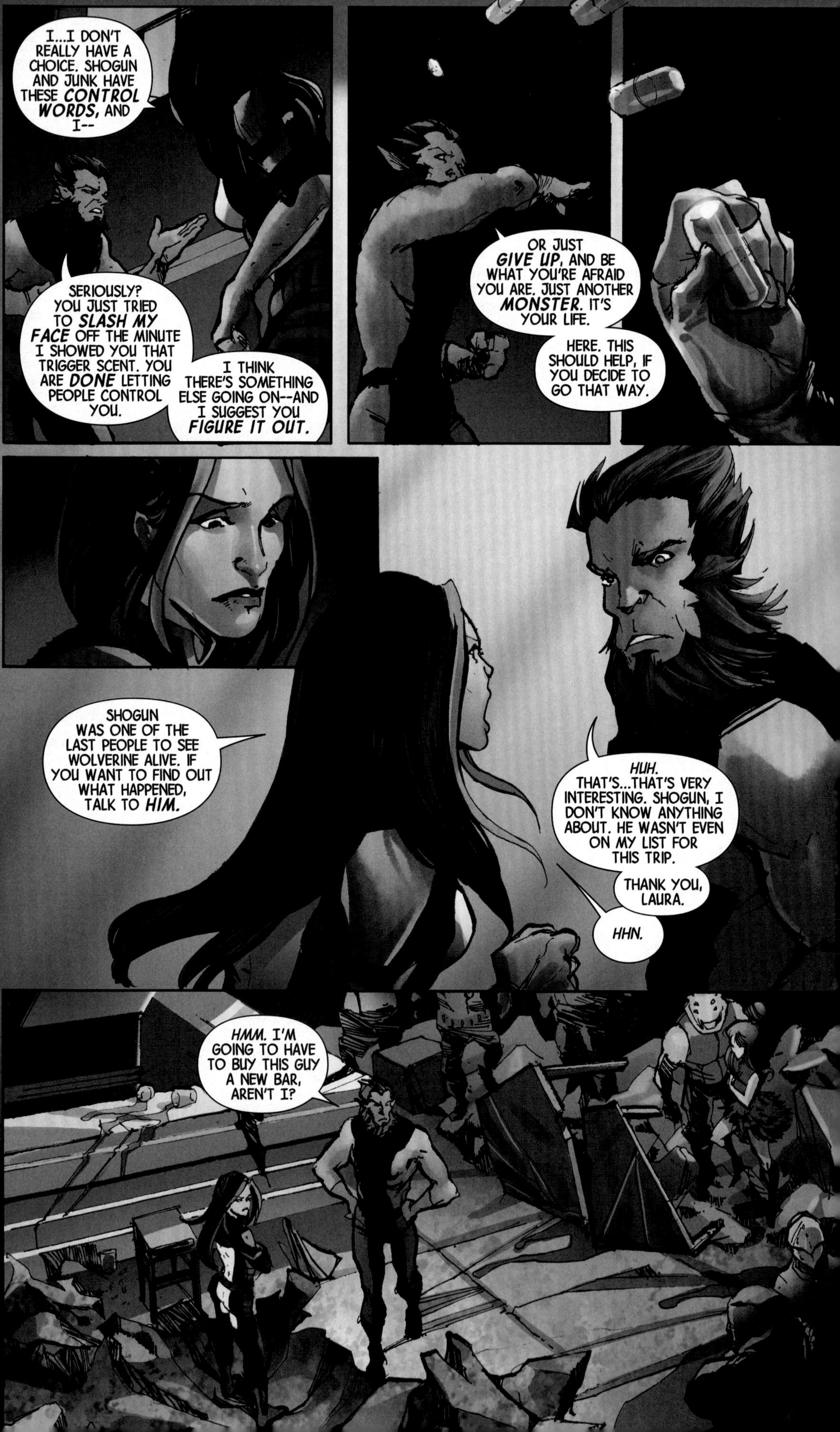

I...I DON'T REALLY HAVE A CHOICE. SHOGUN AND JUNK HAVE THESE CONTROL WORDS, AND I--
SERIOUSLY? YOU JUST TRIED TO SLASH MY FACE OFF THE MINUTE I SHOWED YOU THAT TRIGGER SCENT. YOU ARE DONE LETTING PEOPLE CONTROL YOU.
I THINK THERE'S SOMETHING ELSE GOING ON--AND I SUGGEST YOU FIGURE IT OUT.
OR JUST GIVE UP, AND BE WHAT YOU'RE AFRAID YOU ARE. JUST ANOTHER MONSTER. IT'S YOUR LIFE.
HERE. THIS SHOULD HELP, IF YOU DECIDE TO GO THAT WAY.
SHOGUN WAS ONE OF THE LAST PEOPLE TO SEE WOLVERINE ALIVE. IF YOU WANT TO FIND OUT WHAT HAPPENED, TALK TO HIM.
HUH. THAT'S...THAT'S VERY INTERESTING. SHOGUN, I DON'T KNOW ANYTHING ABOUT. HE WASN'T EVEN ON MY LIST FOR THIS TRIP.
THANK YOU, LAURA.
HHN.
HMM. I'M GOING TO HAVE TO BUY THIS GUY A NEW BAR, AREN'T I?

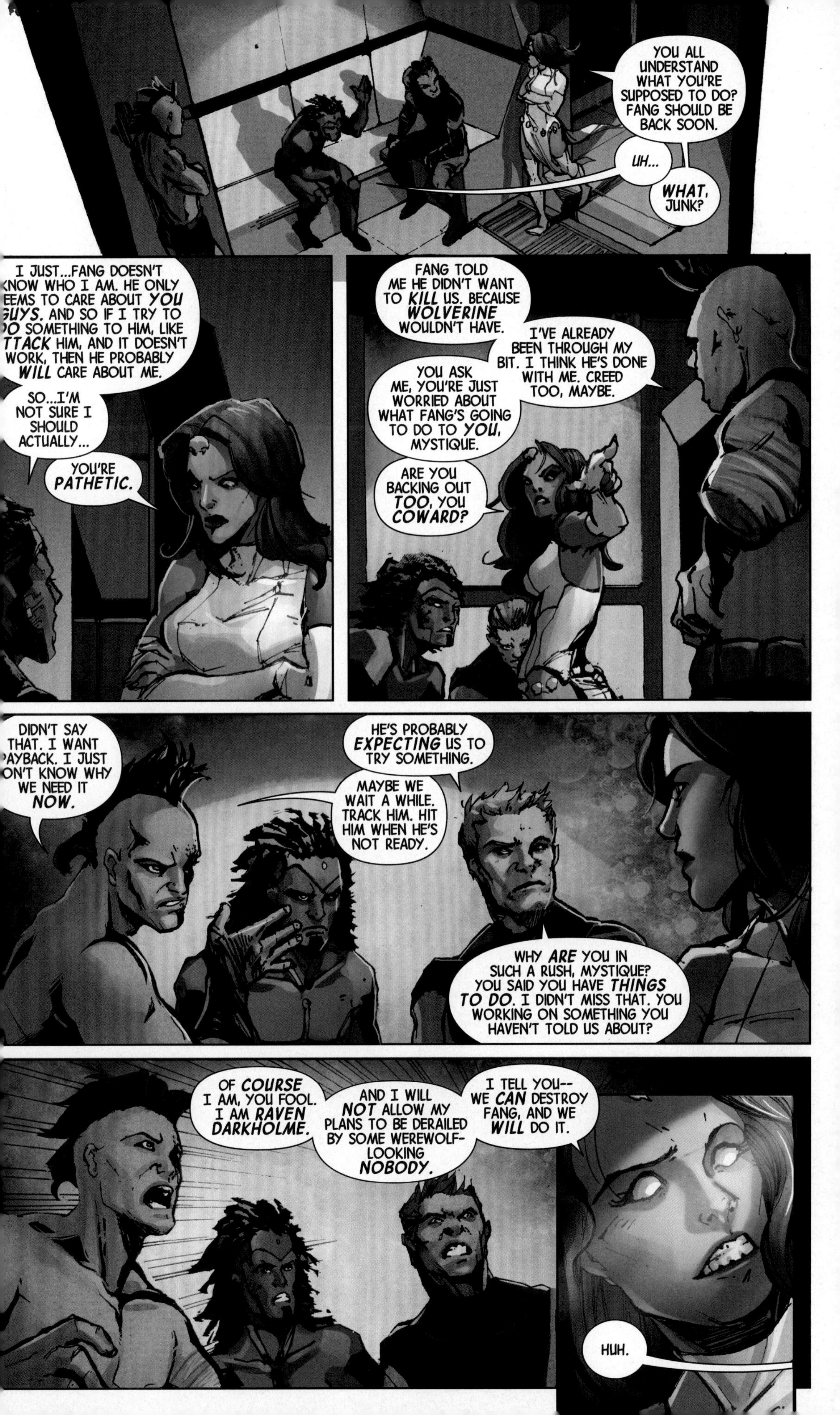
YOU ALL UNDERSTAND WHAT YOU'RE SUPPOSED TO DO? FANG SHOULD BE BACK SOON.
UH...
WHAT, JUNK?
I JUST...FANG DOESN'T KNOW WHO I AM. HE ONLY SEEMS TO CARE ABOUT YOU GUYS. AND SO IF I TRY TO DO SOMETHING TO HIM, LIKE ATTACK HIM, AND IT DOESN'T WORK, THEN HE PROBABLY WILL CARE ABOUT ME.
SO...I'M NOT SURE I SHOULD ACTUALLY...
YOU'RE PATHETIC.
FANG TOLD ME HE DIDN'T WANT TO KILL US. BECAUSE WOLVERINE WOULDN'T HAVE.
I'VE ALREADY BEEN THROUGH MY BIT. I THINK HE'S DONE WITH ME. CREED TOO, MAYBE.
YOU ASK ME, YOU'RE JUST WORRIED ABOUT WHAT FANG'S GOING TO DO TO YOU, MYSTIQUE.
ARE YOU BACKING OUT TOO, YOU COWARD?
DIDN'T SAY THAT. I WANT PAYBACK. I JUST DON'T KNOW WHY WE NEED IT NOW.
HE'S PROBABLY EXPECTING US TO TRY SOMETHING.
MAYBE WE WAIT A WHILE. TRACK HIM. HIT HIM WHEN HE'S NOT READY.
WHY ARE YOU IN SUCH A RUSH, MYSTIQUE? YOU SAID YOU HAVE THINGS TO DO. I DIDN'T MISS THAT. YOU WORKING ON SOMETHING YOU HAVEN'T TOLD US ABOUT?
OF COURSE I AM, YOU FOOL. I AM RAVEN DARKHOLME.
AND I WILL NOT ALLOW MY PLANS TO BE DERAILED BY SOME WEREWOLF-LOOKING NOBODY.
I TELL YOU-- WE CAN DESTROY FANG, AND WE WILL DO IT.
HUH.

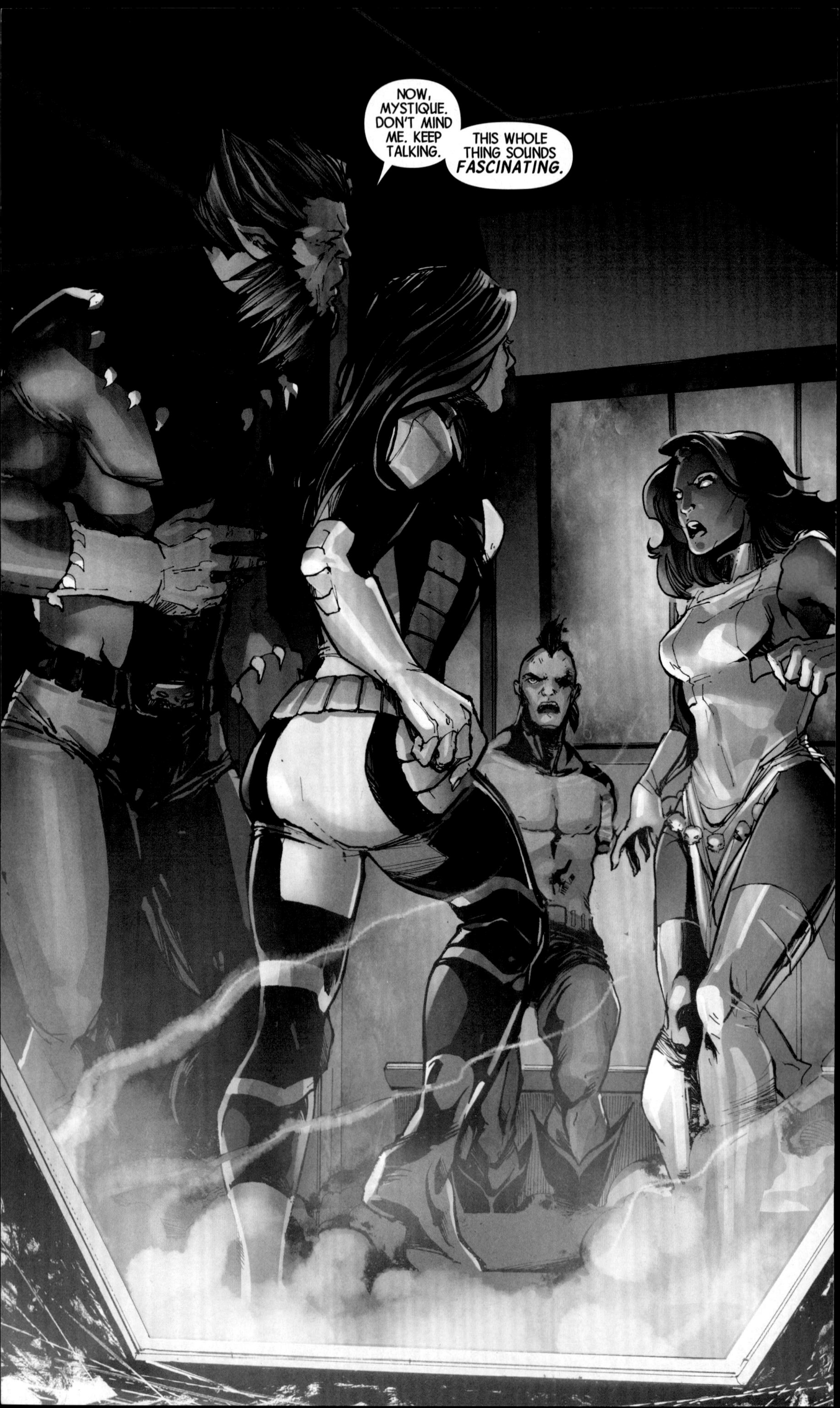
NOW, MYSTIQUE. DON'T MIND ME. KEEP TALKING.
THIS WHOLE THING SOUNDS FASCINATING.

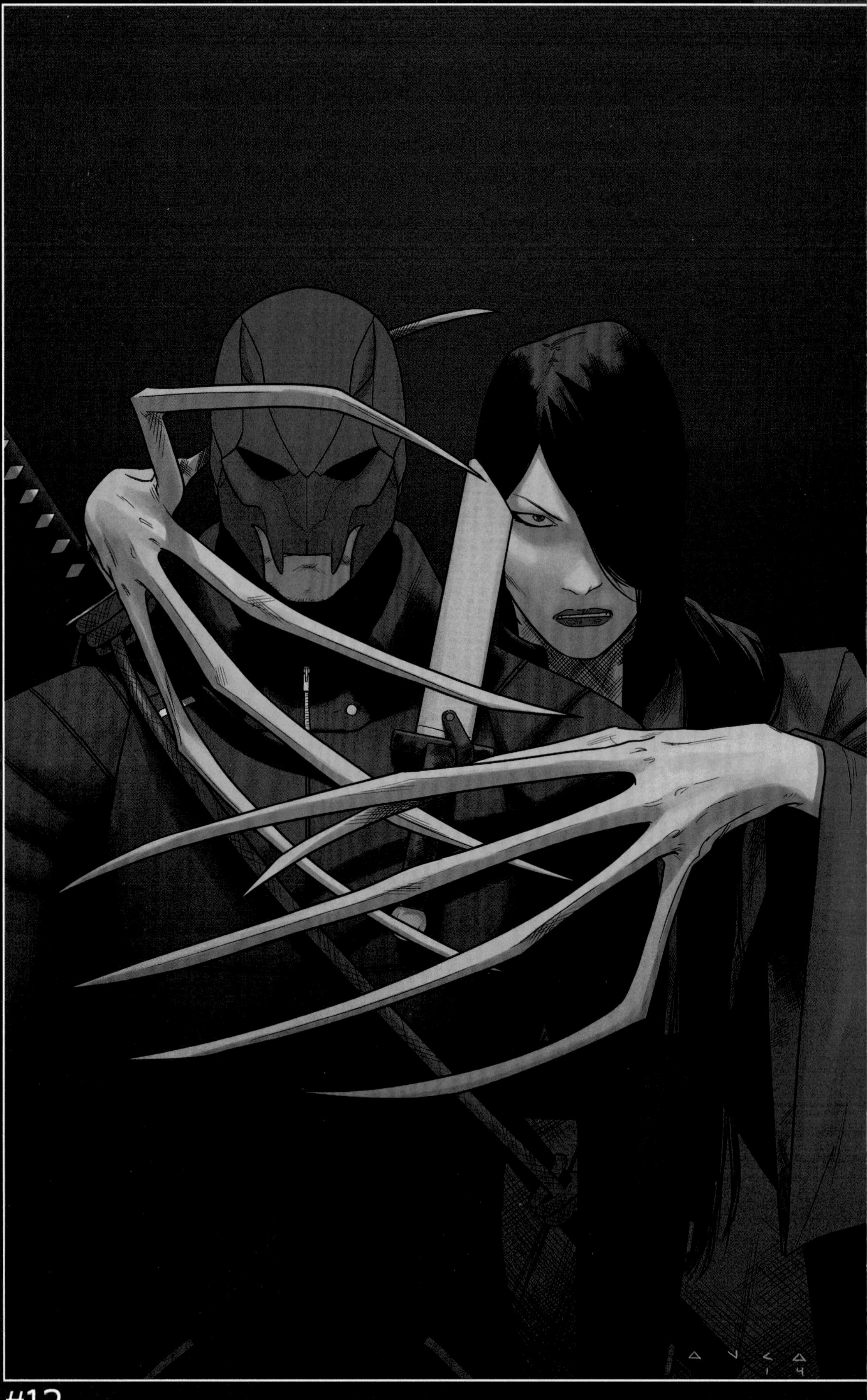

#12

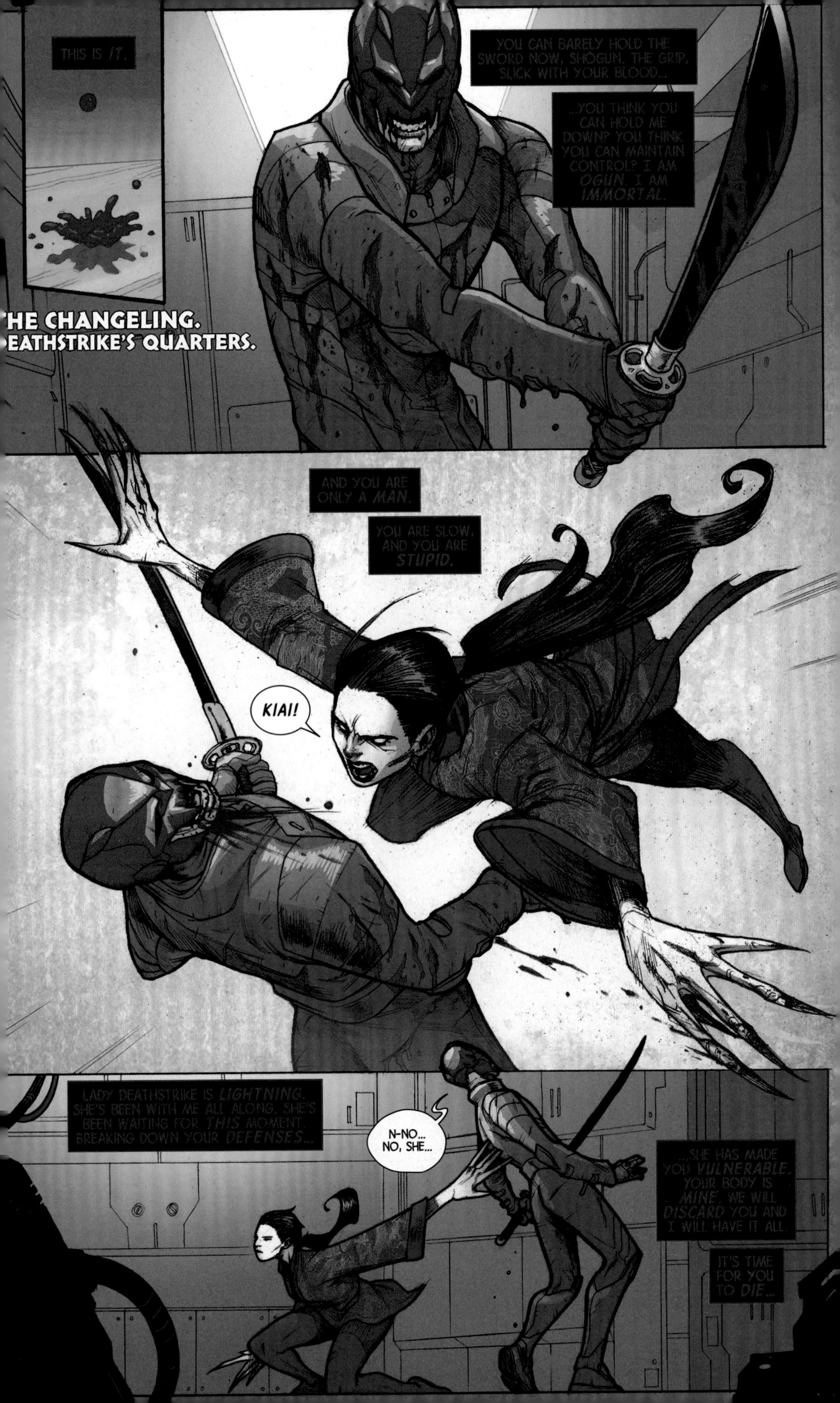
THIS IS IT.
YOU CAN BARELY HOLD THE SWORD NOW, SHŌGUN. THE GRIP, SLICK WITH YOUR BLOOD...
...YOU THINK YOU CAN HOLD ME DOWN? YOU THINK YOU CAN MAINTAIN CONTROL? I AM OGUN. I AM IMMORTAL.
HE CHANGELING.
EATHSTRIKE'S QUARTERS.
AND YOU ARE ONLY A MAN.
YOU ARE SLOW, AND YOU ARE STUPID.
KIAI!
LADY DEATHSTRIKE IS LIGHTNING. SHE'S BEEN WITH ME ALL ALONG. SHE'S BEEN WAITING FOR THIS MOMENT. BREAKING DOWN YOUR DEFENSES...
N-NO... NO, SHE...
...SHE HAS MADE YOU VULNERABLE. YOUR BODY IS MINE. WE WILL DISCARD YOU AND I WILL HAVE IT ALL.
IT'S TIME FOR YOU TO DIE...

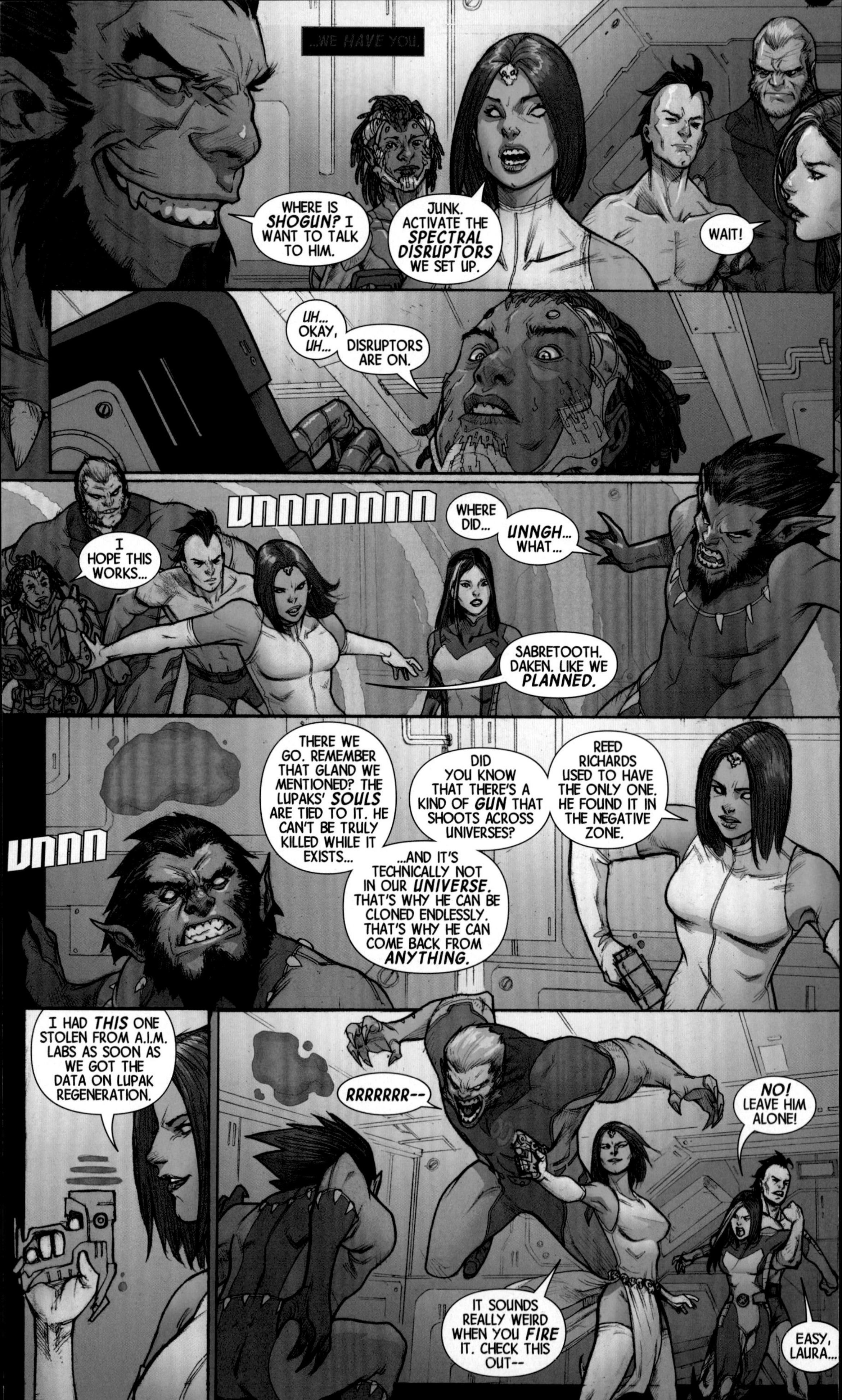
...WE HAVE YOU.
WHERE IS SHOGUN? I WANT TO TALK TO HIM.
JUNK. ACTIVATE THE SPECTRAL DISRUPTORS WE SET UP.
WAIT!
UH... OKAY, UH...
DISRUPTORS ARE ON.
VNNNNNNNN
I HOPE THIS WORKS...
WHERE DID... UNNGH... WHAT...
SABRETOOTH. DAKEN. LIKE WE PLANNED.
VNNN
THERE WE GO. REMEMBER THAT GLAND WE MENTIONED? THE LUPAKS' SOULS ARE TIED TO IT. HE CAN'T BE TRULY KILLED WHILE IT EXISTS...
...AND IT'S TECHNICALLY NOT IN OUR UNIVERSE. THAT'S WHY HE CAN BE CLONED ENDLESSLY. THAT'S WHY HE CAN COME BACK FROM ANYTHING.
DID YOU KNOW THAT THERE'S A KIND OF GUN THAT SHOOTS ACROSS UNIVERSES?
REED RICHARDS USED TO HAVE THE ONLY ONE. HE FOUND IT IN THE NEGATIVE ZONE.
I HAD THIS ONE STOLEN FROM A.I.M. LABS AS SOON AS WE GOT THE DATA ON LUPAK REGENERATION.
RRRRRRR--
NO! LEAVE HIM ALONE!
IT SOUNDS REALLY WEIRD WHEN YOU FIRE IT. CHECK THIS OUT--
EASY, LAURA...

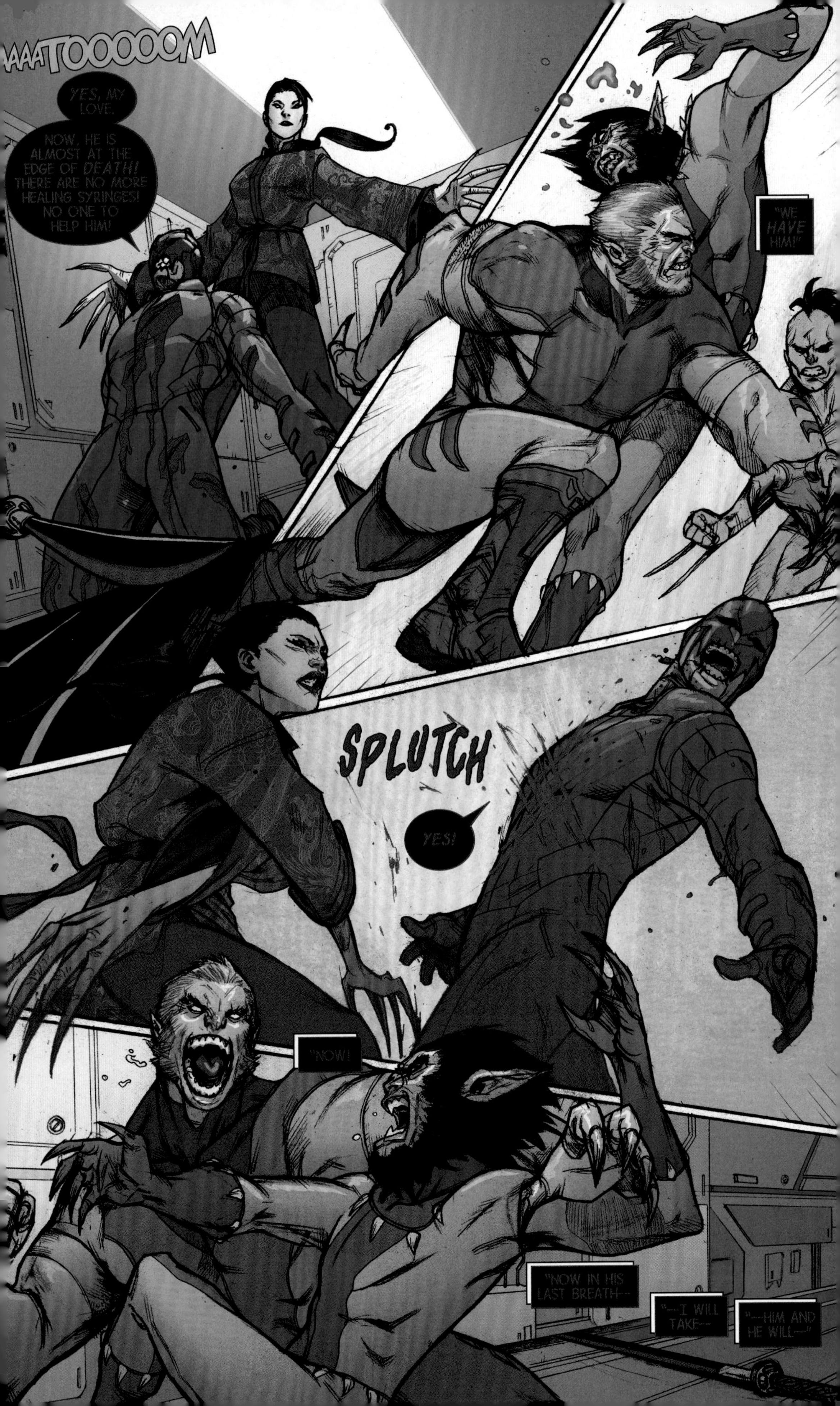
AAAATOOOOOM
YES, MY LOVE.
NOW, HE IS ALMOST AT THE EDGE OF *DEATH!* THERE ARE NO MORE HEALING SYRINGES! NO ONE TO HELP HIM!
"WE *HAVE* HIM!"
SPLUTCH
YES!
"NOW!
"NOW IN HIS LAST BREATH--
"--I WILL TAKE--
"--HIM AND HE WILL--"

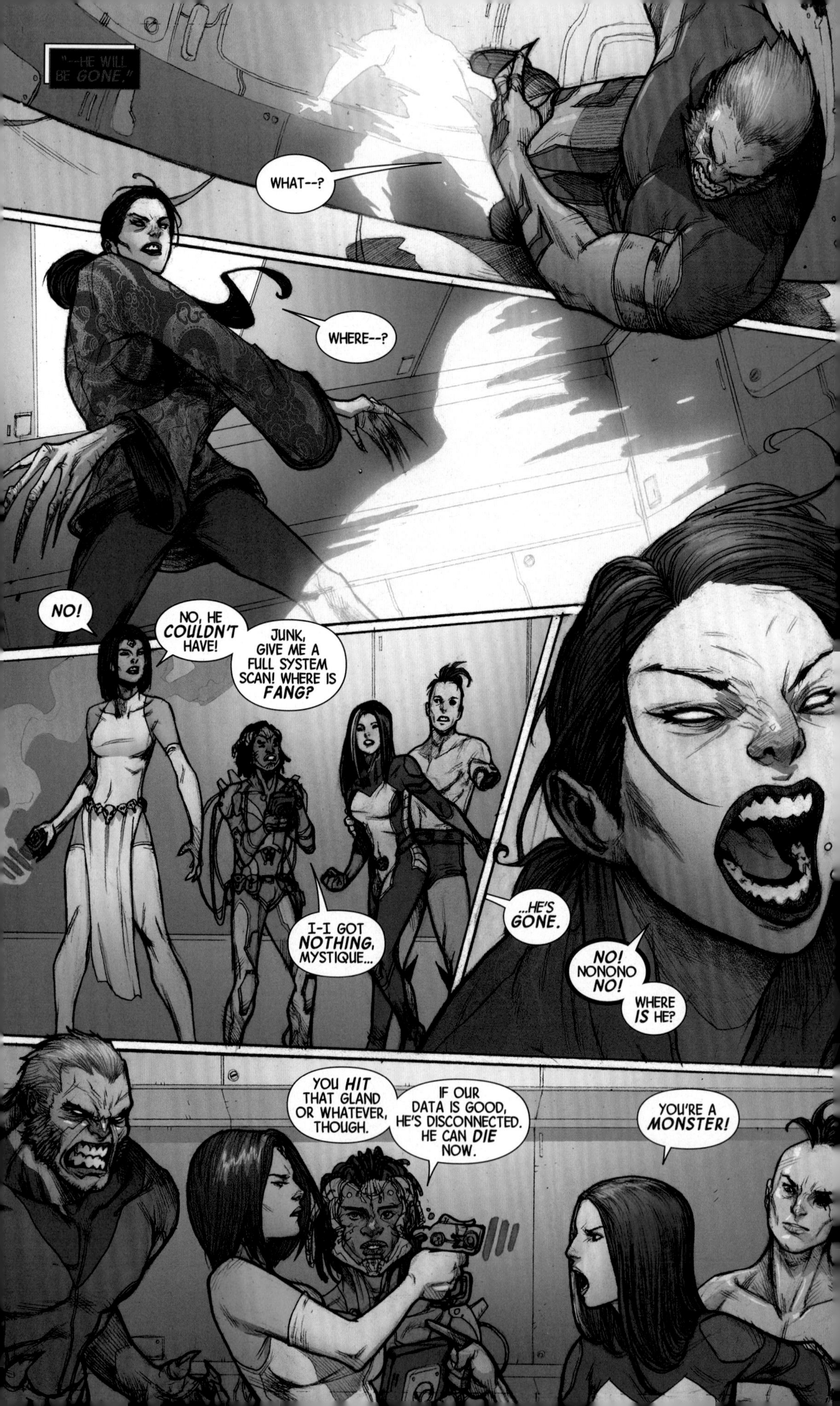
"--HE WILL BE GONE."
WHAT--?
WHERE--?
NO!
NO, HE COULDN'T HAVE!
JUNK, GIVE ME A FULL SYSTEM SCAN! WHERE IS FANG?
I-I GOT NOTHING, MYSTIQUE...
...HE'S GONE.
NO! NONONO NO!
WHERE IS HE?
YOU HIT THAT GLAND OR WHATEVER, THOUGH.
IF OUR DATA IS GOOD, HE'S DISCONNECTED. HE CAN DIE NOW.
YOU'RE A MONSTER!

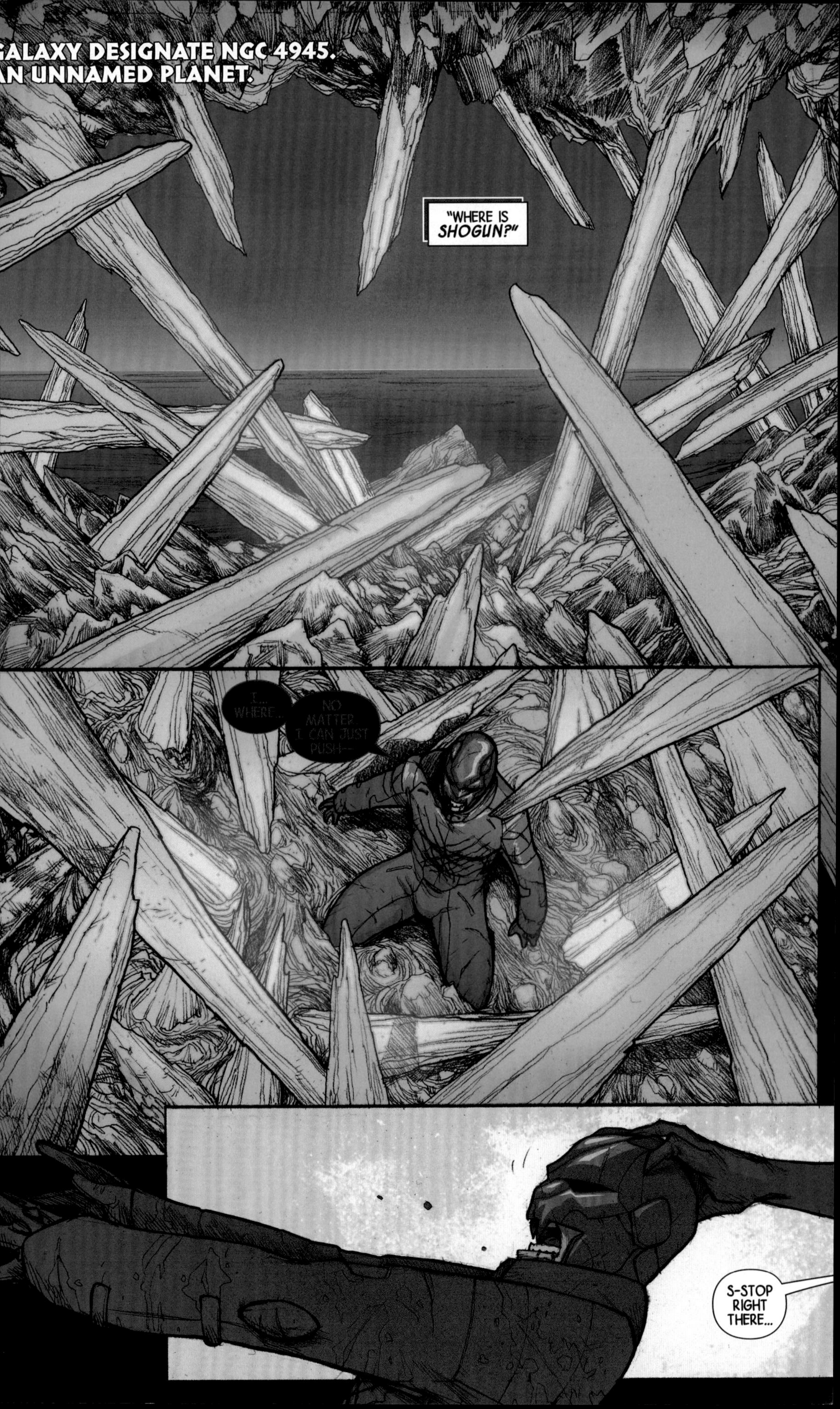
GALAXY DESIGNATE NGC 4945.
AN UNNAMED PLANET.
"WHERE IS SHOGUN?"
I... WHERE...
NO MATTER. I CAN JUST PUSH--
S-STOP RIGHT THERE...

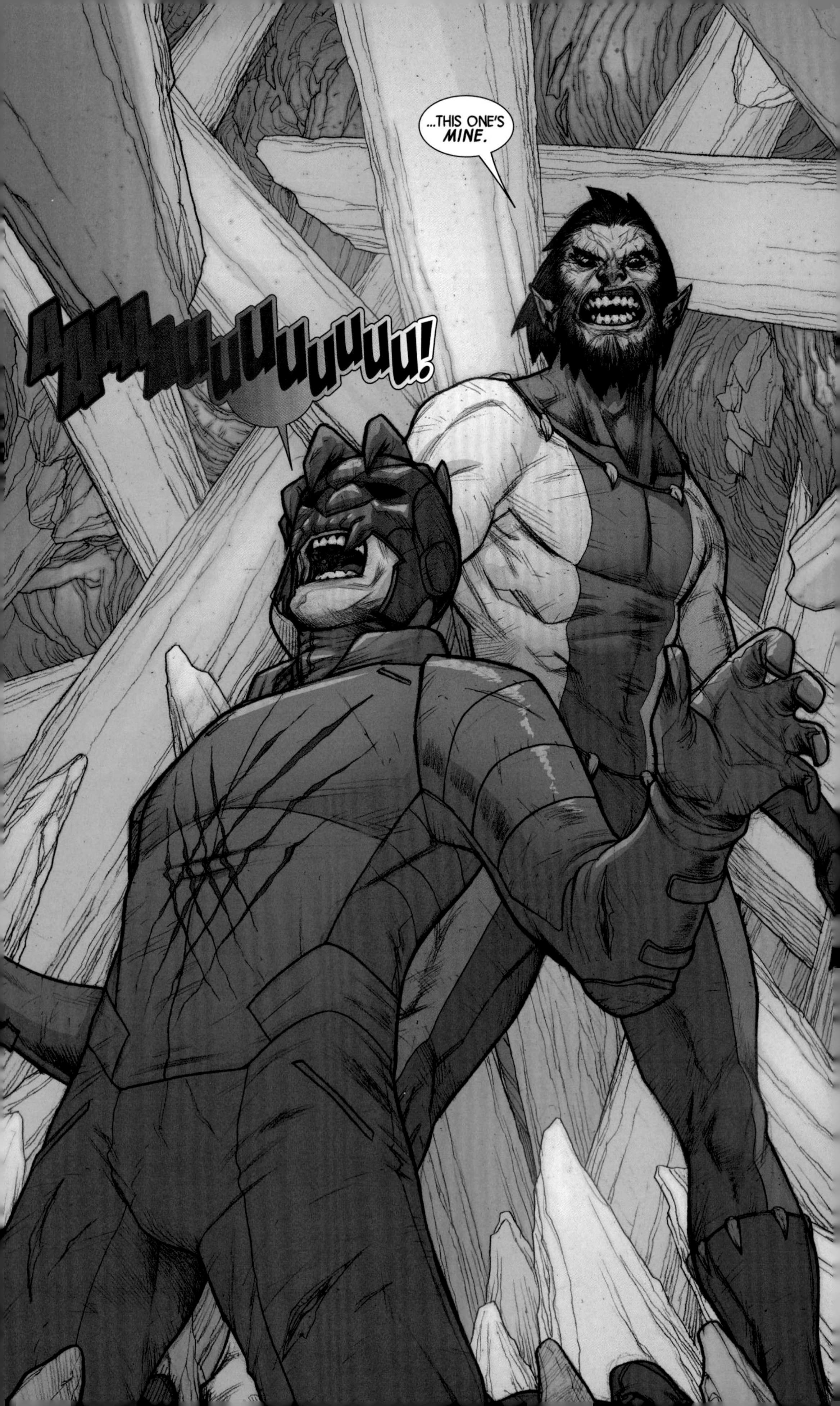
...THIS ONE'S MINE.
AAAAUUUUUUUUU!

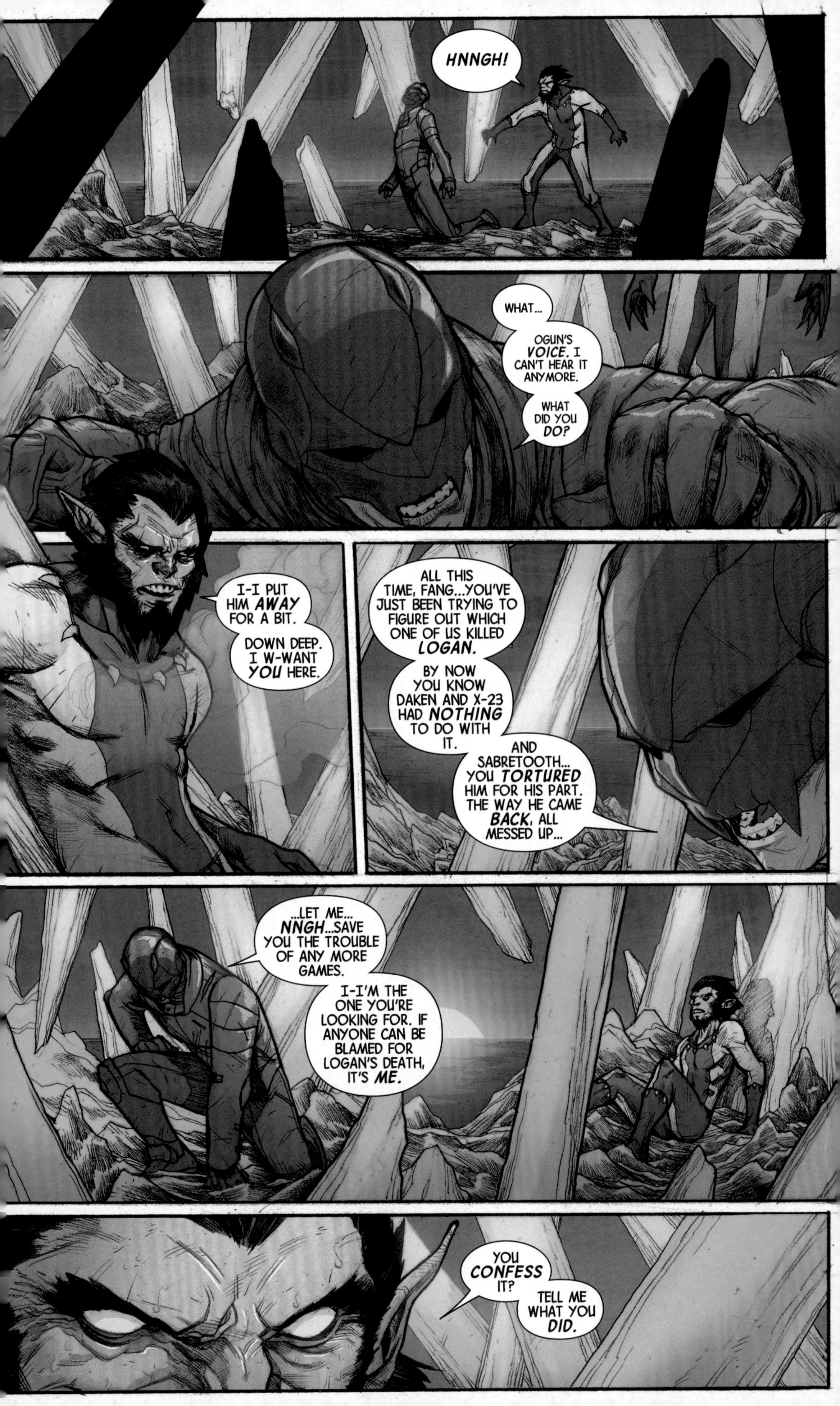
HNNGH!
WHAT...
OGUN'S VOICE. I CAN'T HEAR IT ANYMORE.
WHAT DID YOU DO?
I-I PUT HIM AWAY FOR A BIT.
DOWN DEEP. I W-WANT YOU HERE.
ALL THIS TIME, FANG...YOU'VE JUST BEEN TRYING TO FIGURE OUT WHICH ONE OF US KILLED LOGAN.
BY NOW YOU KNOW DAKEN AND X-23 HAD NOTHING TO DO WITH IT.
AND SABRETOOTH... YOU TORTURED HIM FOR HIS PART. THE WAY HE CAME BACK, ALL MESSED UP...
...LET ME... NNGH...SAVE YOU THE TROUBLE OF ANY MORE GAMES.
I-I'M THE ONE YOU'RE LOOKING FOR. IF ANYONE CAN BE BLAMED FOR LOGAN'S DEATH, IT'S ME.
YOU CONFESS IT?
TELL ME WHAT YOU DID.

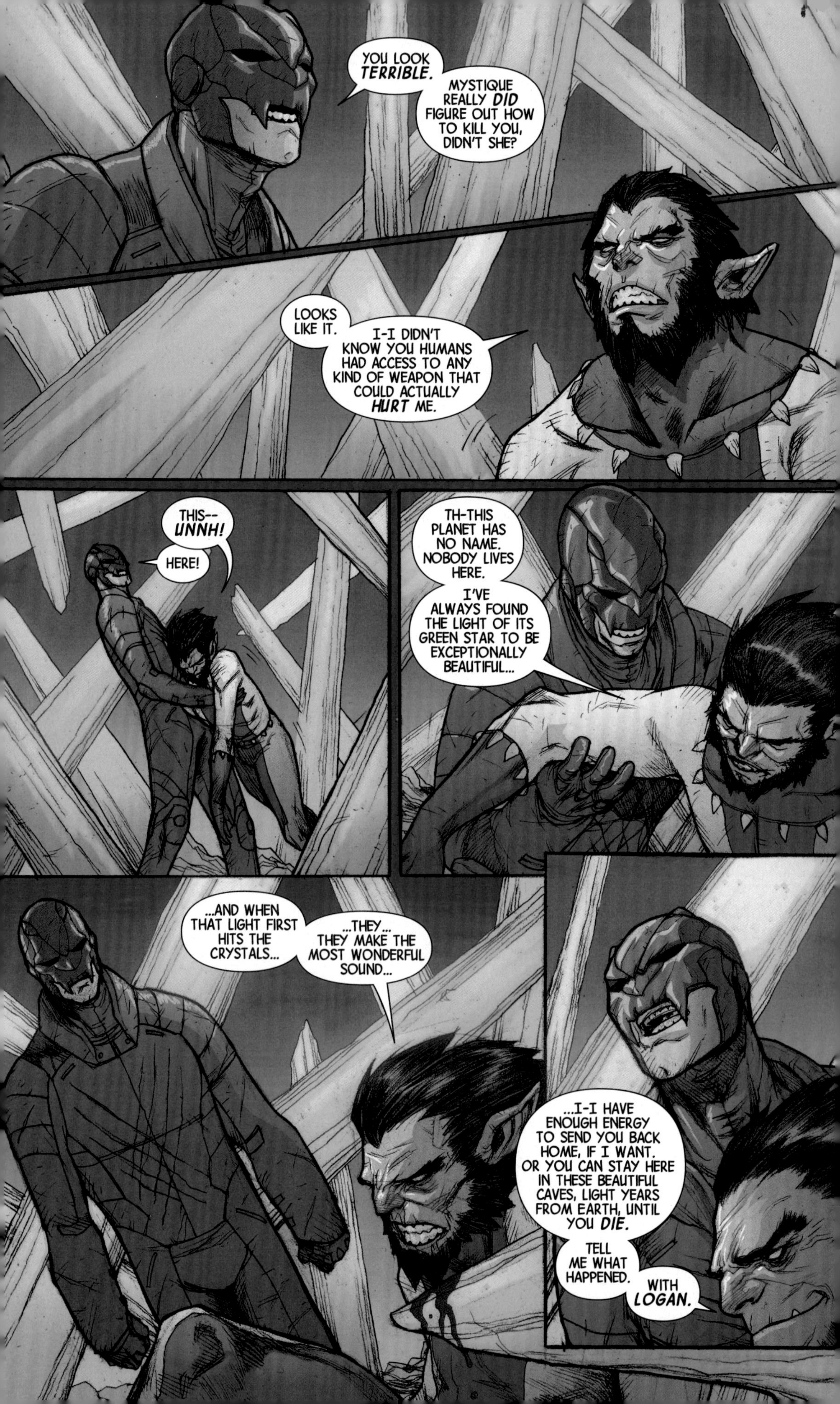
YOU LOOK TERRIBLE.
MYSTIQUE REALLY DID FIGURE OUT HOW TO KILL YOU, DIDN'T SHE?
LOOKS LIKE IT.
I-I DIDN'T KNOW YOU HUMANS HAD ACCESS TO ANY KIND OF WEAPON THAT COULD ACTUALLY HURT ME.
THIS-- UNNH!
HERE!
TH-THIS PLANET HAS NO NAME. NOBODY LIVES HERE.
I'VE ALWAYS FOUND THE LIGHT OF ITS GREEN STAR TO BE EXCEPTIONALLY BEAUTIFUL...
...AND WHEN THAT LIGHT FIRST HITS THE CRYSTALS...
...THEY... THEY MAKE THE MOST WONDERFUL SOUND...
...I-I HAVE ENOUGH ENERGY TO SEND YOU BACK HOME, IF I WANT. OR YOU CAN STAY HERE IN THESE BEAUTIFUL CAVES, LIGHT YEARS FROM EARTH, UNTIL YOU DIE.
TELL ME WHAT HAPPENED.
WITH LOGAN.

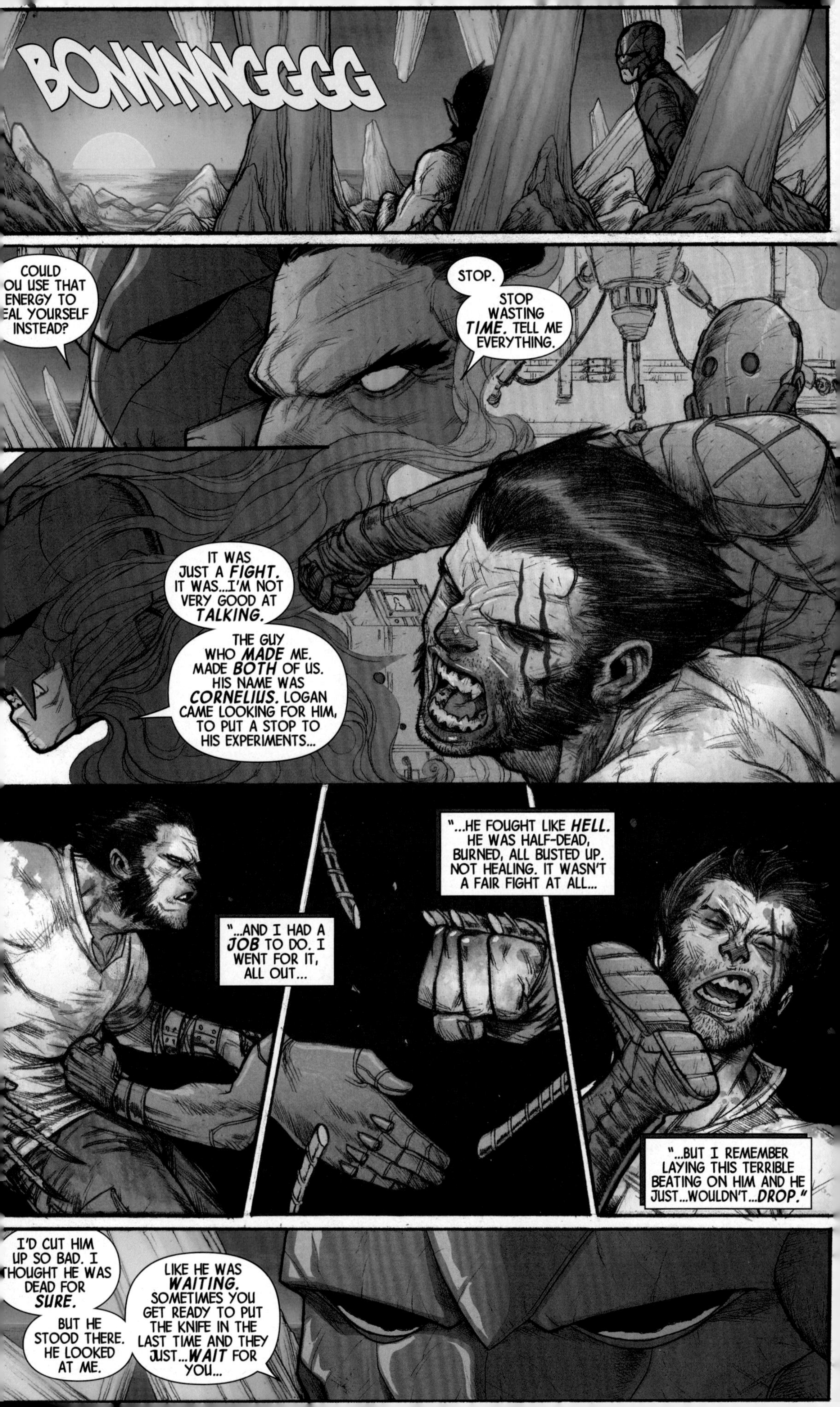

BONNNNGGGG
COULD OU USE THAT ENERGY TO EAL YOURSELF INSTEAD?
STOP.
STOP WASTING TIME. TELL ME EVERYTHING.
IT WAS JUST A FIGHT. IT WAS...I'M NOT VERY GOOD AT TALKING.
THE GUY WHO MADE ME. MADE BOTH OF US. HIS NAME WAS CORNELIUS. LOGAN CAME LOOKING FOR HIM, TO PUT A STOP TO HIS EXPERIMENTS...
"...AND I HAD A JOB TO DO. I WENT FOR IT, ALL OUT...
"...HE FOUGHT LIKE HELL. HE WAS HALF-DEAD, BURNED, ALL BUSTED UP. NOT HEALING. IT WASN'T A FAIR FIGHT AT ALL...
"...BUT I REMEMBER LAYING THIS TERRIBLE BEATING ON HIM AND HE JUST...WOULDN'T...DROP."
I'D CUT HIM UP SO BAD. I THOUGHT HE WAS DEAD FOR SURE.
BUT HE STOOD THERE. HE LOOKED AT ME.
LIKE HE WAS WAITING. SOMETIMES YOU GET READY TO PUT THE KNIFE IN THE LAST TIME AND THEY JUST...WAIT FOR YOU...

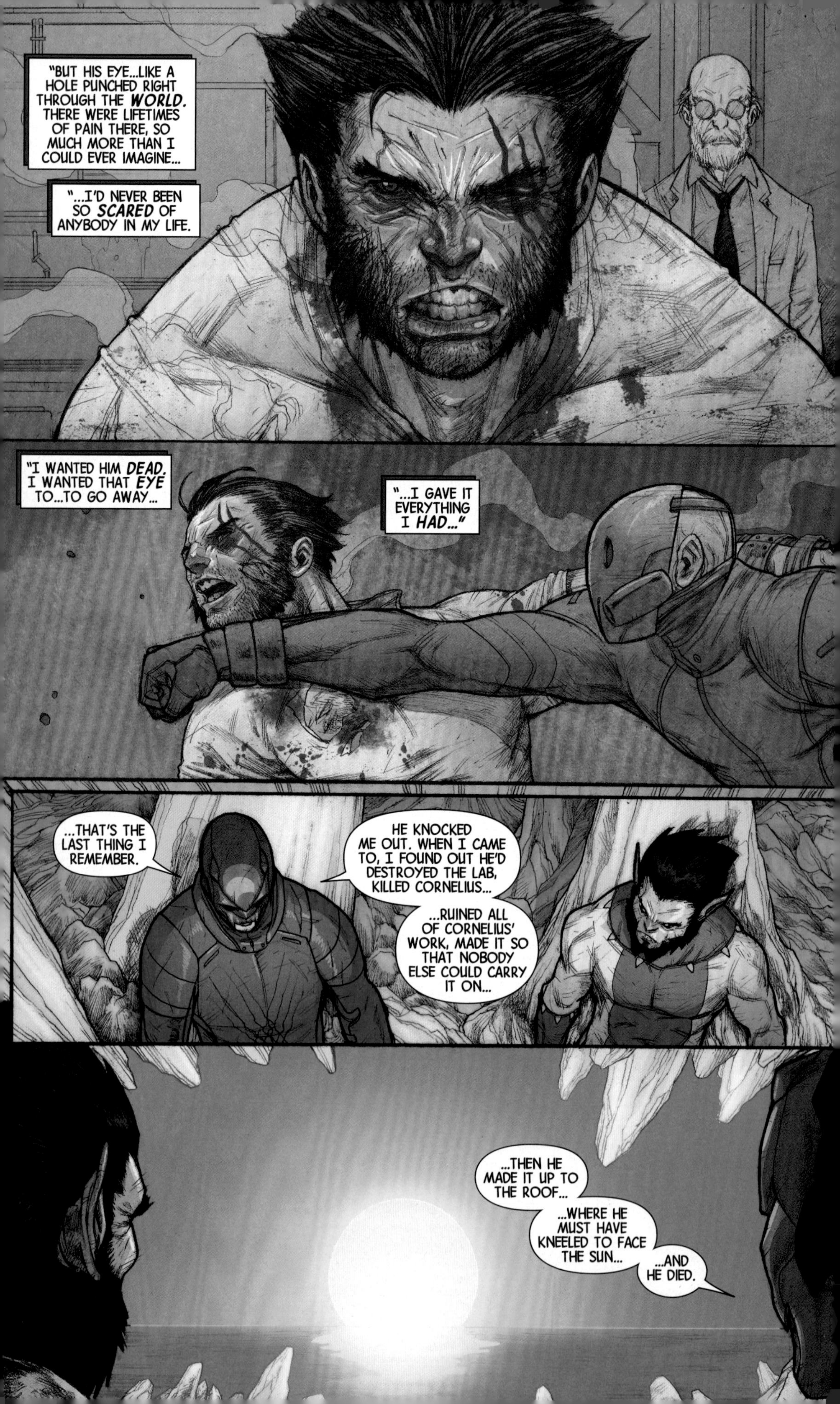
"BUT HIS EYE...LIKE A HOLE PUNCHED RIGHT THROUGH THE WORLD. THERE WERE LIFETIMES OF PAIN THERE, SO MUCH MORE THAN I COULD EVER IMAGINE...
"...I'D NEVER BEEN SO SCARED OF ANYBODY IN MY LIFE.
"I WANTED HIM DEAD. I WANTED THAT EYE TO...TO GO AWAY...
"...I GAVE IT EVERYTHING I HAD..."
...THAT'S THE LAST THING I REMEMBER.
HE KNOCKED ME OUT. WHEN I CAME TO, I FOUND OUT HE'D DESTROYED THE LAB, KILLED CORNELIUS...
...RUINED ALL OF CORNELIUS' WORK, MADE IT SO THAT NOBODY ELSE COULD CARRY IT ON...
...THEN HE MADE IT UP TO THE ROOF...
...WHERE HE MUST HAVE KNEELED TO FACE THE SUN...
...AND HE DIED.

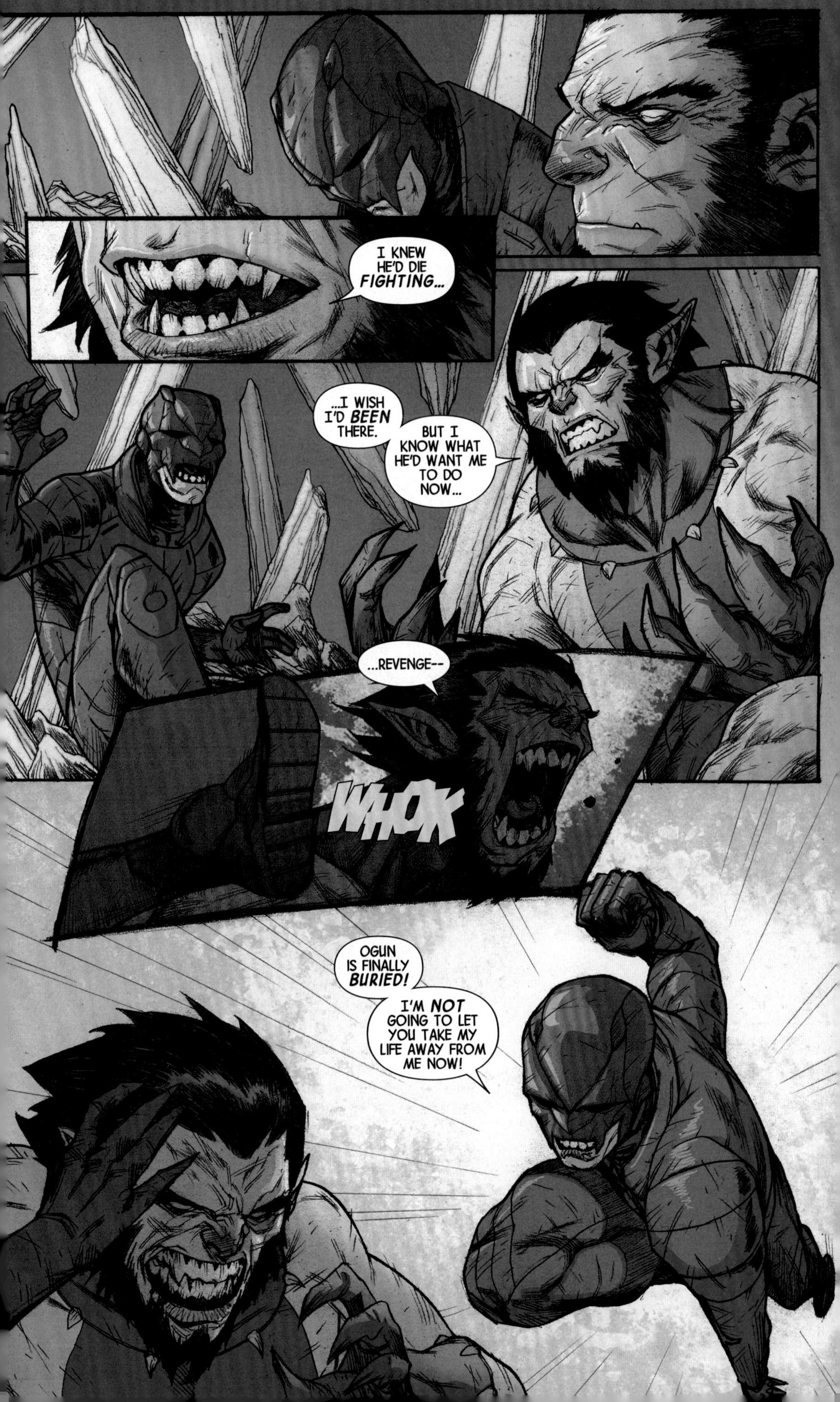

I KNEW HE'D DIE *FIGHTING*...
...I WISH I'D *BEEN* THERE.
BUT I KNOW WHAT HE'D WANT ME TO DO NOW...
...REVENGE--
WHOK
OGUN IS FINALLY *BURIED!*
I'M *NOT* GOING TO LET YOU TAKE MY LIFE AWAY FROM ME NOW!

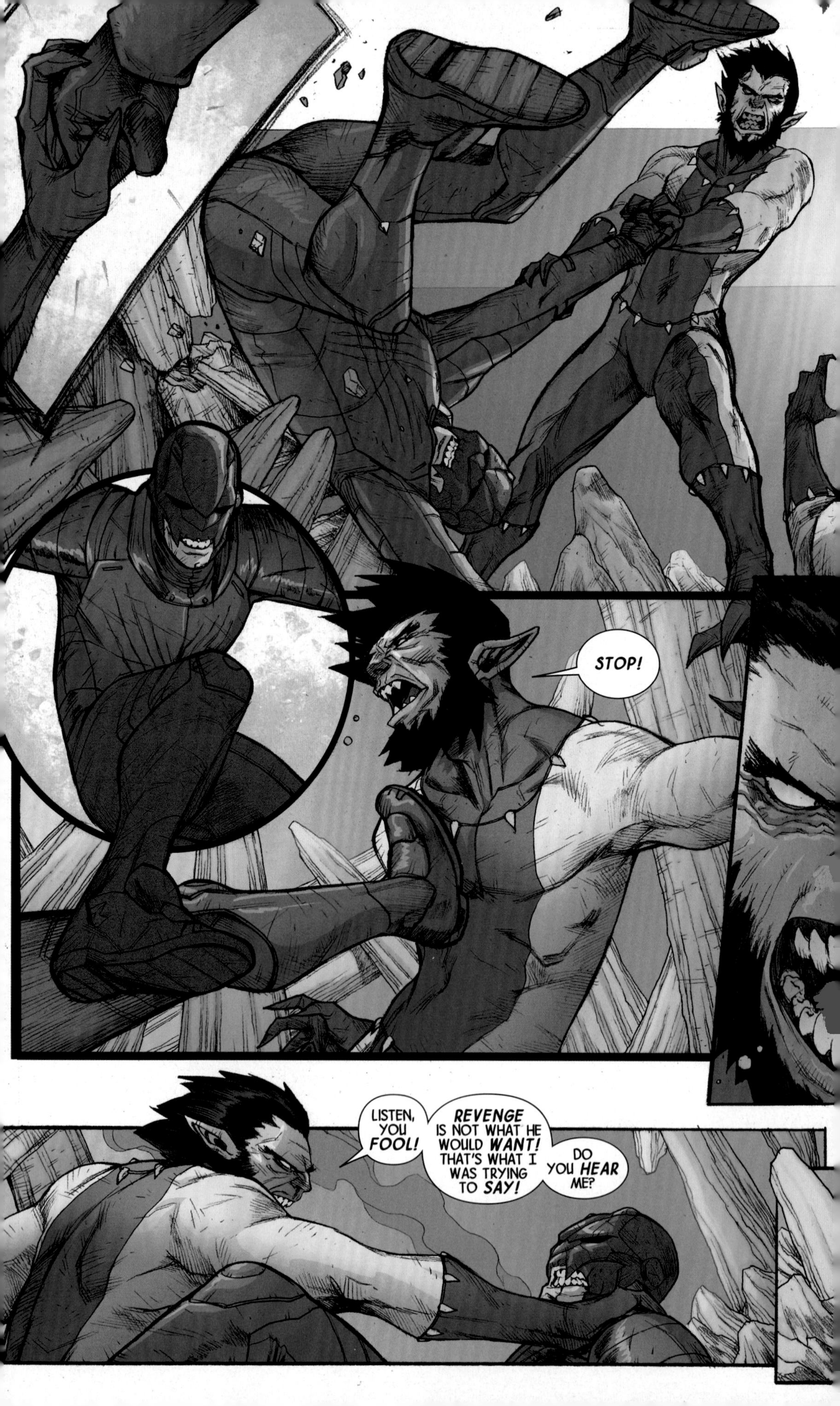
STOP!
LISTEN, YOU FOOL!
REVENGE IS NOT WHAT HE WOULD WANT! THAT'S WHAT I WAS TRYING TO SAY!
DO YOU HEAR ME?

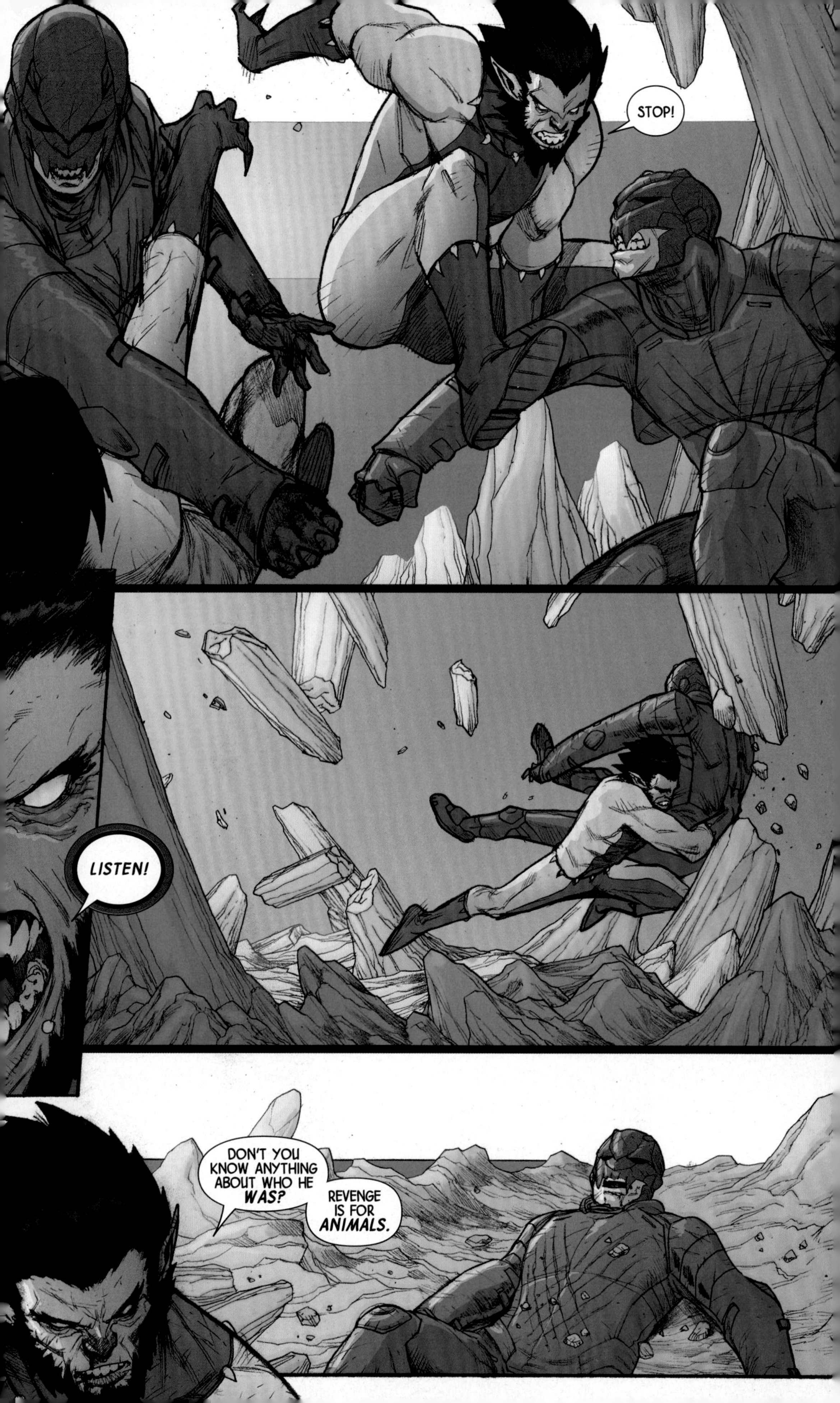
STOP!
LISTEN!
DON'T YOU KNOW ANYTHING ABOUT WHO HE WAS?
REVENGE IS FOR ANIMALS.

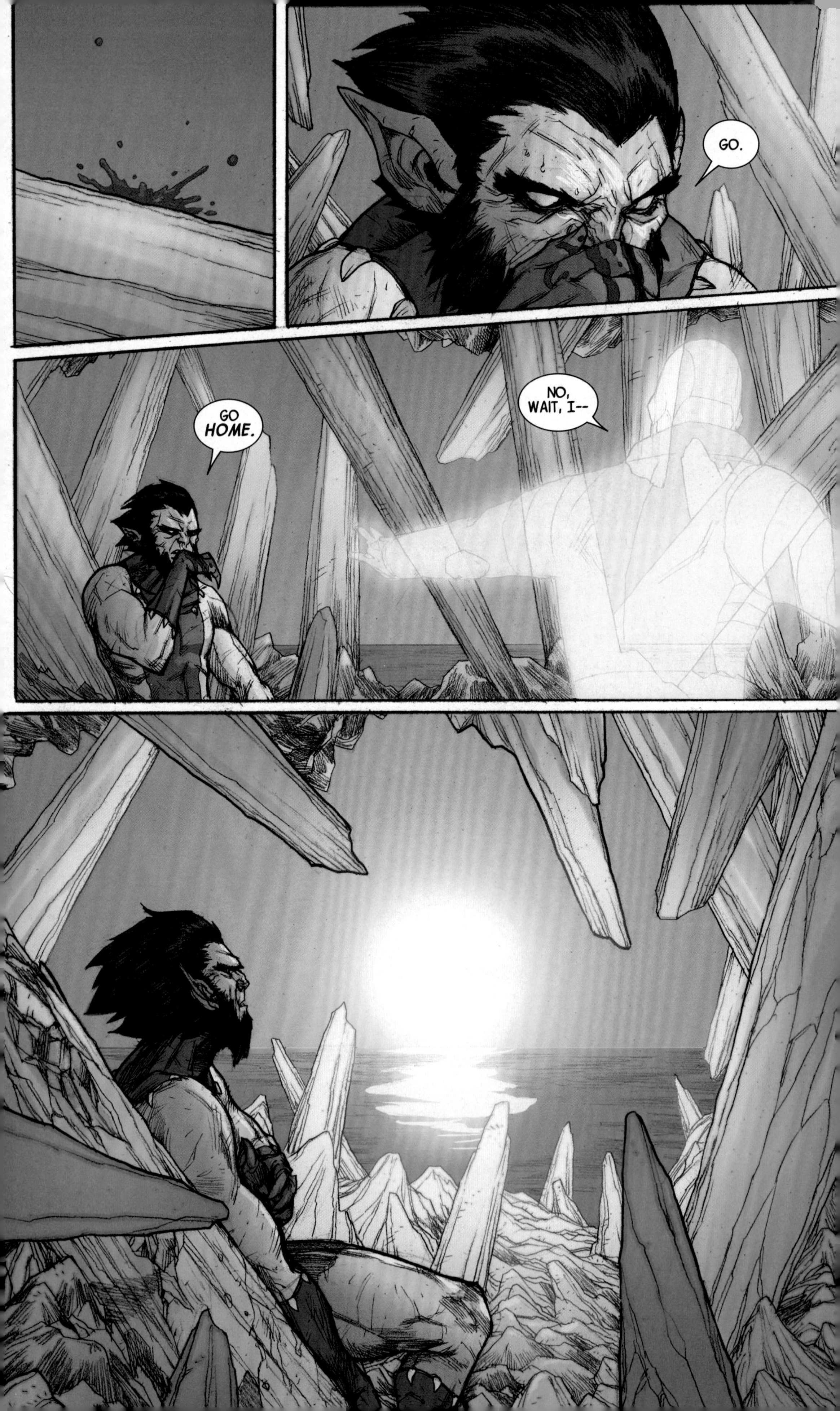
GO.
GO HOME.
NO, WAIT, I--

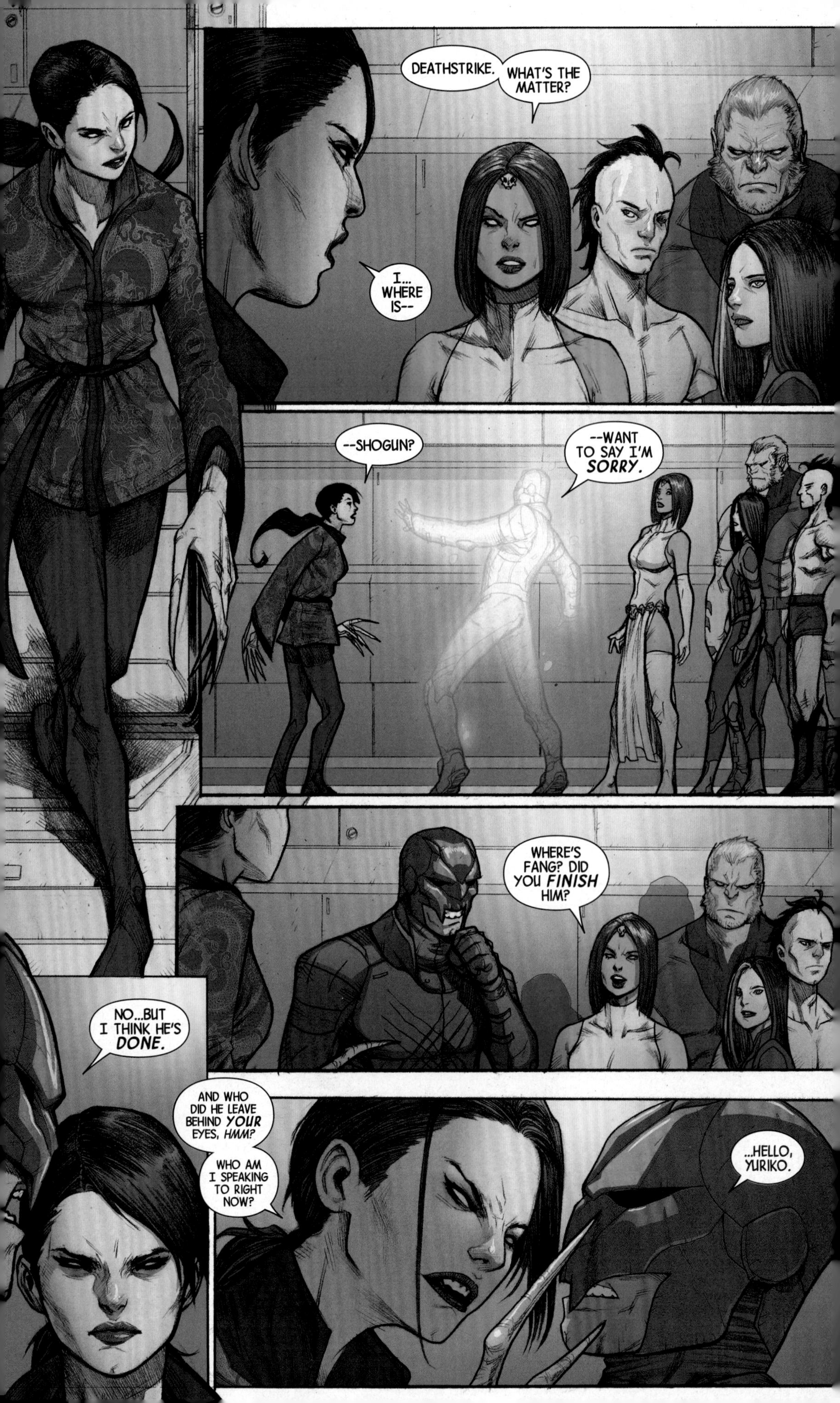
DEATHSTRIKE.
WHAT'S THE MATTER?
I... WHERE IS--
--SHOGUN?
--WANT TO SAY I'M SORRY.
WHERE'S FANG? DID YOU FINISH HIM?
NO...BUT I THINK HE'S DONE.
AND WHO DID HE LEAVE BEHIND YOUR EYES, HMM?
WHO AM I SPEAKING TO RIGHT NOW?
...HELLO, YURIKO.

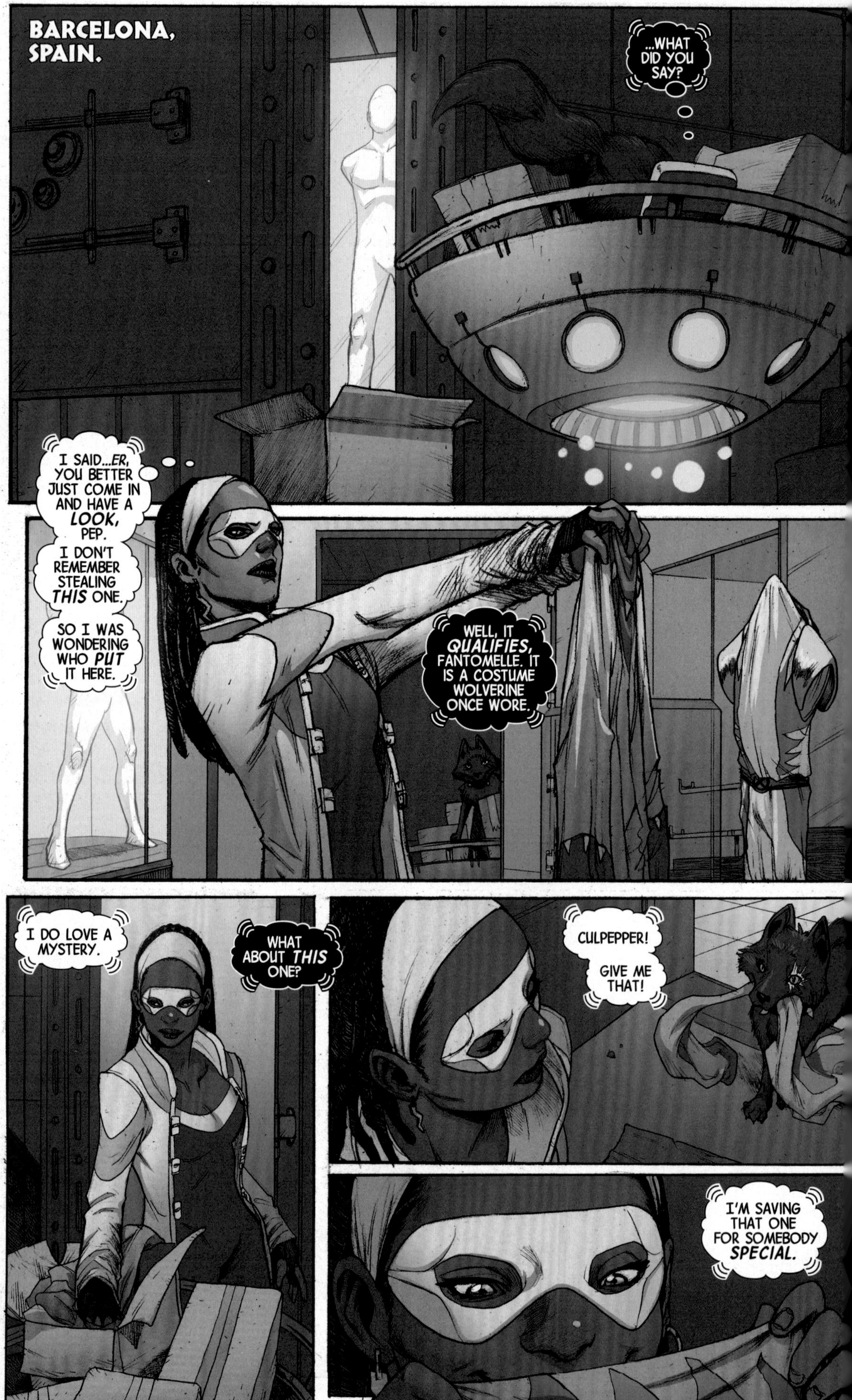
BARCELONA, SPAIN.
...WHAT DID YOU SAY?
I SAID...ER, YOU BETTER JUST COME IN AND HAVE A LOOK, PEP.
I DON'T REMEMBER STEALING THIS ONE.
SO I WAS WONDERING WHO PUT IT HERE.
WELL, IT QUALIFIES, FANTOMELLE. IT IS A COSTUME WOLVERINE ONCE WORE.
I DO LOVE A MYSTERY.
WHAT ABOUT THIS ONE?
CULPEPPER!
GIVE ME THAT!
I'M SAVING THAT ONE FOR SOMEBODY SPECIAL.

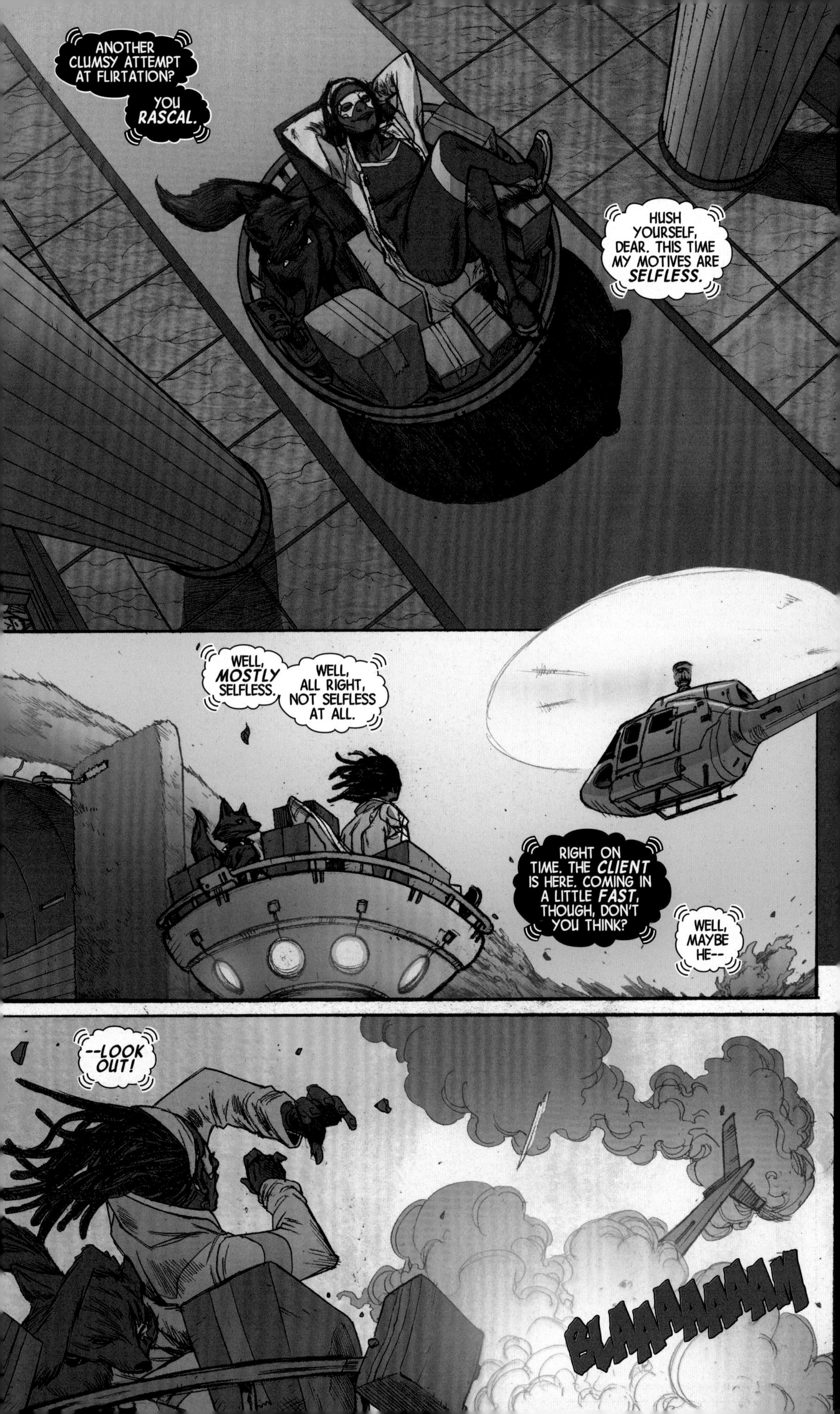
ANOTHER CLUMSY ATTEMPT AT FLIRTATION?
YOU RASCAL.
HUSH YOURSELF, DEAR. THIS TIME MY MOTIVES ARE SELFLESS.
WELL, MOSTLY SELFLESS.
WELL, ALL RIGHT, NOT SELFLESS AT ALL.
RIGHT ON TIME. THE CLIENT IS HERE. COMING IN A LITTLE FAST, THOUGH, DON'T YOU THINK?
WELL, MAYBE HE--
--LOOK OUT!
BLAAAAAAAM

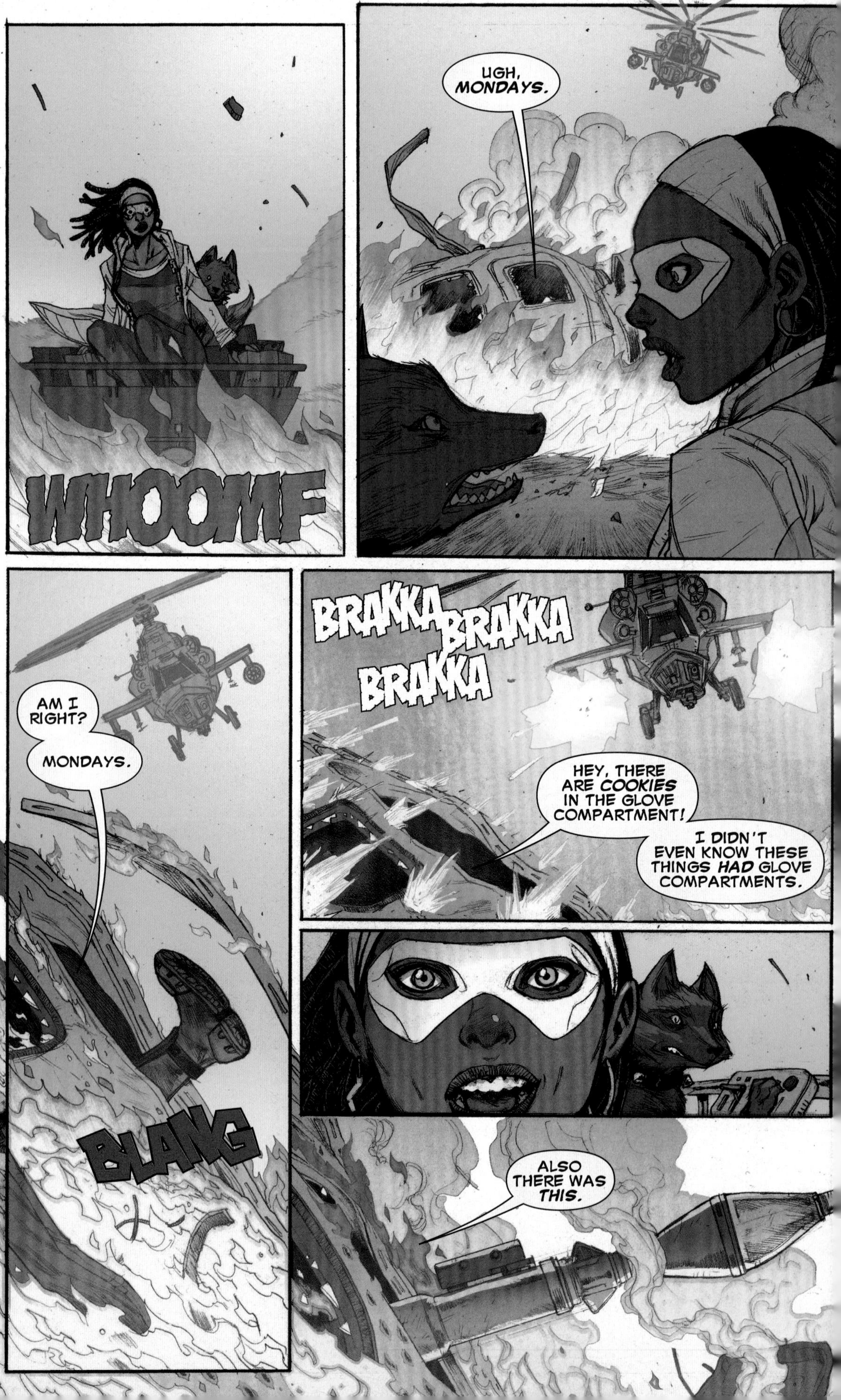
WHOOMF
UGH, MONDAYS.
AM I RIGHT?
MONDAYS.
BRAKKA BRAKKA BRAKKA
HEY, THERE ARE COOKIES IN THE GLOVE COMPARTMENT!
I DIDN'T EVEN KNOW THESE THINGS HAD GLOVE COMPARTMENTS.
BLANG
ALSO THERE WAS THIS.

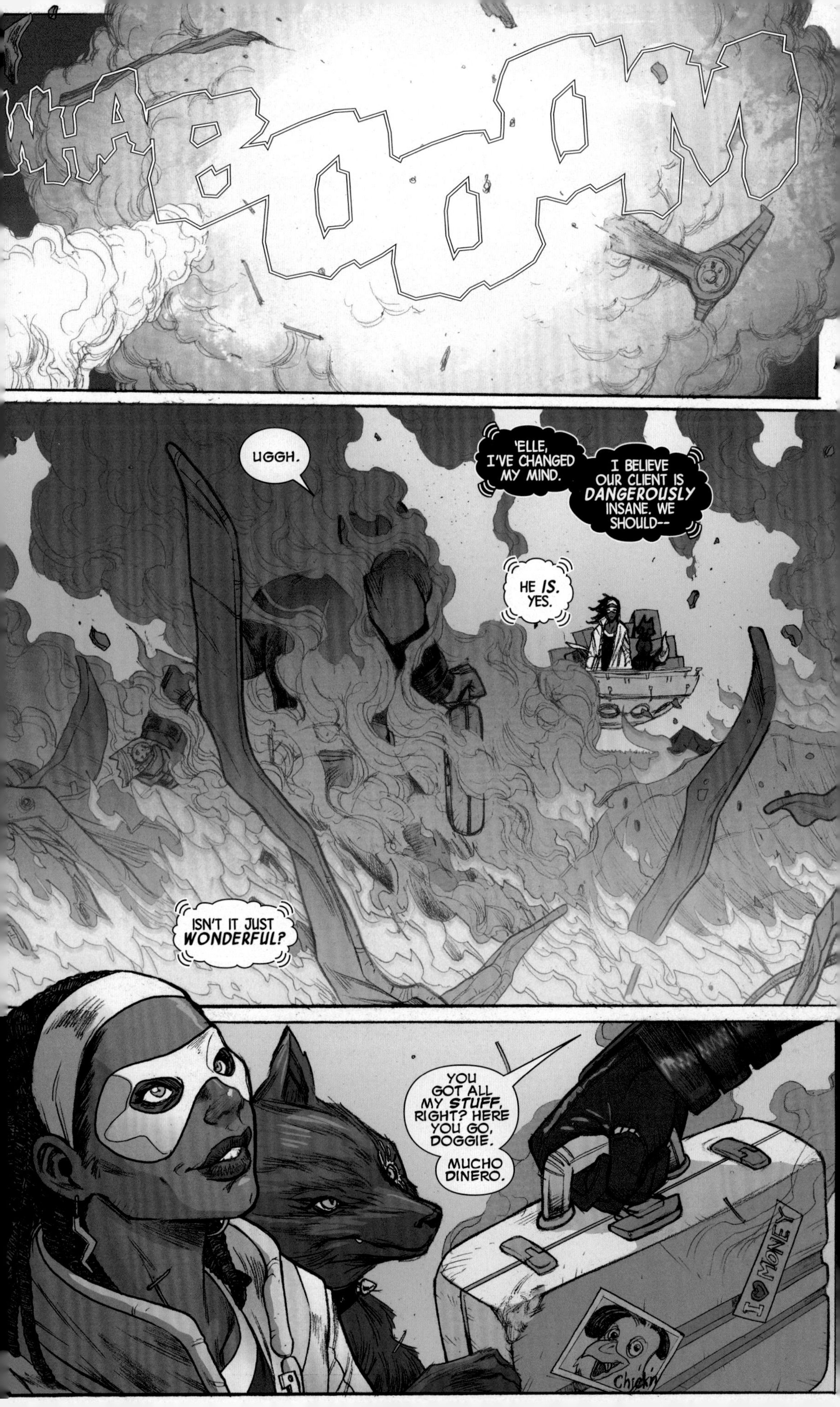
WHA-BOOOM
UGGH.
'ELLE, I'VE CHANGED MY MIND.
I BELIEVE OUR CLIENT IS DANGEROUSLY INSANE. WE SHOULD--
HE IS. YES.
ISN'T IT JUST WONDERFUL?
YOU GOT ALL MY STUFF, RIGHT? HERE YOU GO, DOGGIE.
MUCHO DINERO.
I ♥ MONEY
Chickn

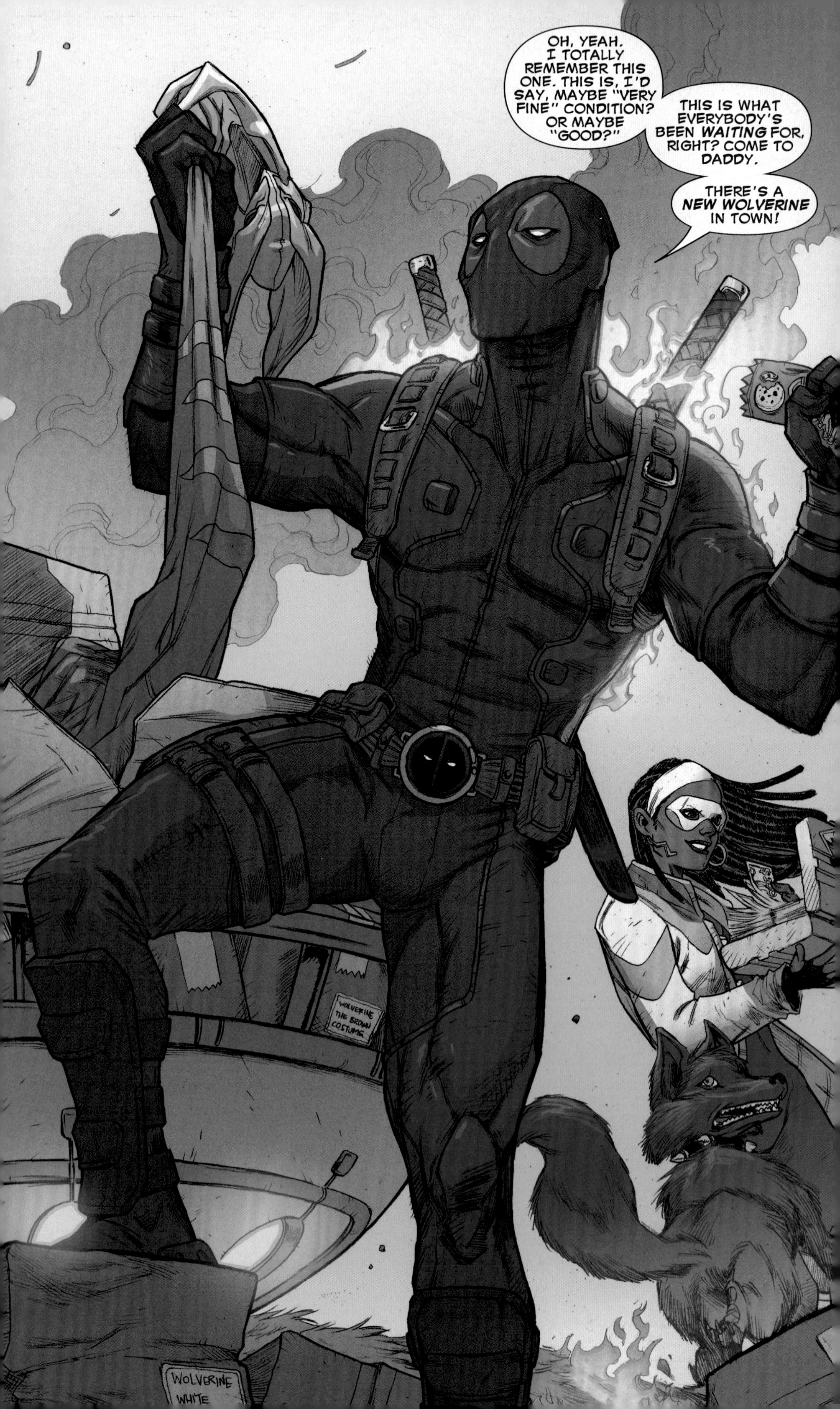
OH, YEAH. I TOTALLY REMEMBER THIS ONE. THIS IS, I'D SAY, MAYBE "VERY FINE" CONDITION? OR MAYBE "GOOD?"
THIS IS WHAT EVERYBODY'S BEEN WAITING FOR, RIGHT? COME TO DADDY.
THERE'S A NEW WOLVERINE IN TOWN!
WOLVERINE THE BROWN COSTUME
WOLVERINE WHITE

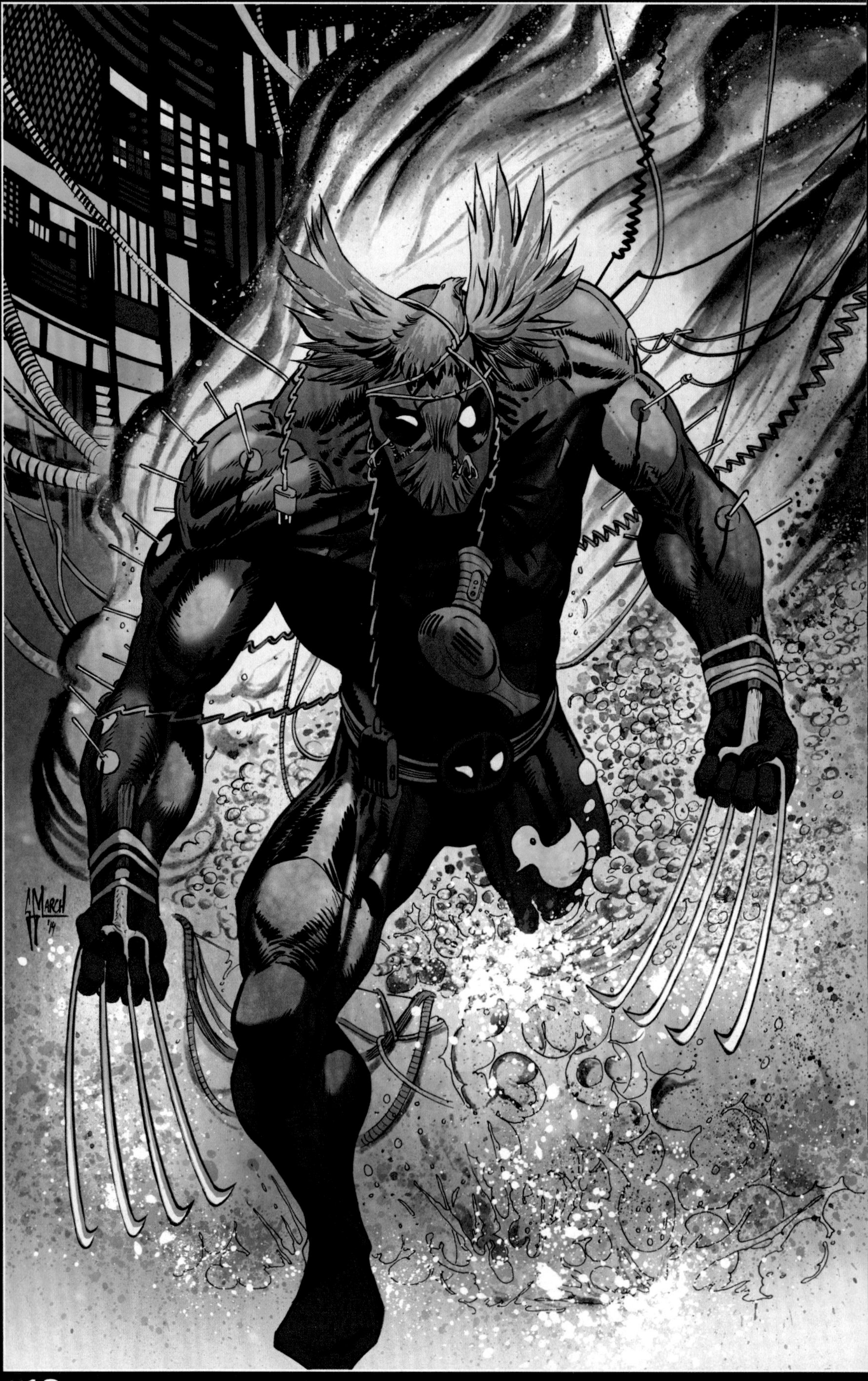

#13

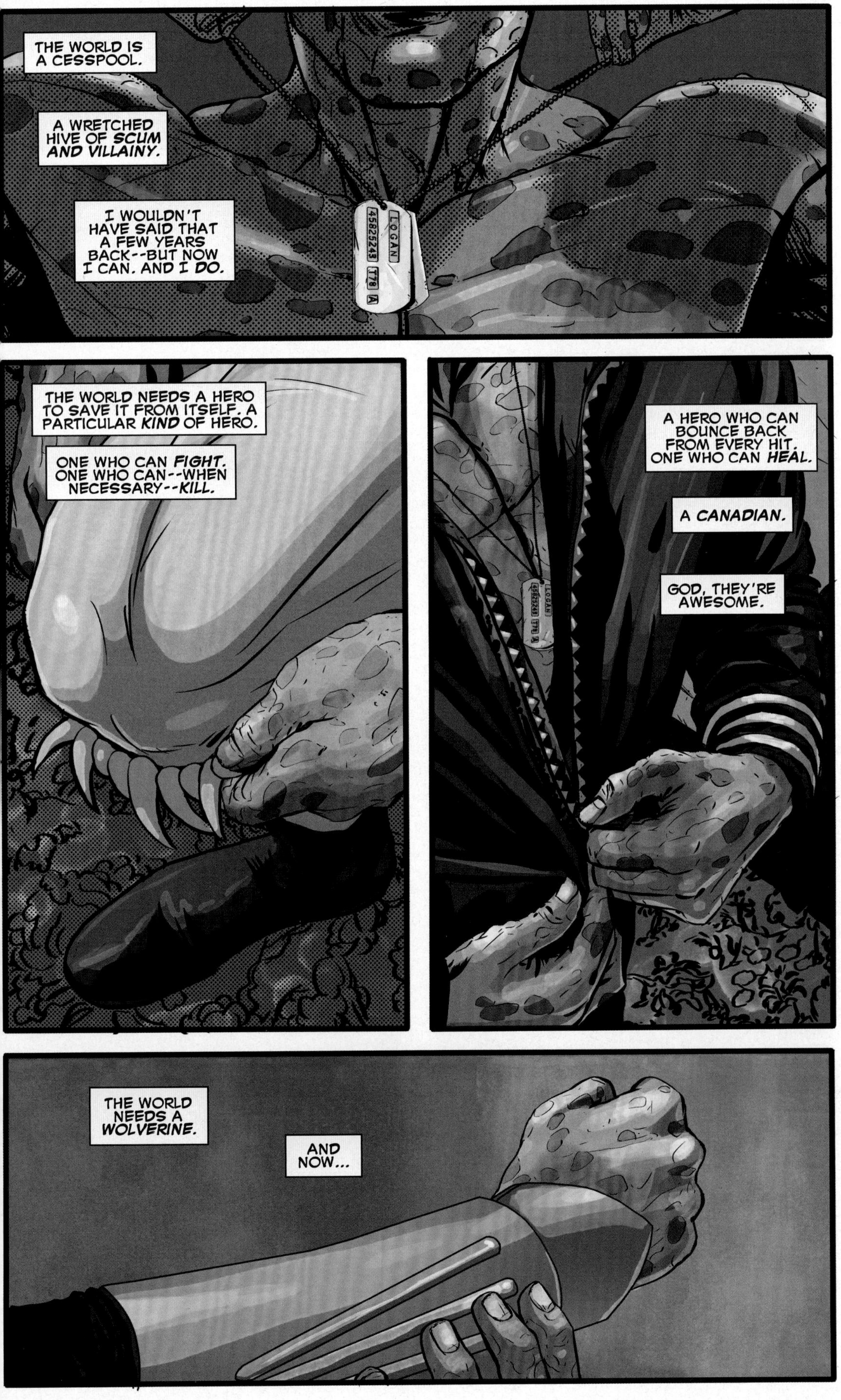
THE WORLD IS A CESSPOOL.
A WRETCHED HIVE OF SCUM AND VILLAINY.
I WOULDN'T HAVE SAID THAT A FEW YEARS BACK--BUT NOW I CAN. AND I DO.
LOGAN
45825243
1T78
A
THE WORLD NEEDS A HERO TO SAVE IT FROM ITSELF. A PARTICULAR KIND OF HERO.
ONE WHO CAN FIGHT. ONE WHO CAN--WHEN NECESSARY--KILL.
A HERO WHO CAN BOUNCE BACK FROM EVERY HIT. ONE WHO CAN HEAL.
A CANADIAN.
GOD, THEY'RE AWESOME.
THE WORLD NEEDS A WOLVERINE.
AND NOW...

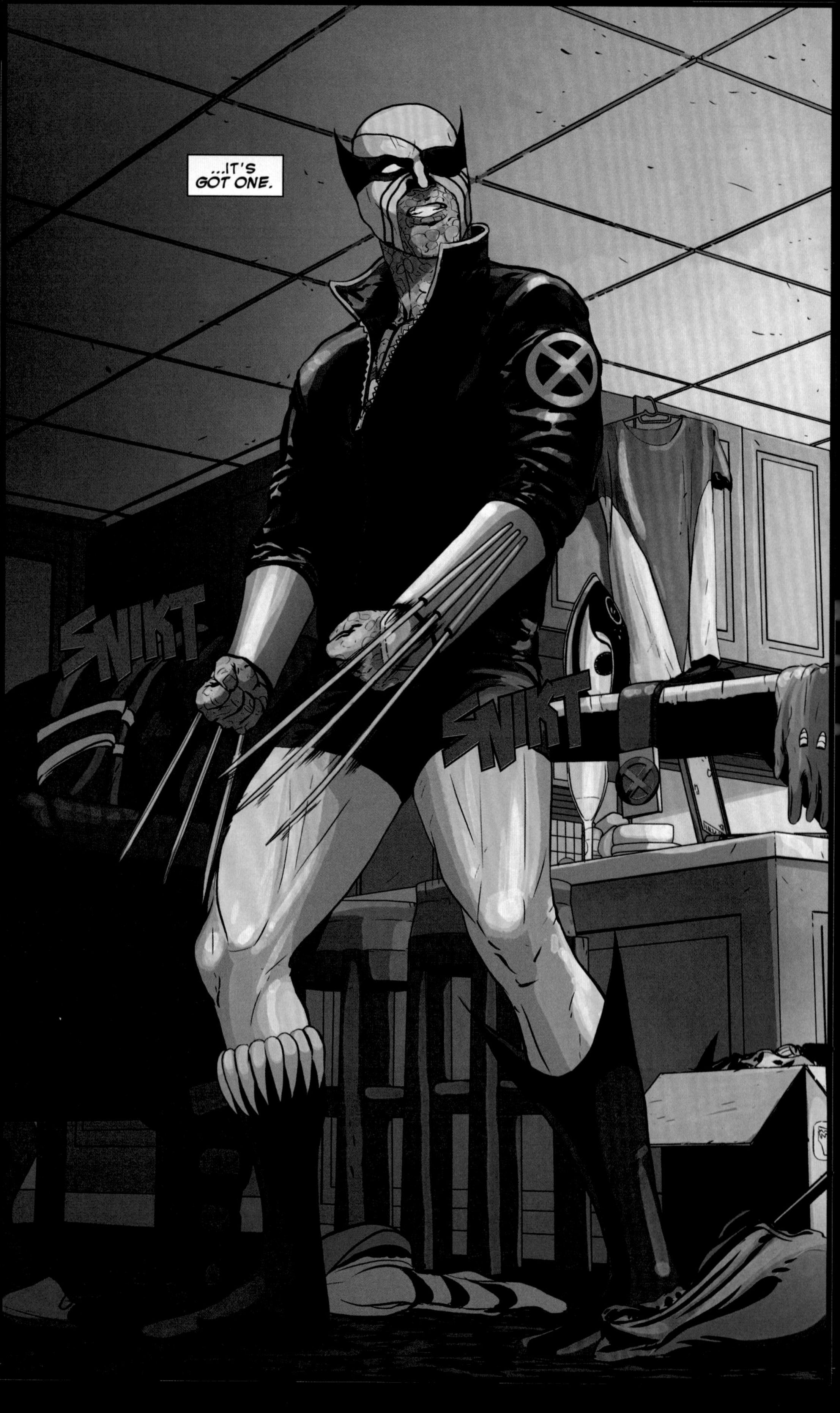
...IT'S
GOT ONE.
SNIKT
SNIKT

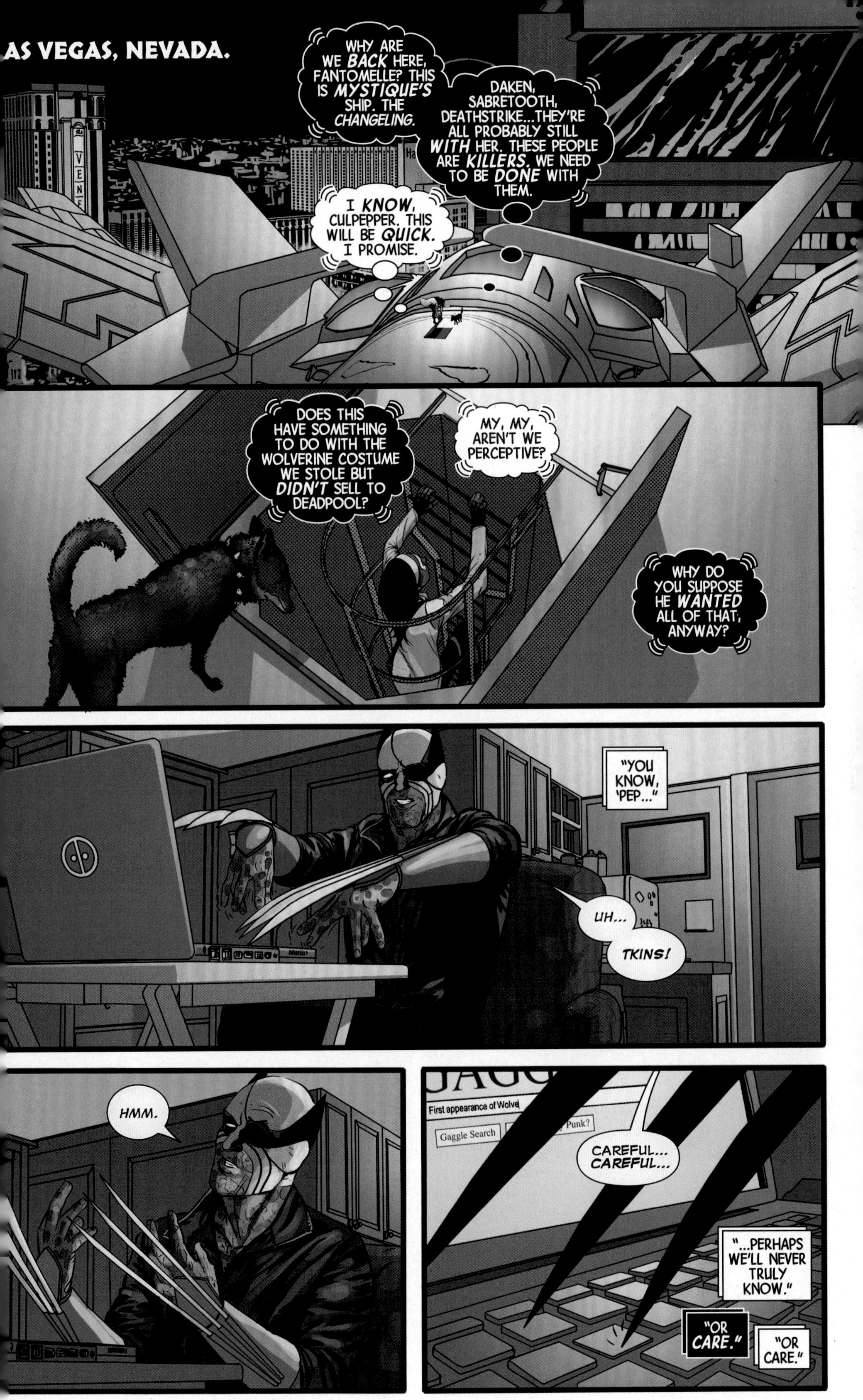
AS VEGAS, NEVADA.
WHY ARE WE BACK HERE, FANTOMELLE? THIS IS MYSTIQUE'S SHIP. THE CHANGELING.
DAKEN, SABRETOOTH, DEATHSTRIKE...THEY'RE ALL PROBABLY STILL WITH HER. THESE PEOPLE ARE KILLERS. WE NEED TO BE DONE WITH THEM.
I KNOW, CULPEPPER. THIS WILL BE QUICK. I PROMISE.
DOES THIS HAVE SOMETHING TO DO WITH THE WOLVERINE COSTUME WE STOLE BUT DIDN'T SELL TO DEADPOOL?
MY, MY, AREN'T WE PERCEPTIVE?
WHY DO YOU SUPPOSE HE WANTED ALL OF THAT, ANYWAY?
"YOU KNOW, 'PEP..."
UH...
TKINS!
HMM.
First appearance of Wolve
Gaggle Search
CAREFUL... CAREFUL...
"...PERHAPS WE'LL NEVER TRULY KNOW."
"OR CARE."
"OR CARE."

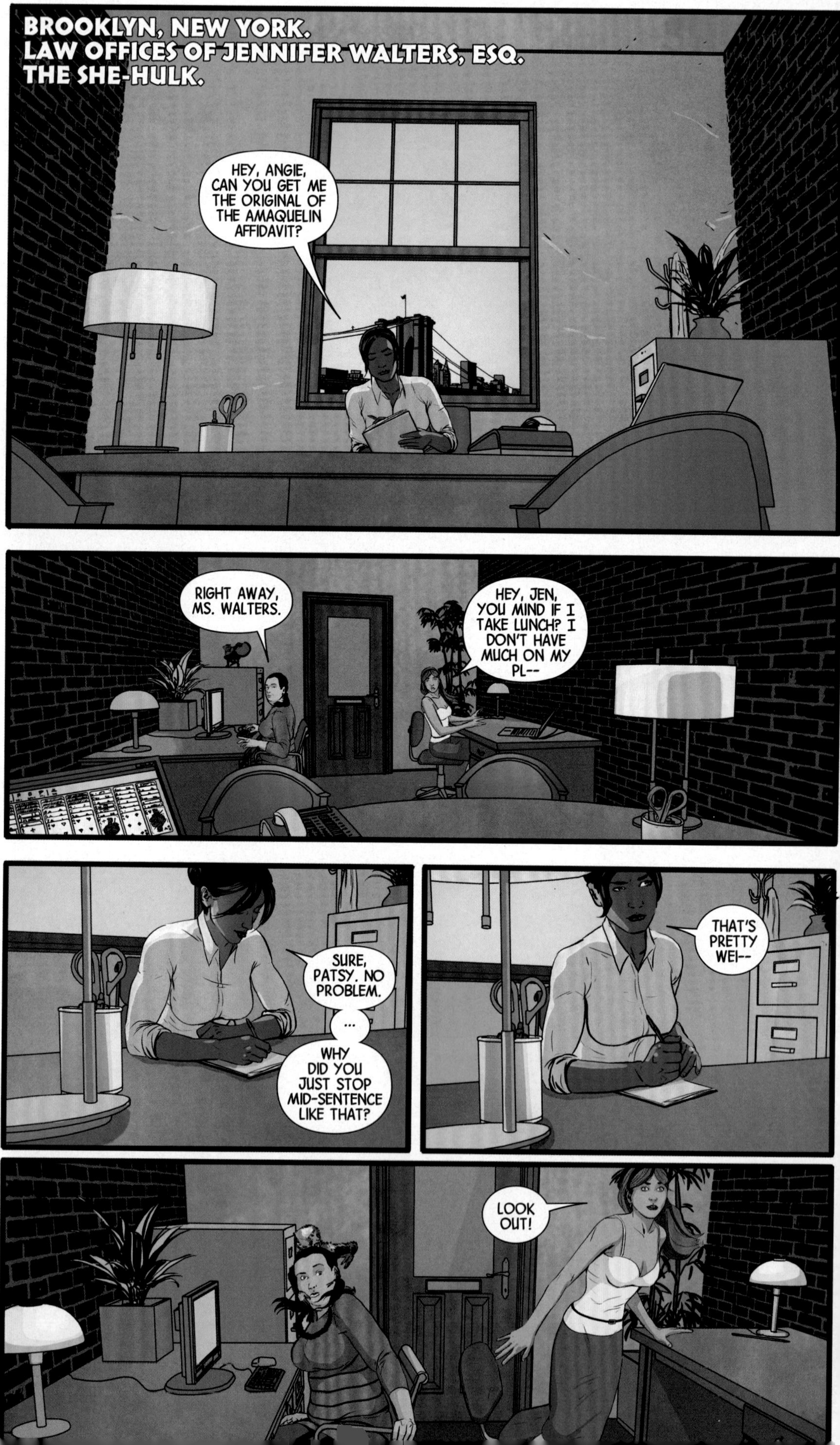
BROOKLYN, NEW YORK.
LAW OFFICES OF JENNIFER WALTERS, ESQ.
THE SHE-HULK.
HEY, ANGIE, CAN YOU GET ME THE ORIGINAL OF THE AMAQUELIN AFFIDAVIT?
RIGHT AWAY, MS. WALTERS.
HEY, JEN, YOU MIND IF I TAKE LUNCH? I DON'T HAVE MUCH ON MY PL--
SURE, PATSY. NO PROBLEM.
...
WHY DID YOU JUST STOP MID-SENTENCE LIKE THAT?
THAT'S PRETTY WEI--
LOOK OUT!

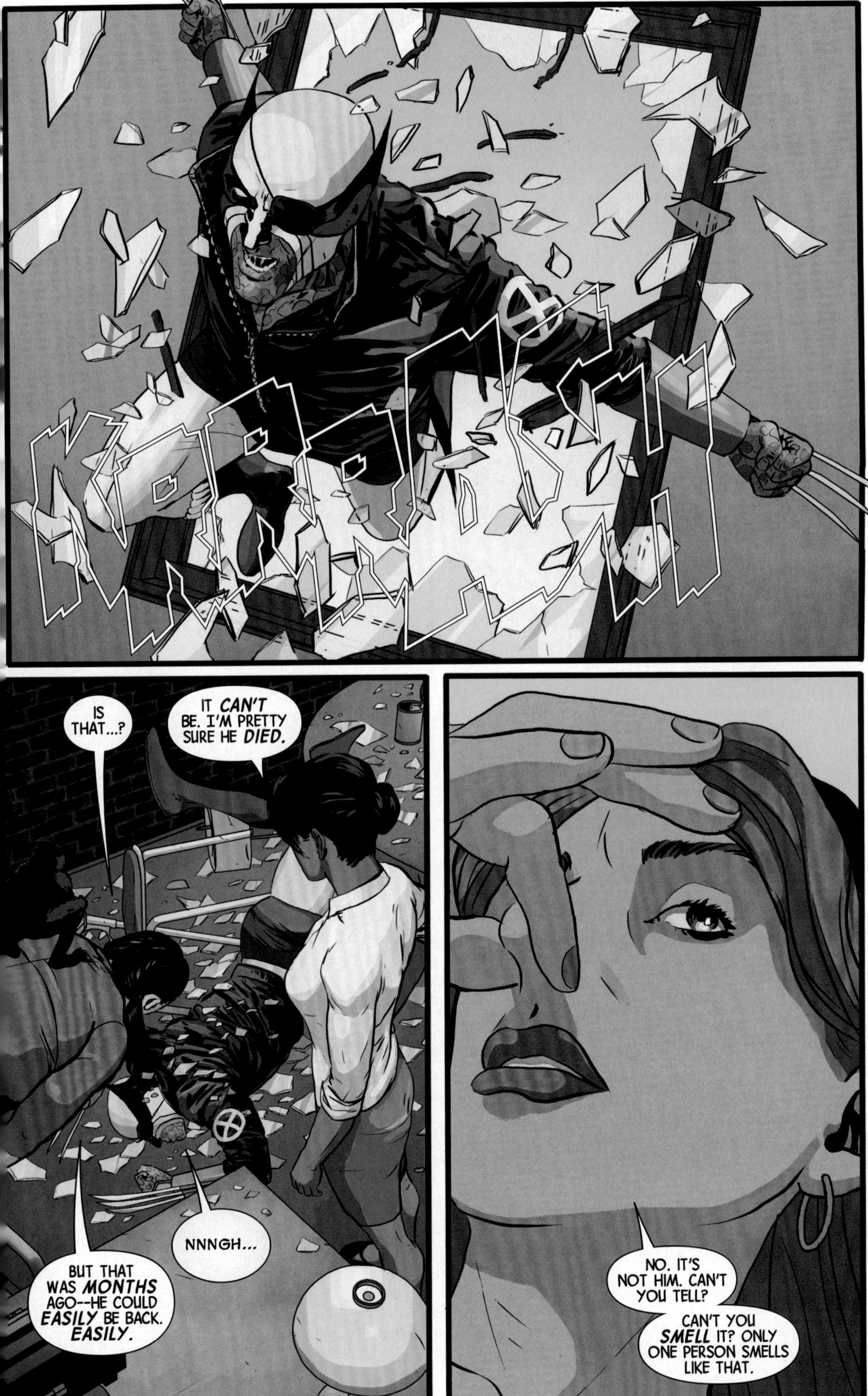
IS THAT...?
IT CAN'T BE. I'M PRETTY SURE HE DIED.
BUT THAT WAS MONTHS AGO--HE COULD EASILY BE BACK. EASILY.
NNNGH...
NO. IT'S NOT HIM. CAN'T YOU TELL?
CAN'T YOU SMELL IT? ONLY ONE PERSON SMELLS LIKE THAT.

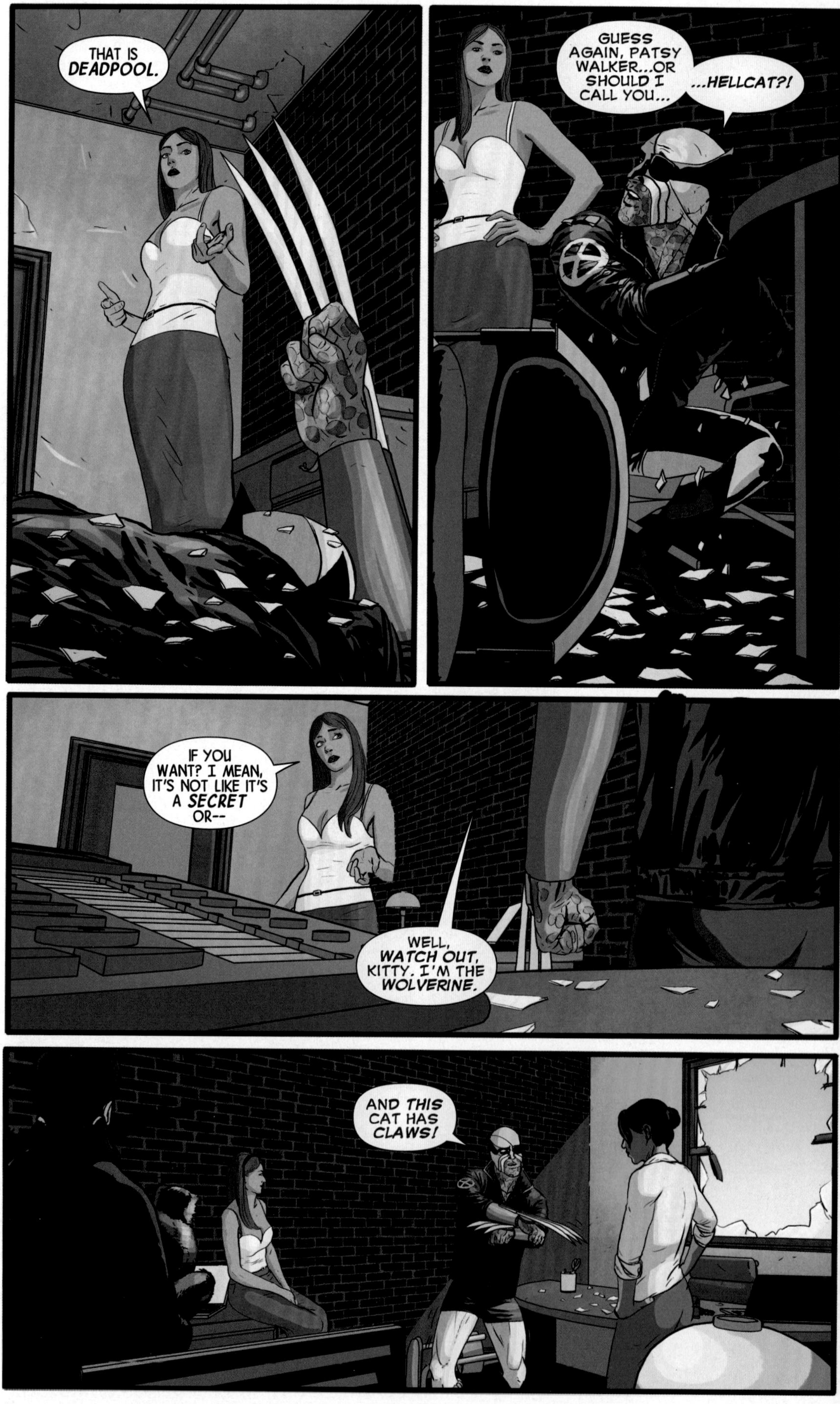

THAT IS DEADPOOL.
GUESS AGAIN, PATSY WALKER...OR SHOULD I CALL YOU...
...HELLCAT?!
IF YOU WANT? I MEAN, IT'S NOT LIKE IT'S A SECRET OR--
WELL, WATCH OUT, KITTY. I'M THE WOLVERINE.
AND THIS CAT HAS CLAWS!

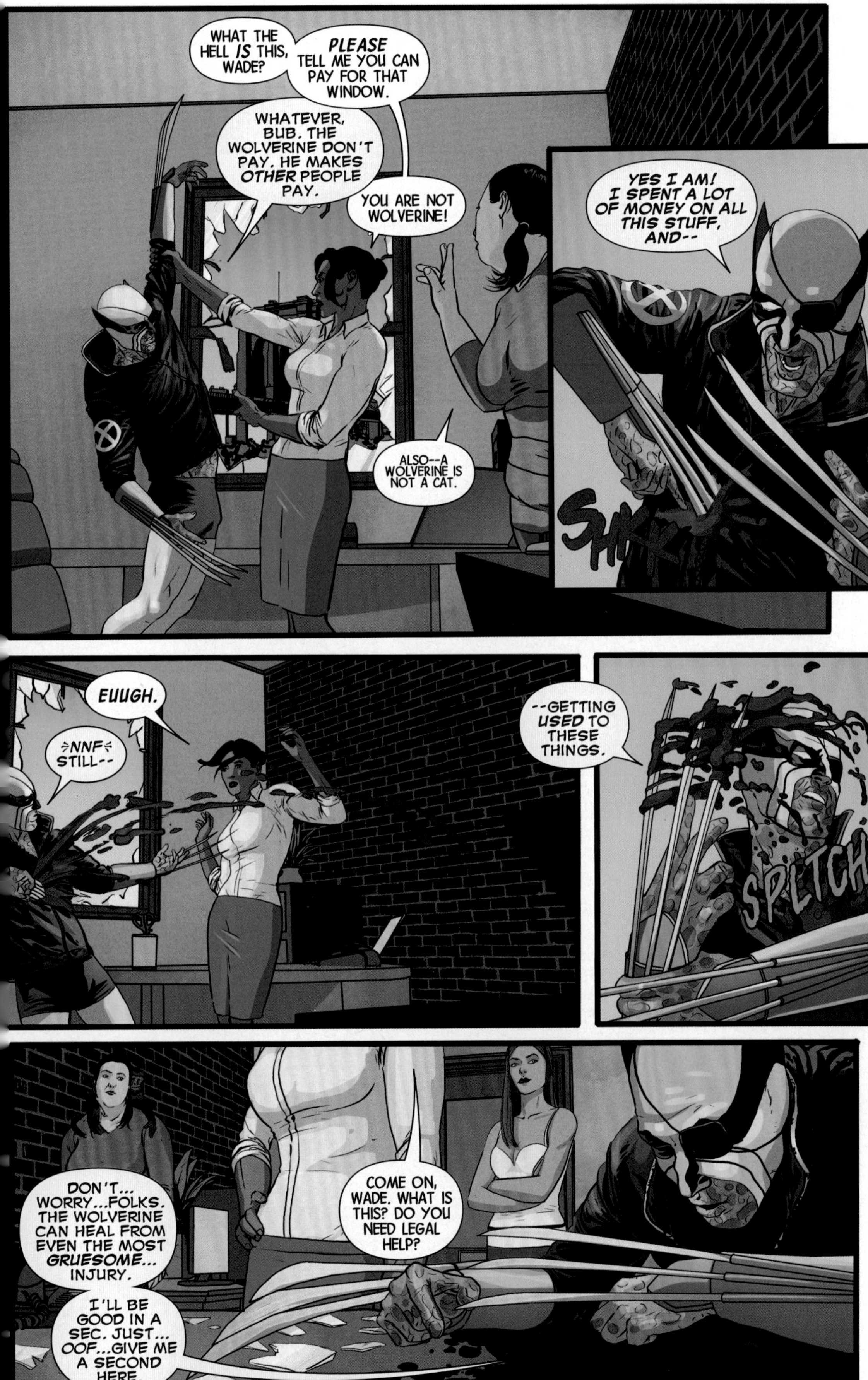
WHAT THE HELL *IS* THIS, WADE?
PLEASE TELL ME YOU CAN PAY FOR THAT WINDOW.
WHATEVER, BUB. THE WOLVERINE DON'T PAY. HE MAKES *OTHER* PEOPLE PAY.
YOU ARE NOT WOLVERINE!
ALSO--A WOLVERINE IS NOT A CAT.
YES I AM! I SPENT A LOT OF MONEY ON ALL THIS STUFF, AND--
SHKK
EUUGH.
NNF STILL--
--GETTING *USED* TO THESE THINGS.
SPLTCH
DON'T... WORRY...FOLKS. THE WOLVERINE CAN HEAL FROM EVEN THE MOST *GRUESOME*... INJURY.
I'LL BE GOOD IN A SEC. JUST... OOF...GIVE ME A SECOND HERE.
COME ON, WADE. WHAT IS THIS? DO YOU NEED LEGAL HELP?

PROBABLY. BUT THAT'S NOT WHY I'M HERE.

THE FIRST THING WOLVERINE EVER DID WAS GET INTO A FIGHT WITH *THE HULK.* I LOOKED IT UP.

IF I'M GOING TO DO THIS, I WANT TO DO IT *RIGHT.*

YOU CAN'T BE SERIOUS.

WHY DOES EVERYONE ALWAYS *SAY* THAT TO ME?

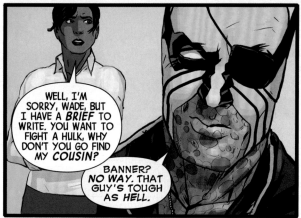

WELL, I'M SORRY, WADE, BUT I HAVE A *BRIEF* TO WRITE. YOU WANT TO FIGHT A HULK, WHY DON'T YOU GO FIND MY *COUSIN?*

BANNER? *NO WAY.* THAT GUY'S TOUGH AS *HELL.*

AND *WHAT...I'M NOT?*

UHH...

WHOA, WHOA, HOLD ON NOW--

YOU KNOW, WHY NOT?

WINDOW'S BUSTED ANYWAY.

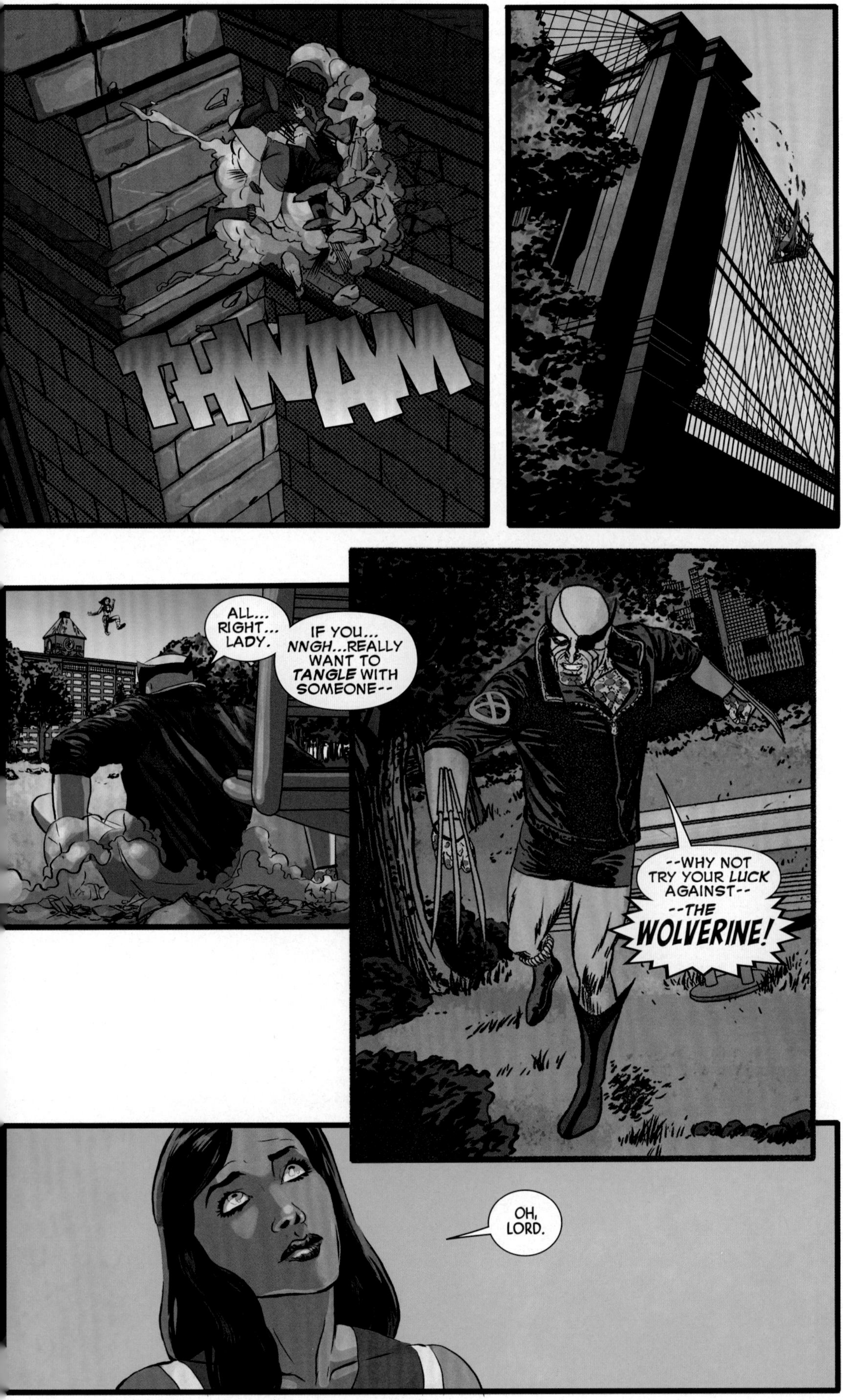
THWAM
ALL... RIGHT... LADY.
IF YOU... NNGH...REALLY WANT TO TANGLE WITH SOMEONE--
--WHY NOT TRY YOUR LUCK AGAINST--
--THE WOLVERINE!
OH, LORD.

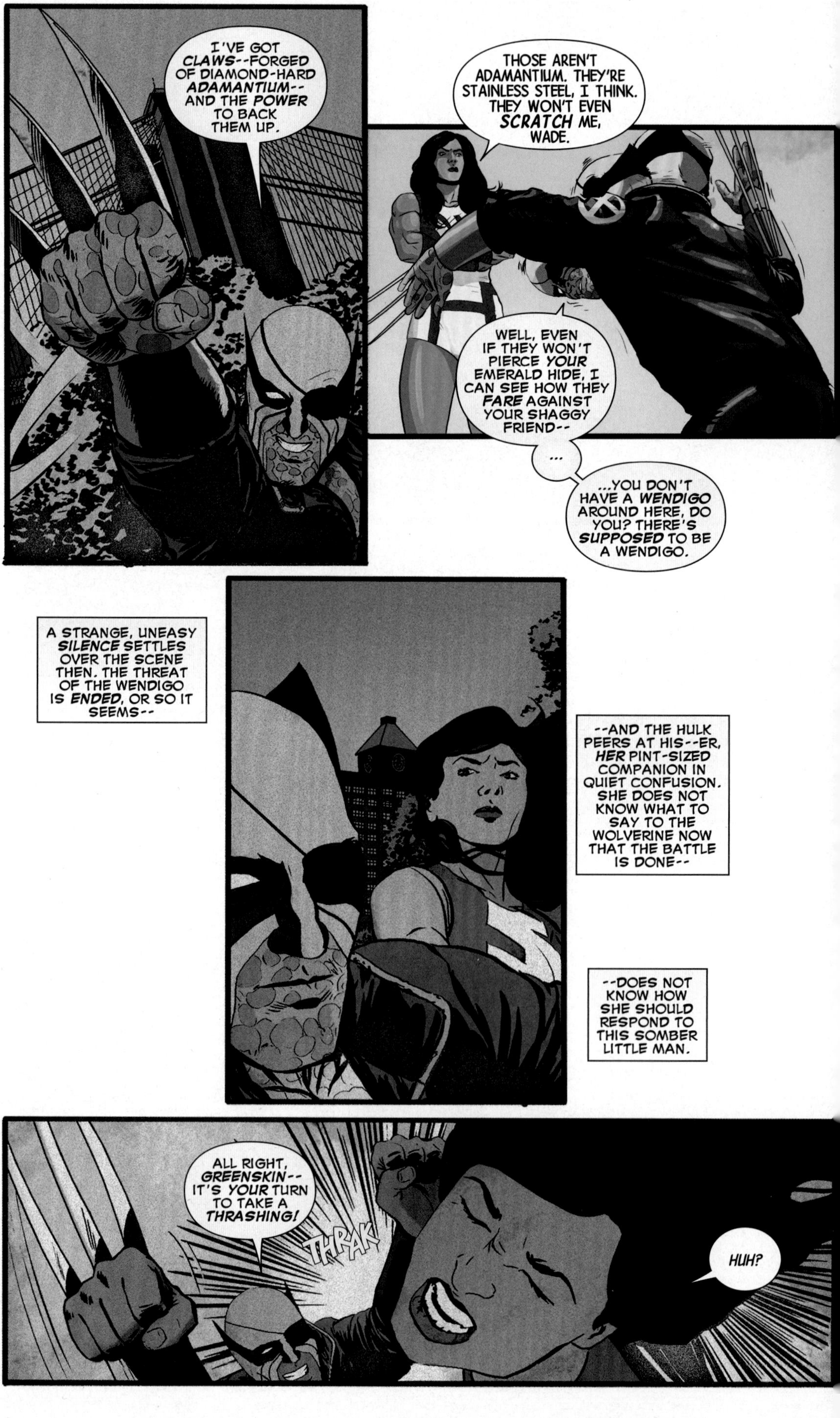

I'VE GOT CLAWS--FORGED OF DIAMOND-HARD ADAMANTIUM--AND THE POWER TO BACK THEM UP.
THOSE AREN'T ADAMANTIUM. THEY'RE STAINLESS STEEL, I THINK. THEY WON'T EVEN SCRATCH ME, WADE.
WELL, EVEN IF THEY WON'T PIERCE YOUR EMERALD HIDE, I CAN SEE HOW THEY FARE AGAINST YOUR SHAGGY FRIEND--
...
...YOU DON'T HAVE A WENDIGO AROUND HERE, DO YOU? THERE'S SUPPOSED TO BE A WENDIGO.
A STRANGE, UNEASY SILENCE SETTLES OVER THE SCENE THEN. THE THREAT OF THE WENDIGO IS ENDED, OR SO IT SEEMS--
--AND THE HULK PEERS AT HIS--ER, HER PINT-SIZED COMPANION IN QUIET CONFUSION. SHE DOES NOT KNOW WHAT TO SAY TO THE WOLVERINE NOW THAT THE BATTLE IS DONE--
--DOES NOT KNOW HOW SHE SHOULD RESPOND TO THIS SOMBER LITTLE MAN.
ALL RIGHT, GREENSKIN--IT'S YOUR TURN TO TAKE A THRASHING!
THRAK
HUH?

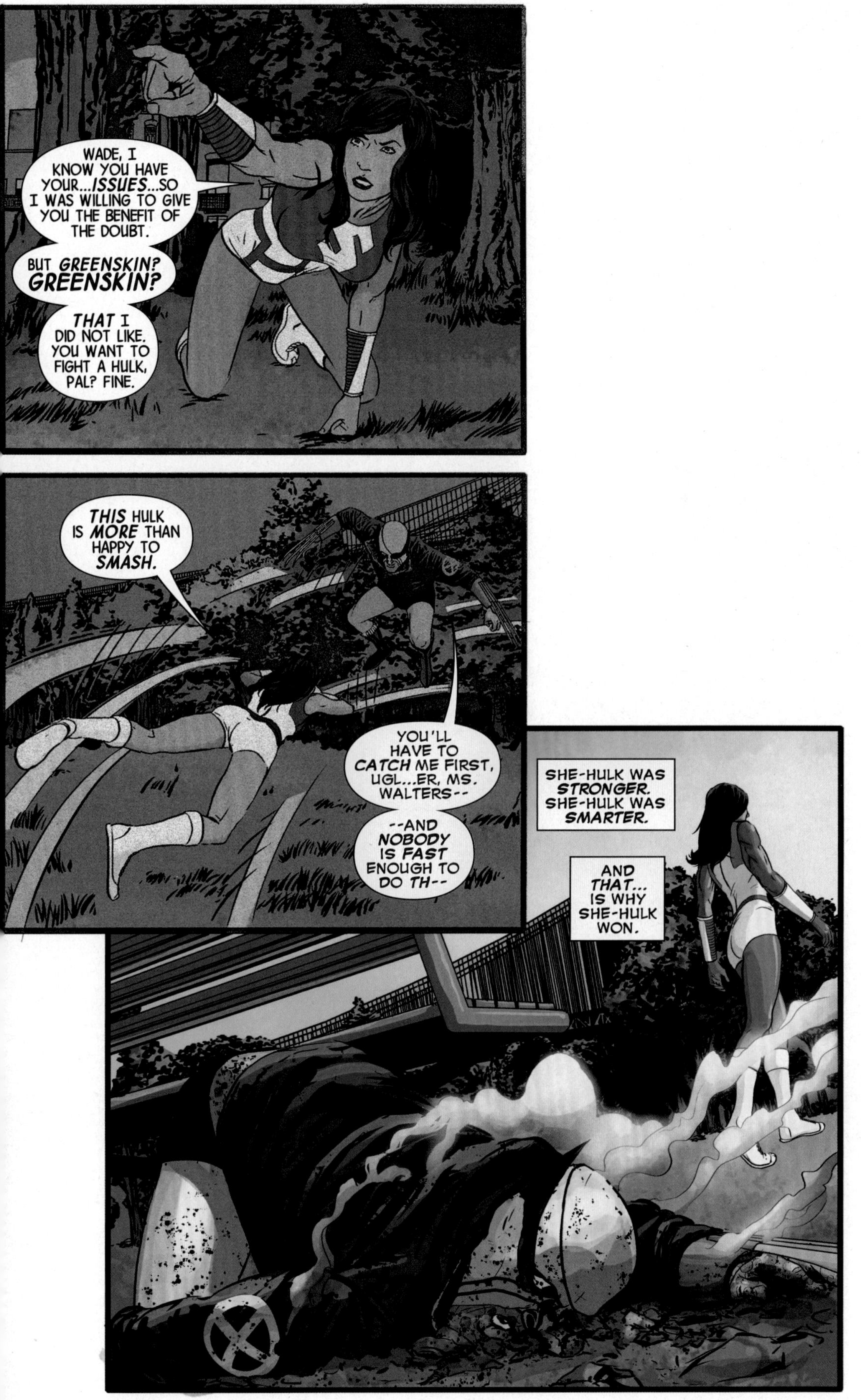
WADE, I KNOW YOU HAVE YOUR...ISSUES...SO I WAS WILLING TO GIVE YOU THE BENEFIT OF THE DOUBT.
BUT GREENSKIN? GREENSKIN?
THAT I DID NOT LIKE. YOU WANT TO FIGHT A HULK, PAL? FINE.
THIS HULK IS MORE THAN HAPPY TO SMASH.
YOU'LL HAVE TO CATCH ME FIRST, UGL...ER, MS. WALTERS--
--AND NOBODY IS FAST ENOUGH TO DO TH--
SHE-HULK WAS STRONGER. SHE-HULK WAS SMARTER.
AND THAT... IS WHY SHE-HULK WON.

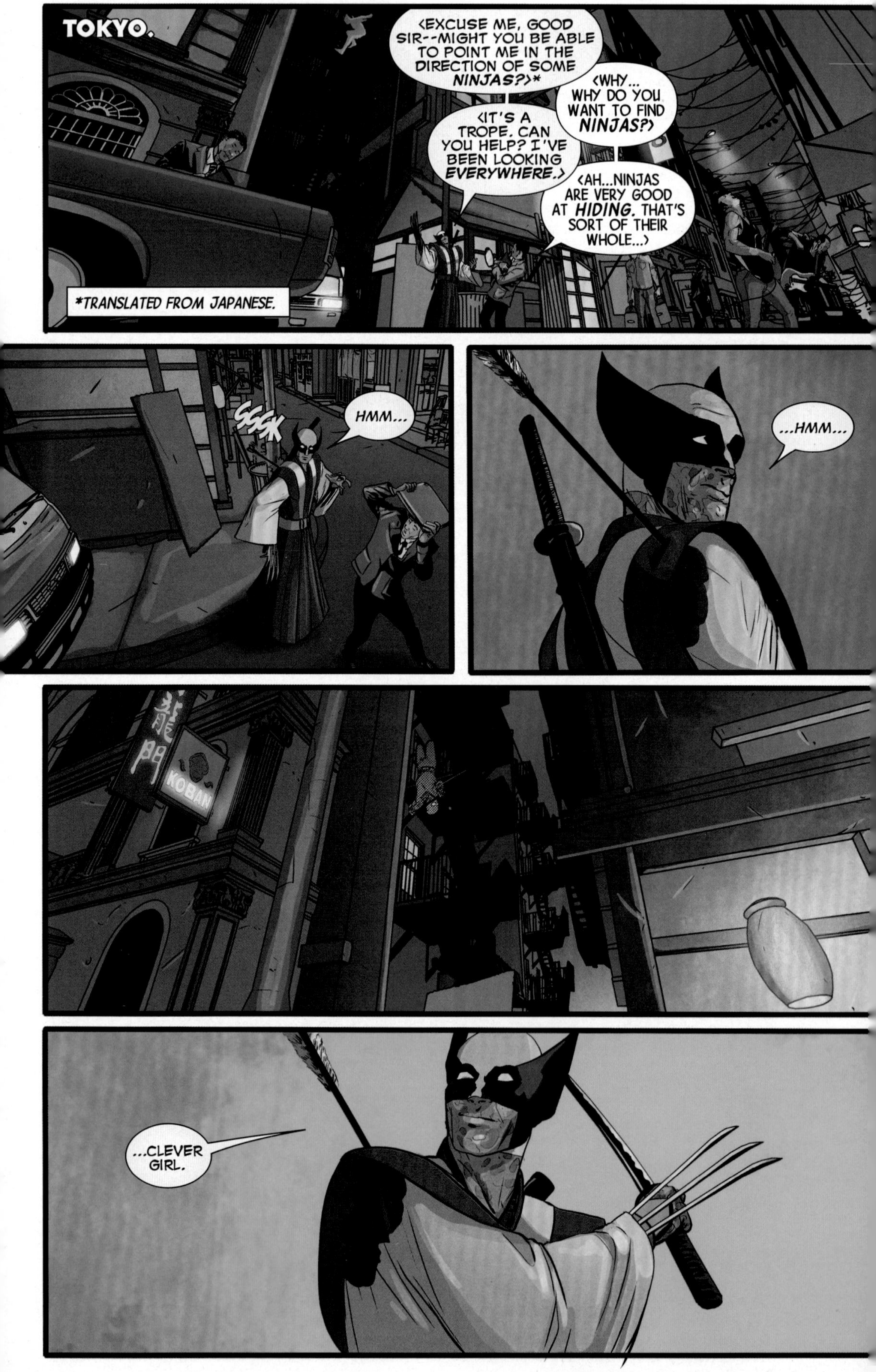
TOKYO.
<EXCUSE ME, GOOD SIR--MIGHT YOU BE ABLE TO POINT ME IN THE DIRECTION OF SOME NINJAS?>*
<WHY... WHY DO YOU WANT TO FIND NINJAS?>
<IT'S A TROPE. CAN YOU HELP? I'VE BEEN LOOKING EVERYWHERE.>
<AH...NINJAS ARE VERY GOOD AT HIDING. THAT'S SORT OF THEIR WHOLE...>
*TRANSLATED FROM JAPANESE.
SSSGK
HMM...
...HMM...
KOBAN
...CLEVER GIRL.

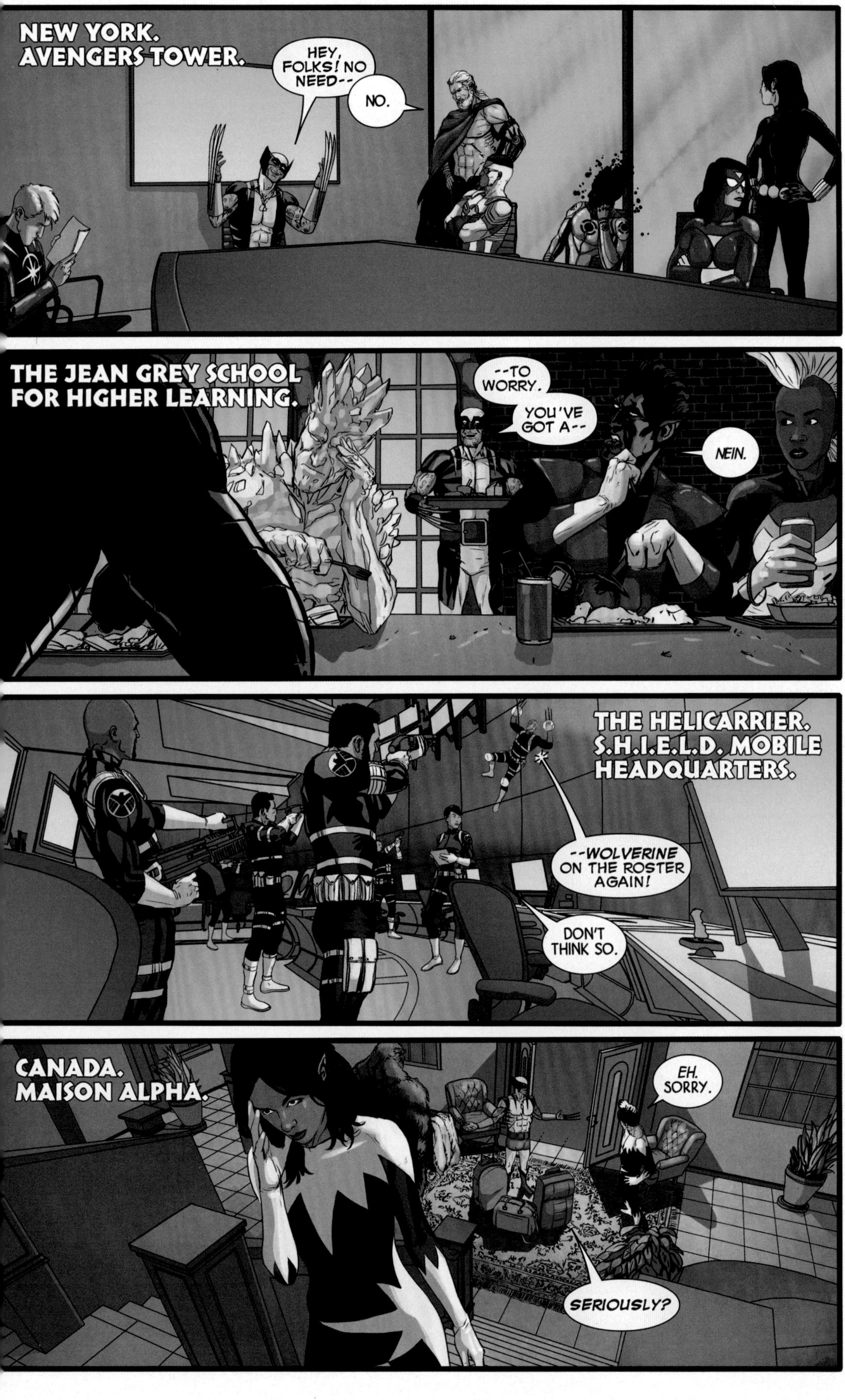
NEW YORK. AVENGERS TOWER.
HEY, FOLKS! NO NEED--
NO.
THE JEAN GREY SCHOOL FOR HIGHER LEARNING.
--TO WORRY.
YOU'VE GOT A--
NEIN.
THE HELICARRIER. S.H.I.E.L.D. MOBILE HEADQUARTERS.
--WOLVERINE ON THE ROSTER AGAIN!
DON'T THINK SO.
CANADA. MAISON ALPHA.
EH. SORRY.
SERIOUSLY?

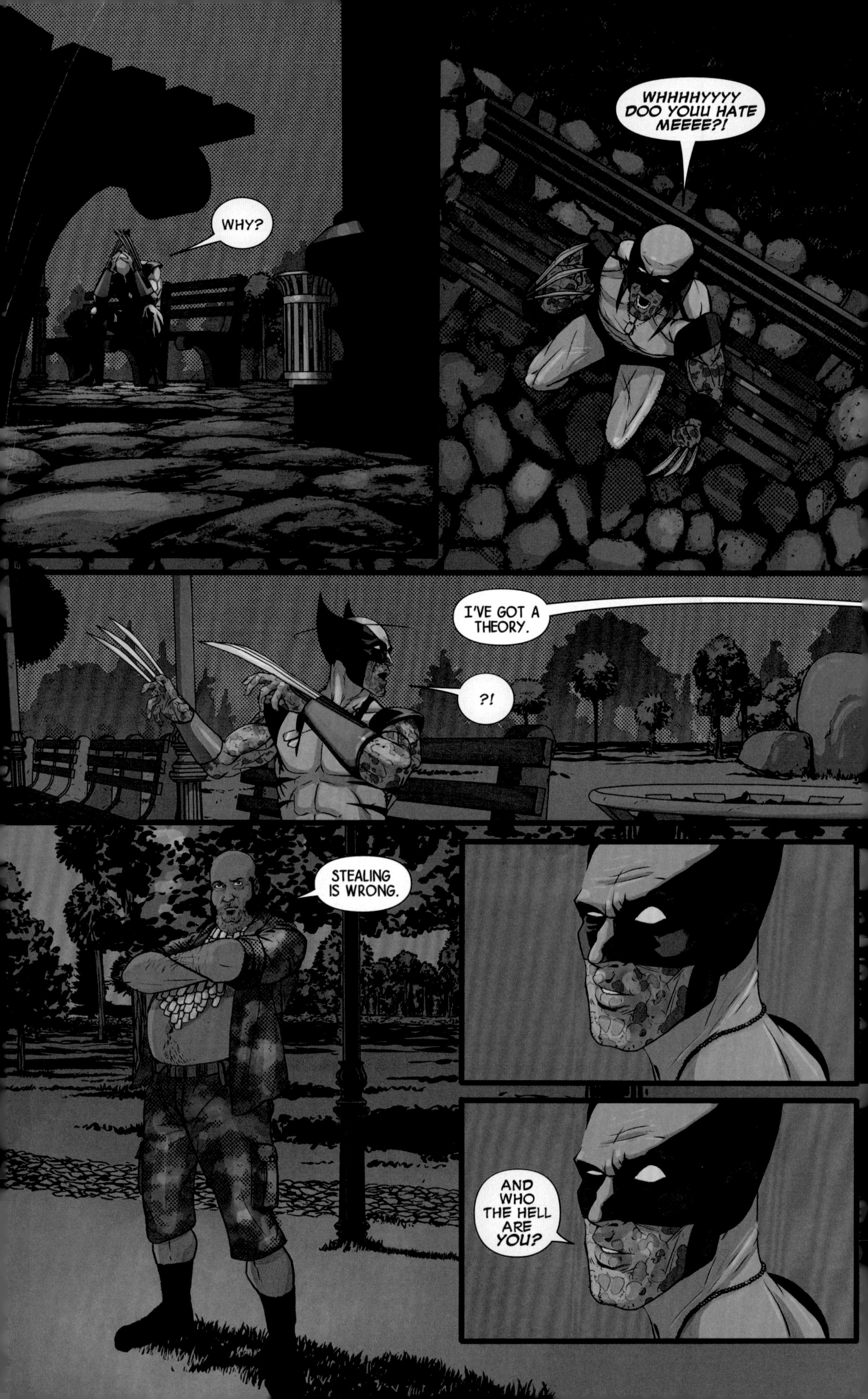
WHY?
WHHHHYYYY DOO YOUU HATE MEEEE?!
I'VE GOT A THEORY.
?!
STEALING IS WRONG.
AND WHO THE HELL ARE YOU?

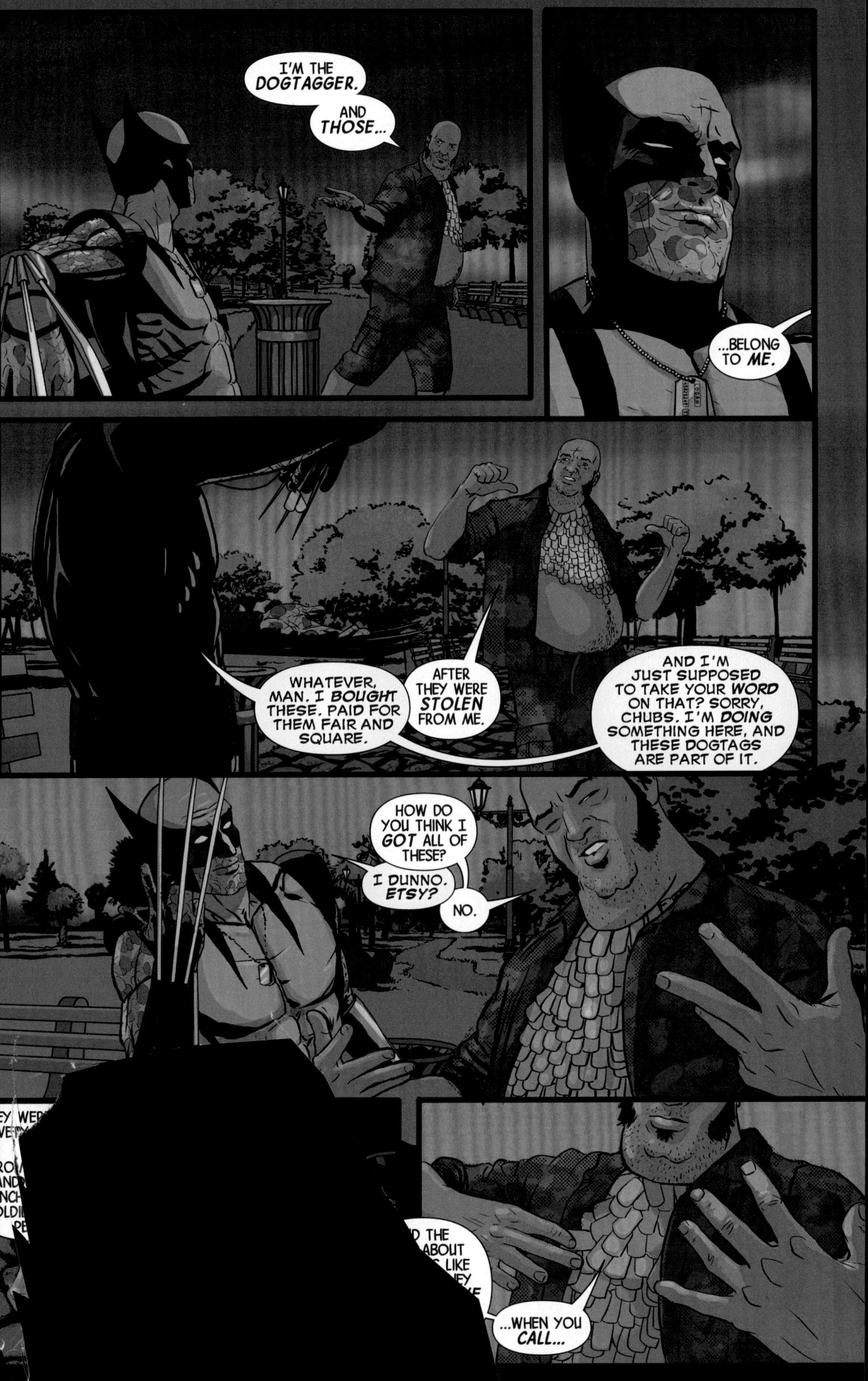
I'M THE DOGTAGGER.
AND THOSE...
...BELONG TO ME.
AFTER THEY WERE STOLEN FROM ME.
WHATEVER, MAN. I BOUGHT THESE. PAID FOR THEM FAIR AND SQUARE.
AND I'M JUST SUPPOSED TO TAKE YOUR WORD ON THAT? SORRY, CHUBS. I'M DOING SOMETHING HERE, AND THESE DOGTAGS ARE PART OF IT.
HOW DO YOU THINK I GOT ALL OF THESE?
I DUNNO. ETSY?
NO.
...WHEN YOU CALL...

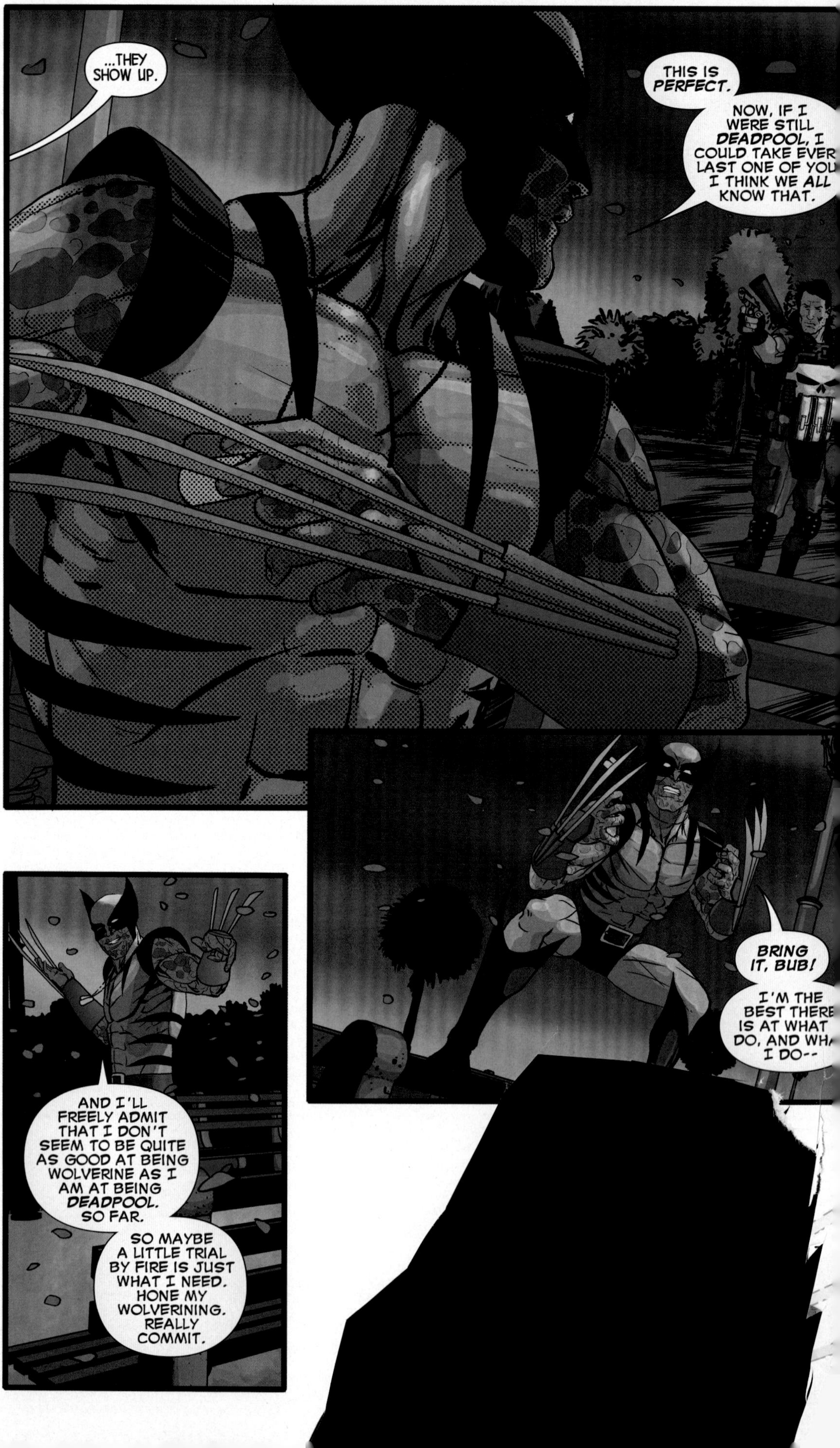
...THEY SHOW UP.
THIS IS PERFECT.
NOW, IF I WERE STILL DEADPOOL, I COULD TAKE EVER LAST ONE OF YOU I THINK WE ALL KNOW THAT.
AND I'LL FREELY ADMIT THAT I DON'T SEEM TO BE QUITE AS GOOD AT BEING WOLVERINE AS I AM AT BEING DEADPOOL. SO FAR.
SO MAYBE A LITTLE TRIAL BY FIRE IS JUST WHAT I NEED. HONE MY WOLVERINING. REALLY COMMIT.
BRING IT, BUB!
I'M THE BEST THERE IS AT WHAT DO, AND WHA I DO--

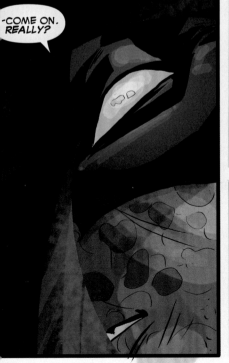

-COME ON. REALLY?

COME ONNNNN.

JUST GIVE ME A SECOND HERE. I'M STILL GETTING *USED* TO THESE TH--

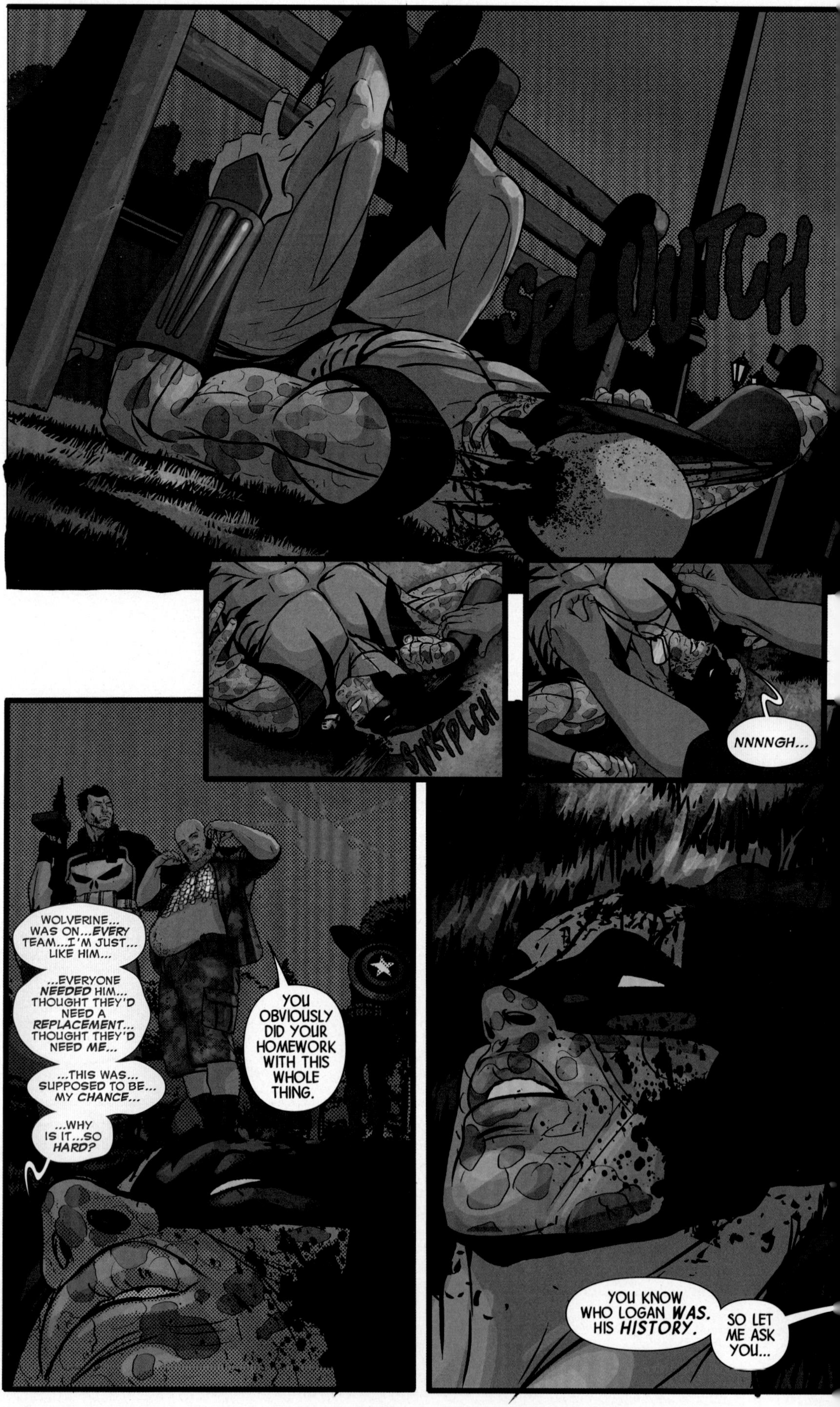
SPLOUTCH
SNKTPLCH
NNNNGH...
WOLVERINE... WAS ON...EVERY TEAM...I'M JUST... LIKE HIM...
...EVERYONE NEEDED HIM... THOUGHT THEY'D NEED A REPLACEMENT... THOUGHT THEY'D NEED ME...
...THIS WAS... SUPPOSED TO BE... MY CHANCE...
...WHY IS IT...SO HARD?
YOU OBVIOUSLY DID YOUR HOMEWORK WITH THIS WHOLE THING.
YOU KNOW WHO LOGAN WAS. HIS HISTORY.
SO LET ME ASK YOU...

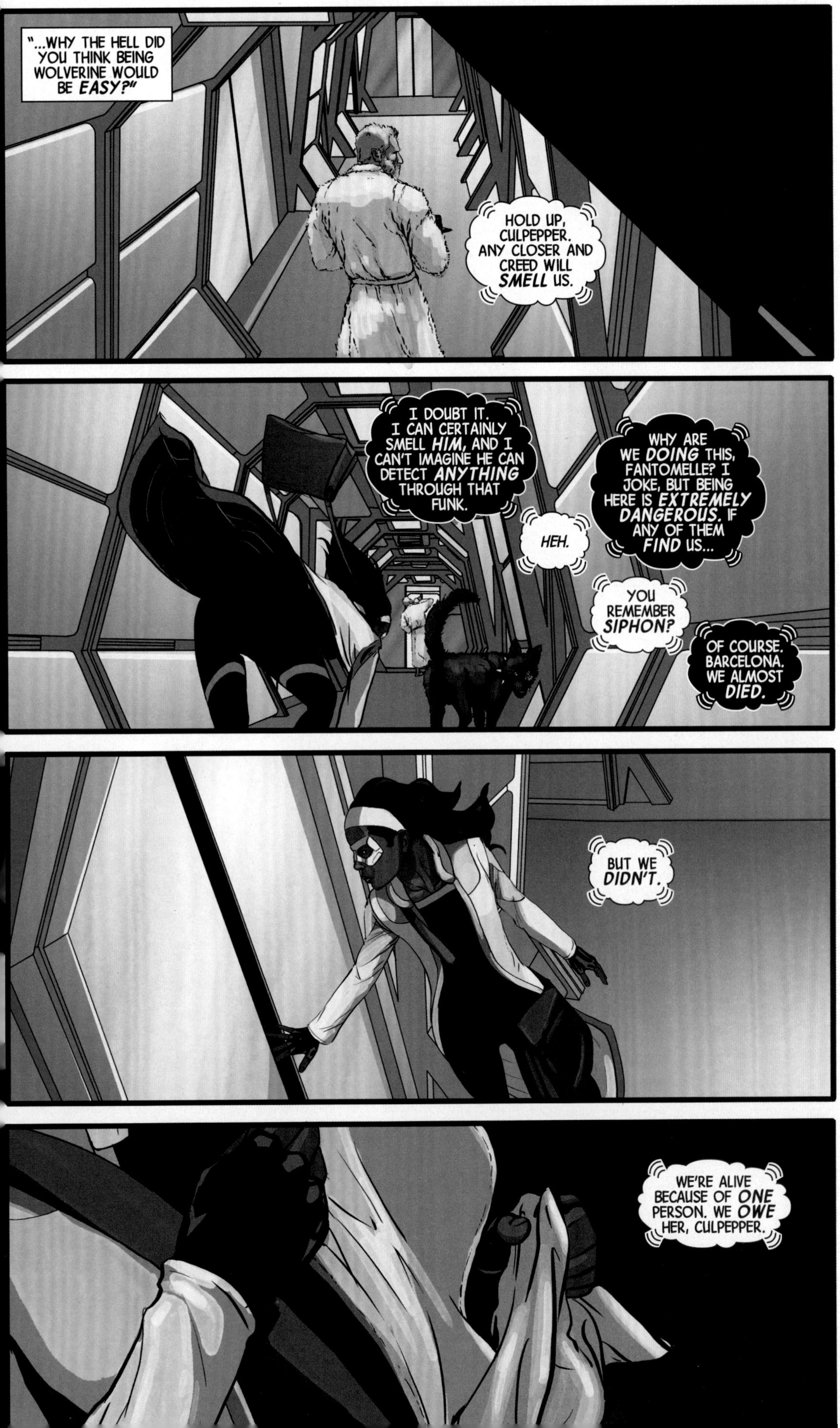
"...WHY THE HELL DID YOU THINK BEING WOLVERINE WOULD BE EASY?"
HOLD UP, CULPEPPER. ANY CLOSER AND CREED WILL SMELL US.
I DOUBT IT. I CAN CERTAINLY SMELL HIM, AND I CAN'T IMAGINE HE CAN DETECT ANYTHING THROUGH THAT FUNK.
HEH.
WHY ARE WE DOING THIS, FANTOMELLE? I JOKE, BUT BEING HERE IS EXTREMELY DANGEROUS. IF ANY OF THEM FIND US...
YOU REMEMBER SIPHON?
OF COURSE. BARCELONA. WE ALMOST DIED.
BUT WE DIDN'T.
WE'RE ALIVE BECAUSE OF ONE PERSON. WE OWE HER, CULPEPPER.

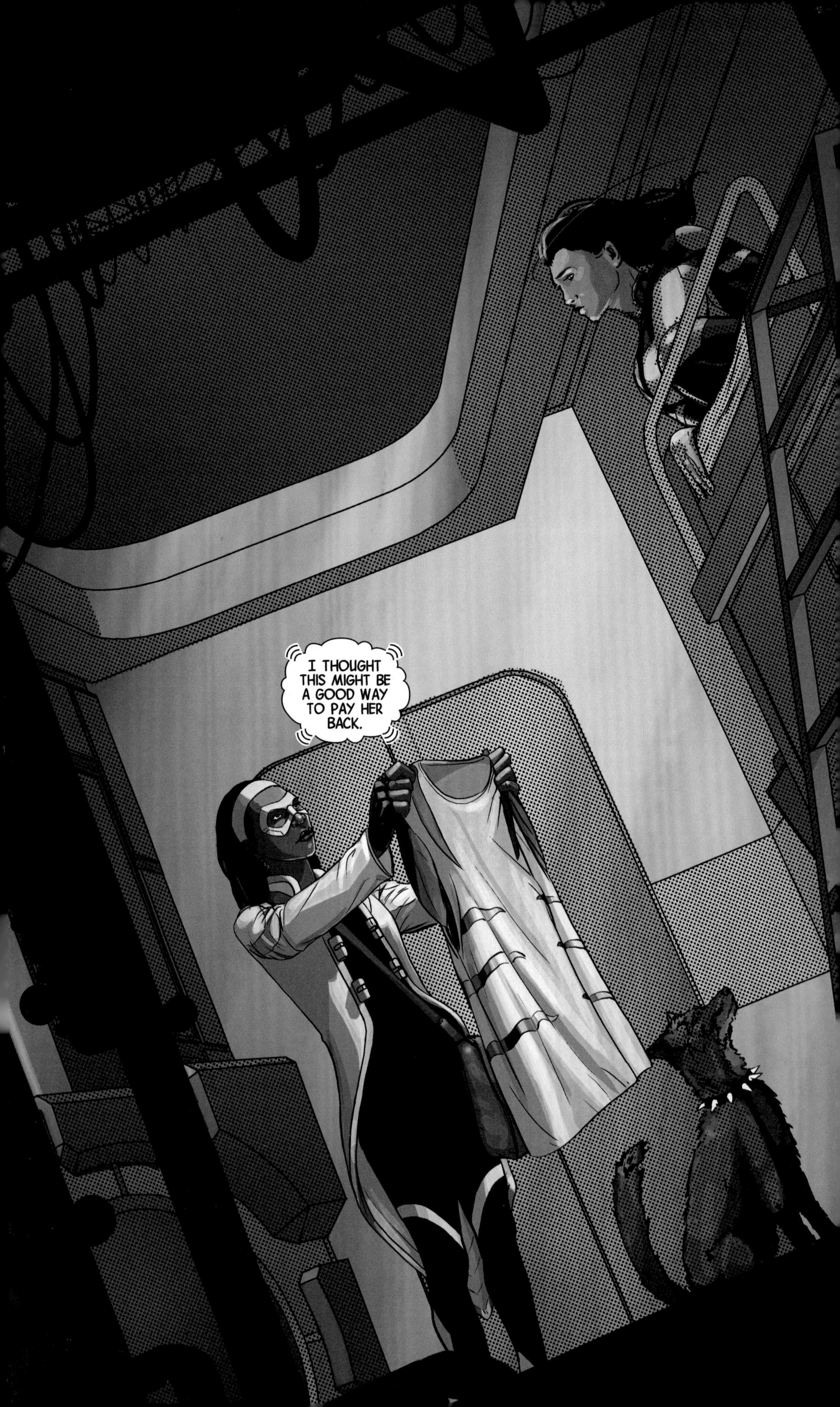
I THOUGHT THIS MIGHT BE A GOOD WAY TO PAY HER BACK.

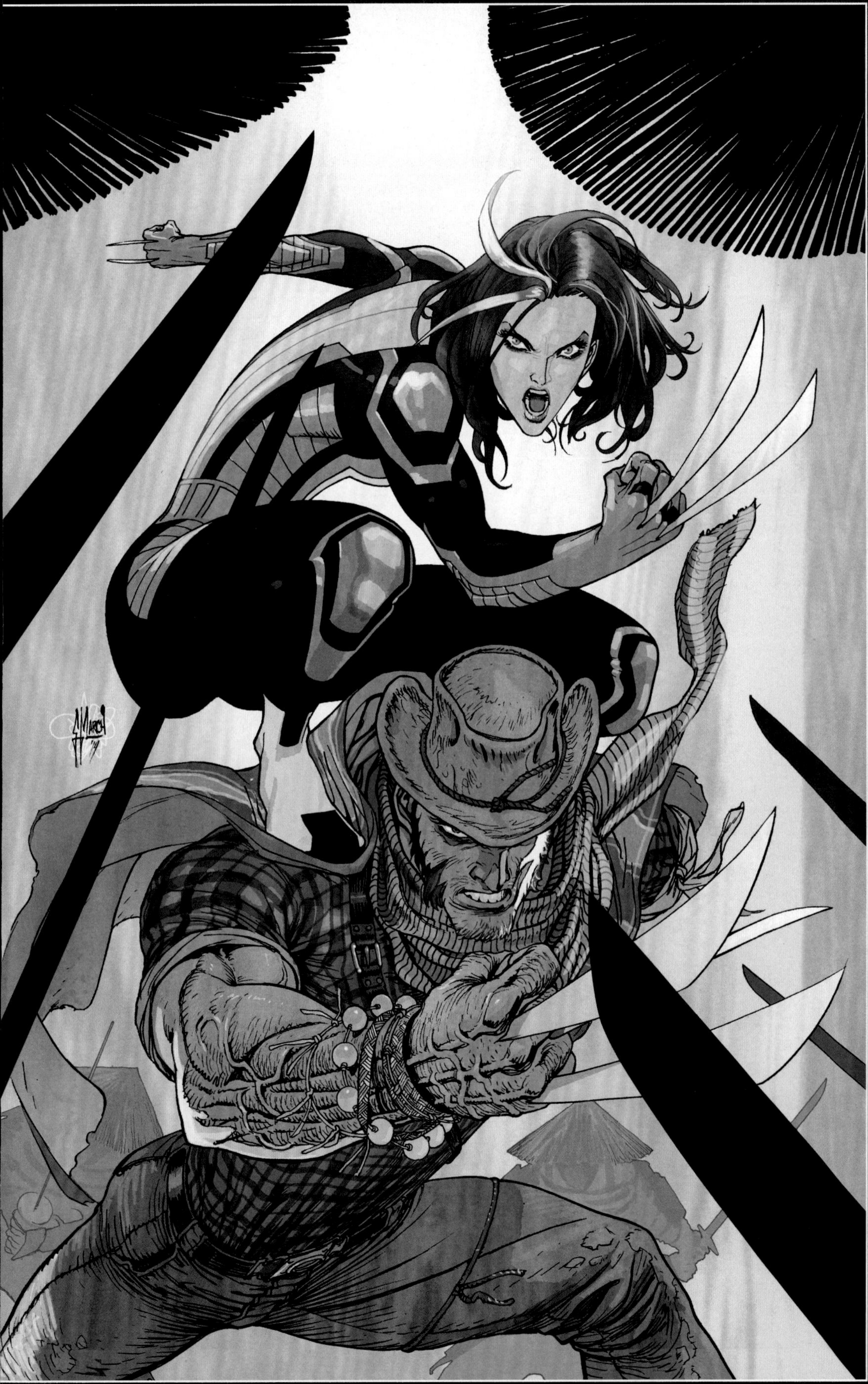

#14

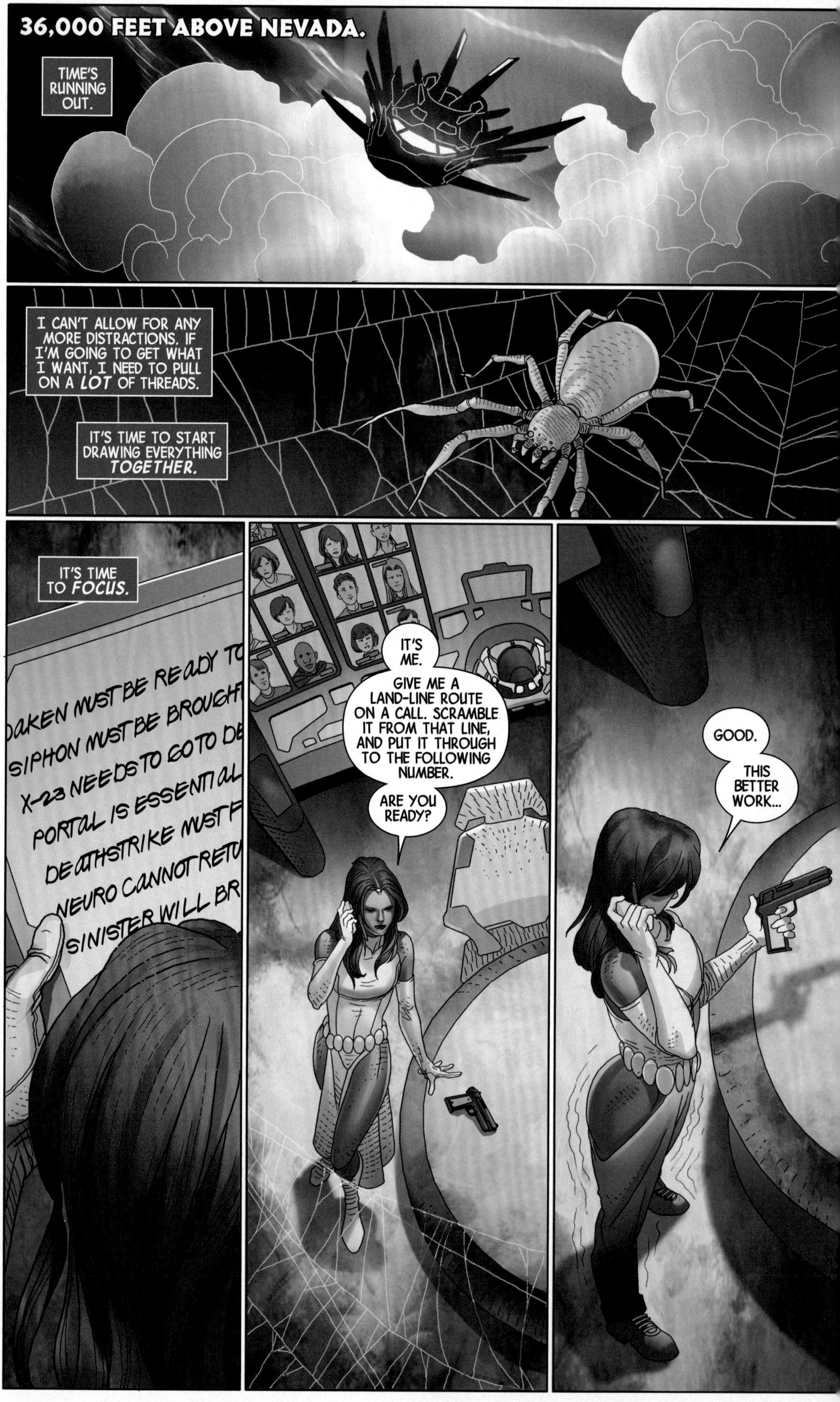

36,000 FEET ABOVE NEVADA.
TIME'S RUNNING OUT.
I CAN'T ALLOW FOR ANY MORE DISTRACTIONS. IF I'M GOING TO GET WHAT I WANT, I NEED TO PULL ON A LOT OF THREADS.
IT'S TIME TO START DRAWING EVERYTHING TOGETHER.
IT'S TIME TO FOCUS.
DAKEN MUST BE READY TO
SIPHON MUST BE BROUGHT
X-23 NEEDS TO GO TO DE
PORTAL IS ESSENTIAL
DEATHSTRIKE MUST F
NEURO CANNOT RETU
SINISTER WILL BR
IT'S ME.
GIVE ME A LAND-LINE ROUTE ON A CALL. SCRAMBLE IT FROM THAT LINE, AND PUT IT THROUGH TO THE FOLLOWING NUMBER.
ARE YOU READY?
GOOD.
THIS BETTER WORK...

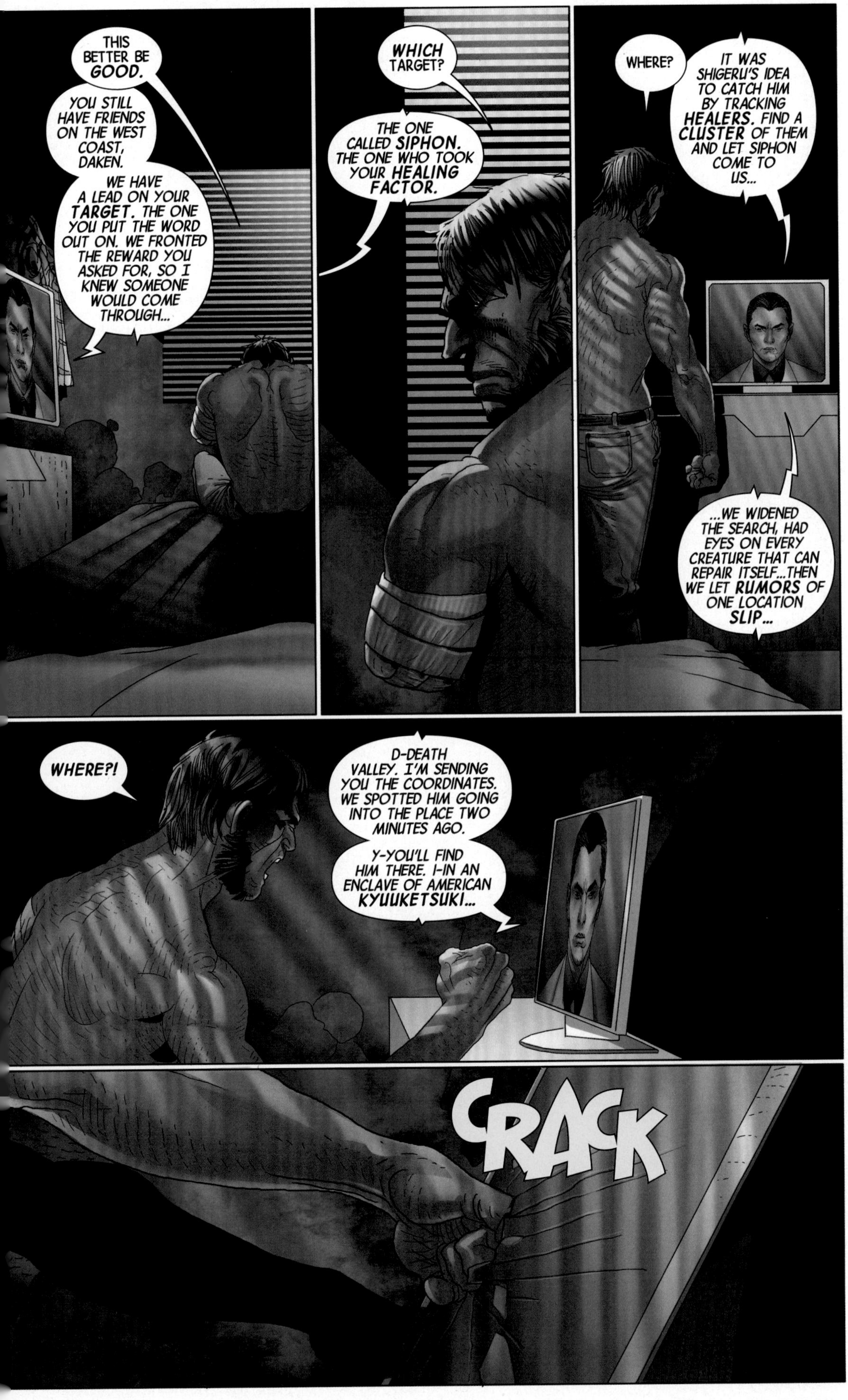
THIS BETTER BE GOOD.
YOU STILL HAVE FRIENDS ON THE WEST COAST, DAKEN.
WE HAVE A LEAD ON YOUR TARGET. THE ONE YOU PUT THE WORD OUT ON. WE FRONTED THE REWARD YOU ASKED FOR, SO I KNEW SOMEONE WOULD COME THROUGH...
WHICH TARGET?
THE ONE CALLED SIPHON. THE ONE WHO TOOK YOUR HEALING FACTOR.
WHERE?
IT WAS SHIGERU'S IDEA TO CATCH HIM BY TRACKING HEALERS. FIND A CLUSTER OF THEM AND LET SIPHON COME TO US...
...WE WIDENED THE SEARCH, HAD EYES ON EVERY CREATURE THAT CAN REPAIR ITSELF...THEN WE LET RUMORS OF ONE LOCATION SLIP...
WHERE?!
D-DEATH VALLEY. I'M SENDING YOU THE COORDINATES. WE SPOTTED HIM GOING INTO THE PLACE TWO MINUTES AGO.
Y-YOU'LL FIND HIM THERE. I-IN AN ENCLAVE OF AMERICAN KYUUKETSUKI...
CRACK

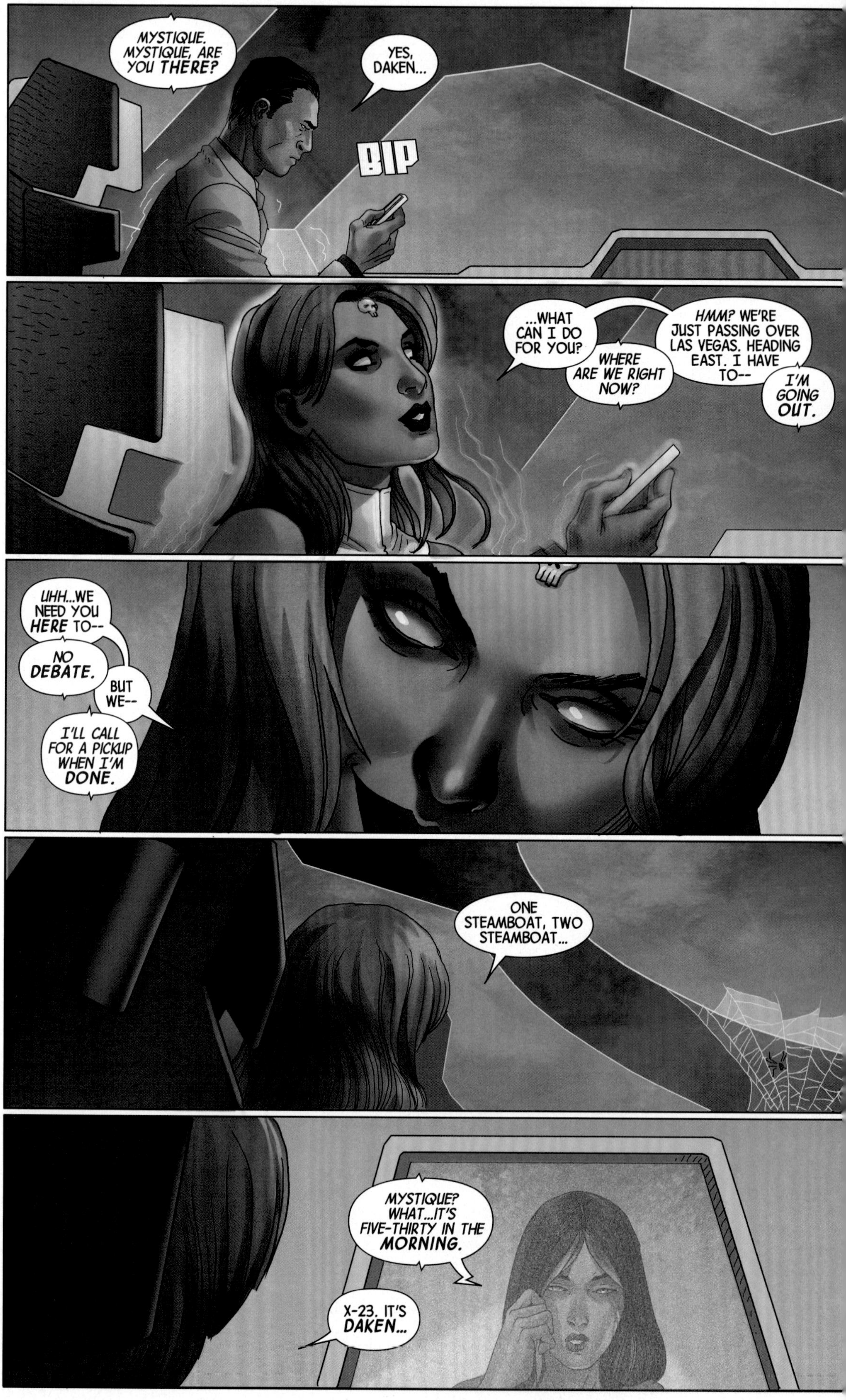
MYSTIQUE. MYSTIQUE, ARE YOU THERE?
YES, DAKEN...
BIP
...WHAT CAN I DO FOR YOU?
WHERE ARE WE RIGHT NOW?
HMM? WE'RE JUST PASSING OVER LAS VEGAS. HEADING EAST. I HAVE TO--
I'M GOING OUT.
UHH...WE NEED YOU HERE TO--
NO DEBATE.
BUT WE--
I'LL CALL FOR A PICKUP WHEN I'M DONE.
ONE STEAMBOAT, TWO STEAMBOAT...
MYSTIQUE? WHAT...IT'S FIVE-THIRTY IN THE MORNING.
X-23. IT'S DAKEN...

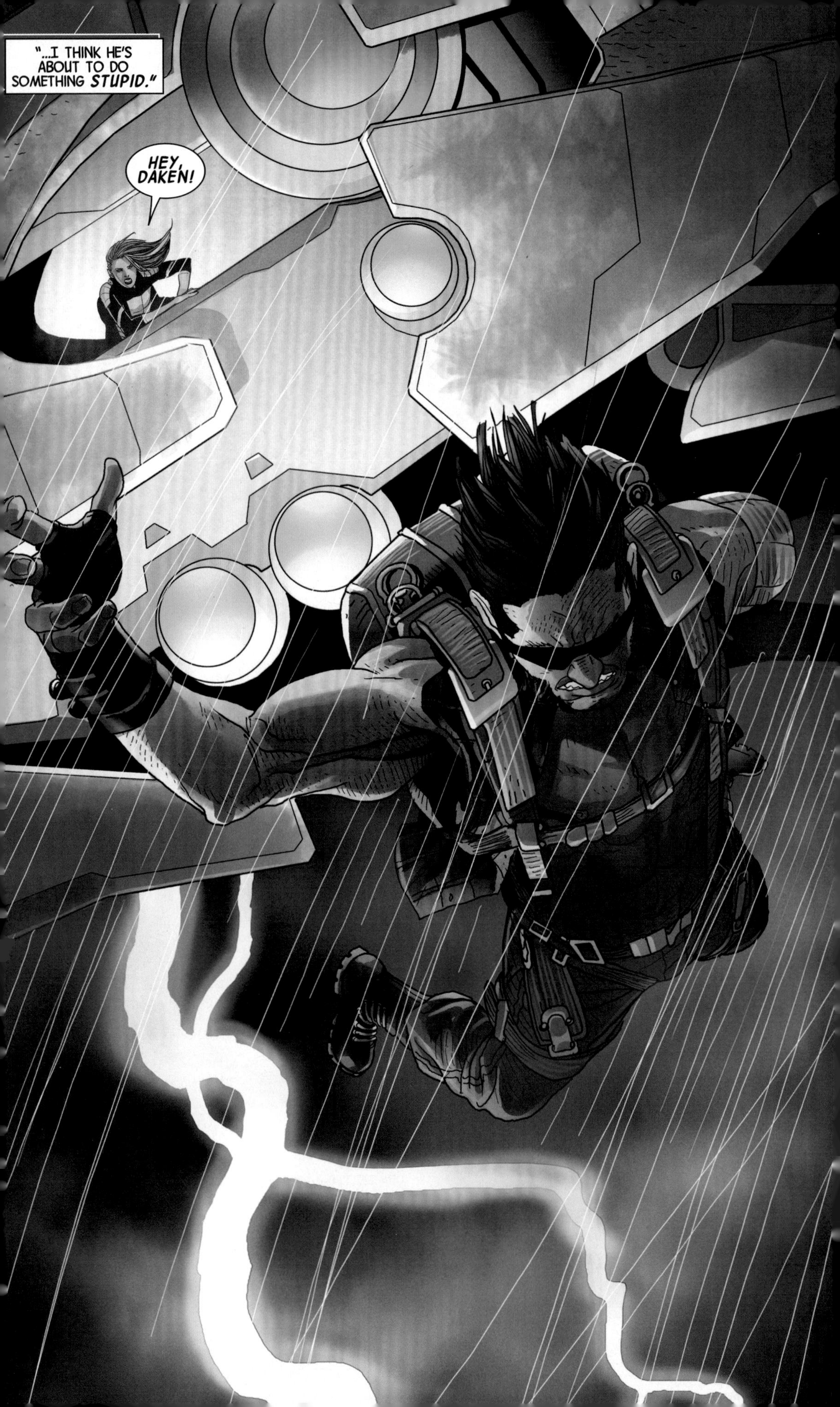
"...I THINK HE'S ABOUT TO DO SOMETHING STUPID."
HEY, DAKEN!

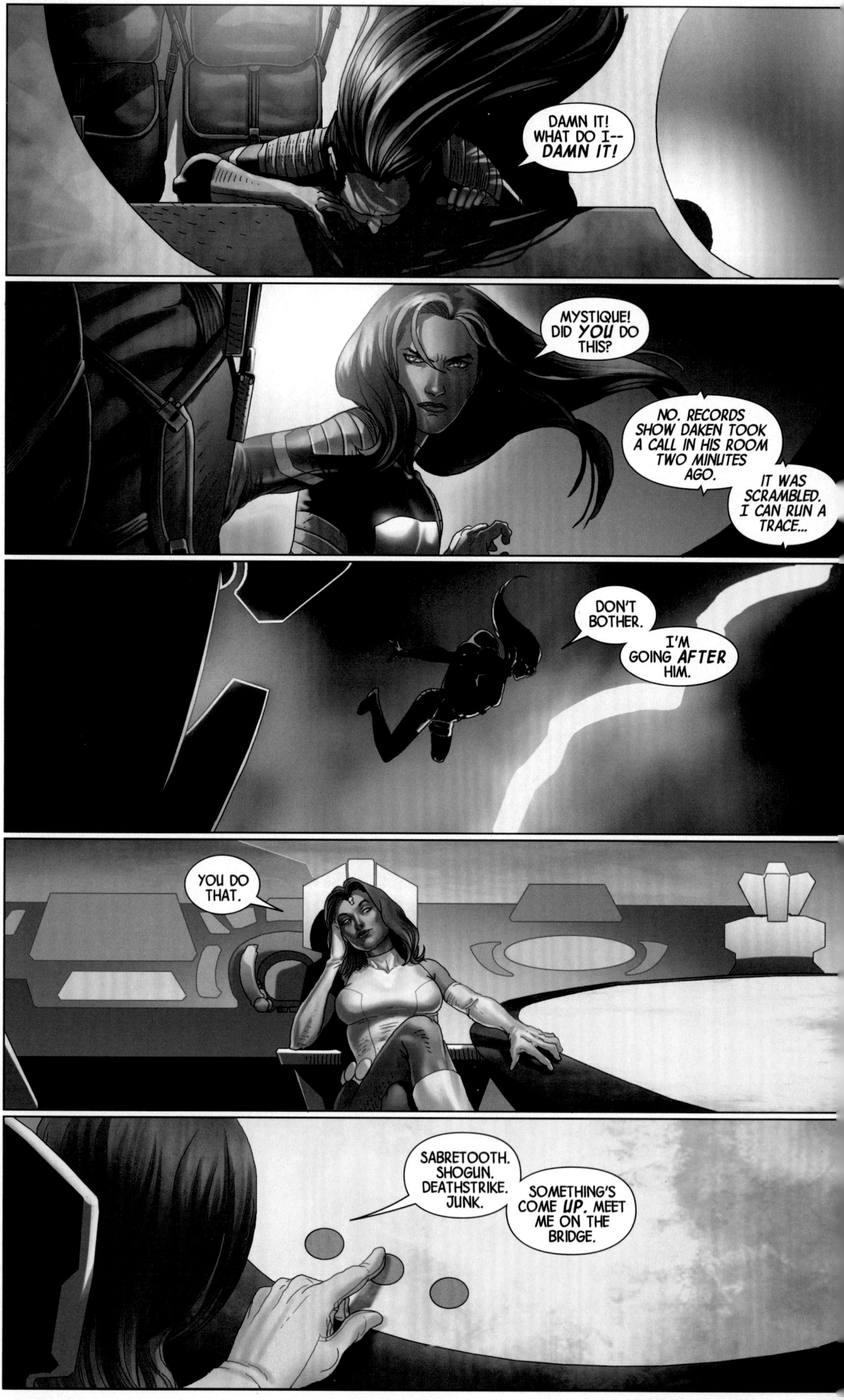
DAMN IT! WHAT DO I-- DAMN IT!
MYSTIQUE! DID YOU DO THIS?
NO. RECORDS SHOW DAKEN TOOK A CALL IN HIS ROOM TWO MINUTES AGO.
IT WAS SCRAMBLED. I CAN RUN A TRACE...
DON'T BOTHER.
I'M GOING AFTER HIM.
YOU DO THAT.
SABRETOOTH. SHOGUN. DEATHSTRIKE. JUNK.
SOMETHING'S COME UP. MEET ME ON THE BRIDGE.

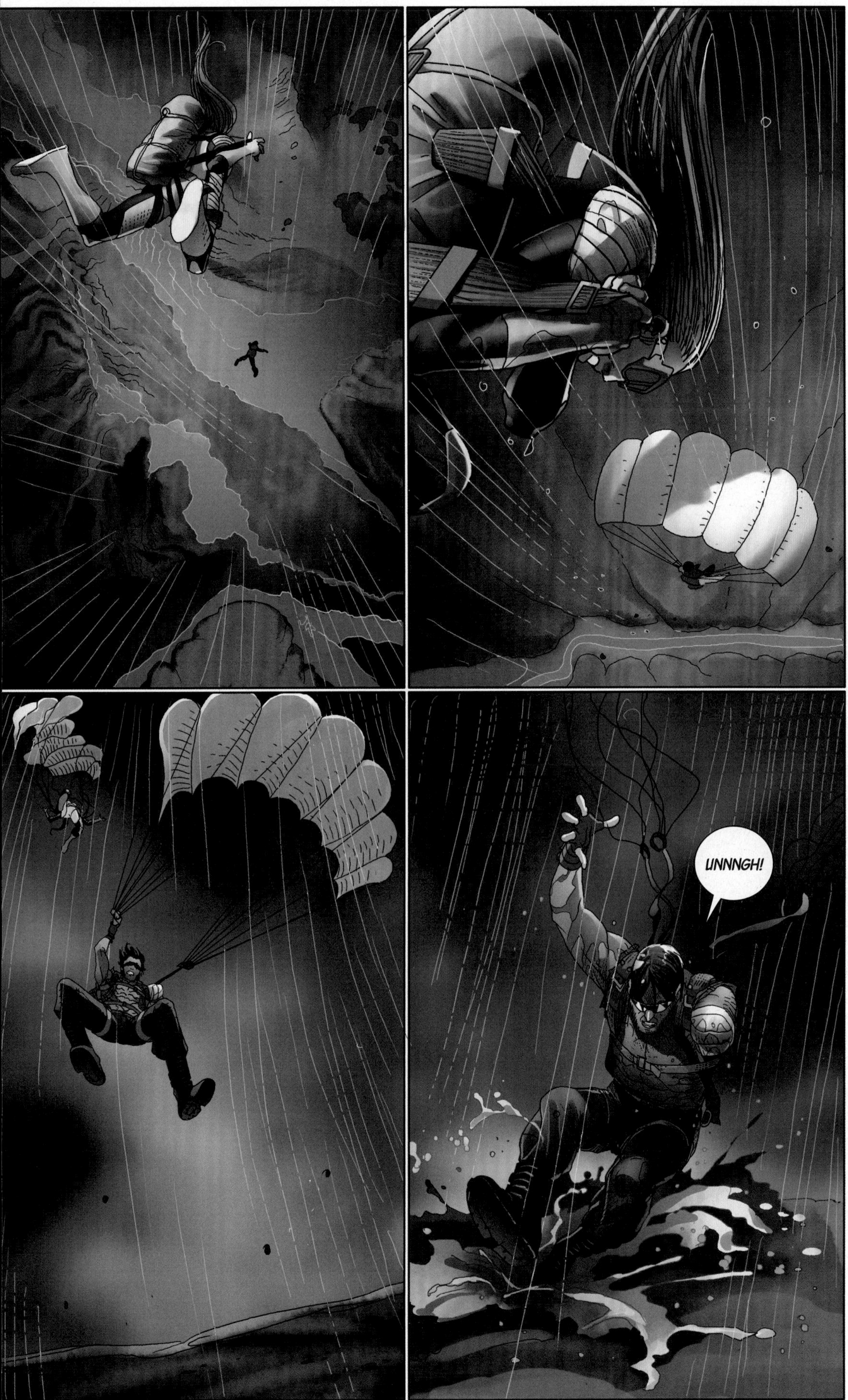
UNNNGH!

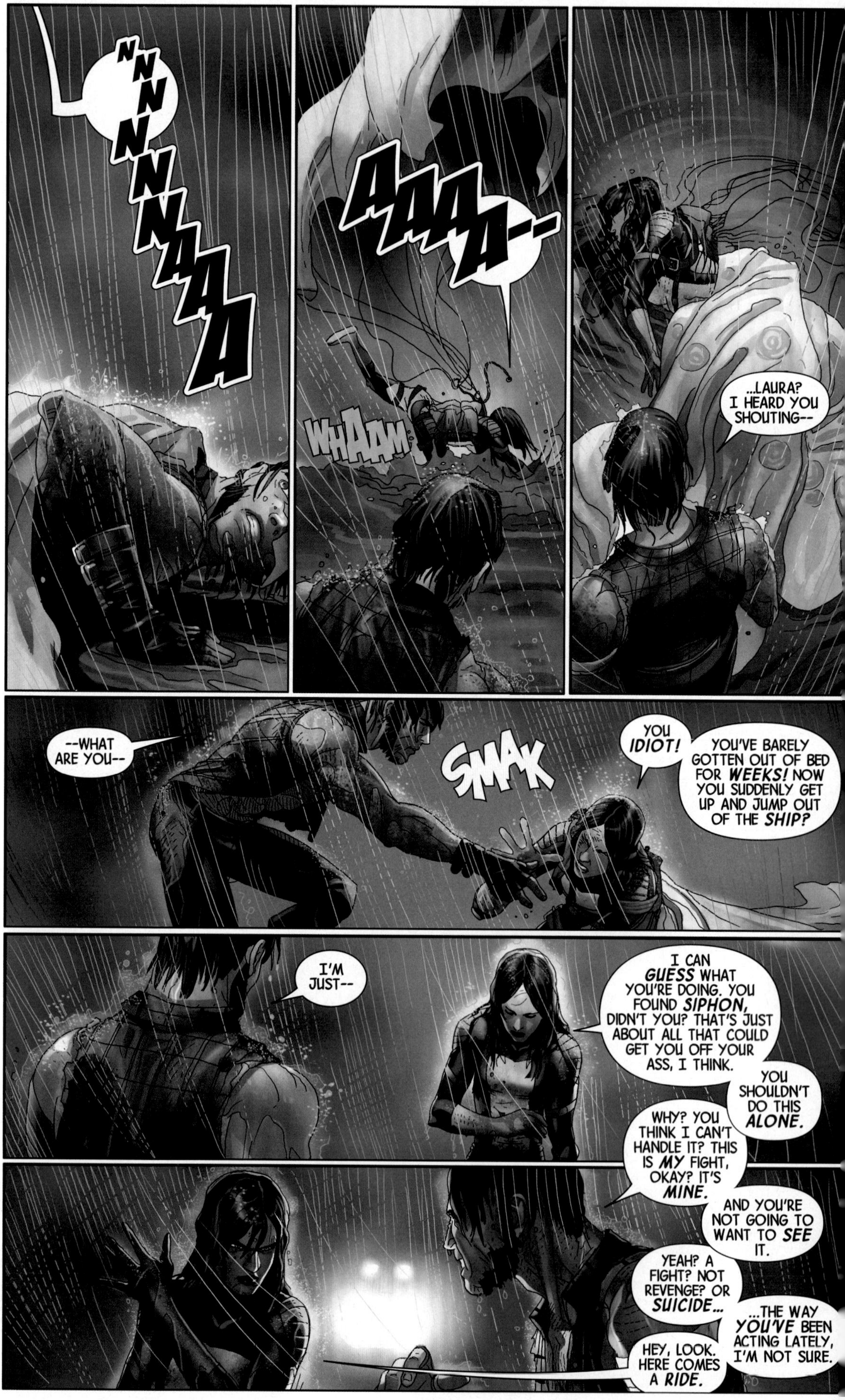
NNNNNAAAA
AAAA--
WHAAM
...LAURA? I HEARD YOU SHOUTING--
--WHAT ARE YOU--
SMAK
YOU IDIOT!
YOU'VE BARELY GOTTEN OUT OF BED FOR WEEKS! NOW YOU SUDDENLY GET UP AND JUMP OUT OF THE SHIP?
I'M JUST--
I CAN GUESS WHAT YOU'RE DOING. YOU FOUND SIPHON, DIDN'T YOU? THAT'S JUST ABOUT ALL THAT COULD GET YOU OFF YOUR ASS, I THINK.
YOU SHOULDN'T DO THIS ALONE.
WHY? YOU THINK I CAN'T HANDLE IT? THIS IS MY FIGHT, OKAY? IT'S MINE.
AND YOU'RE NOT GOING TO WANT TO SEE IT.
YEAH? A FIGHT? NOT REVENGE? OR SUICIDE...
...THE WAY YOU'VE BEEN ACTING LATELY, I'M NOT SURE.
HEY, LOOK. HERE COMES A RIDE.

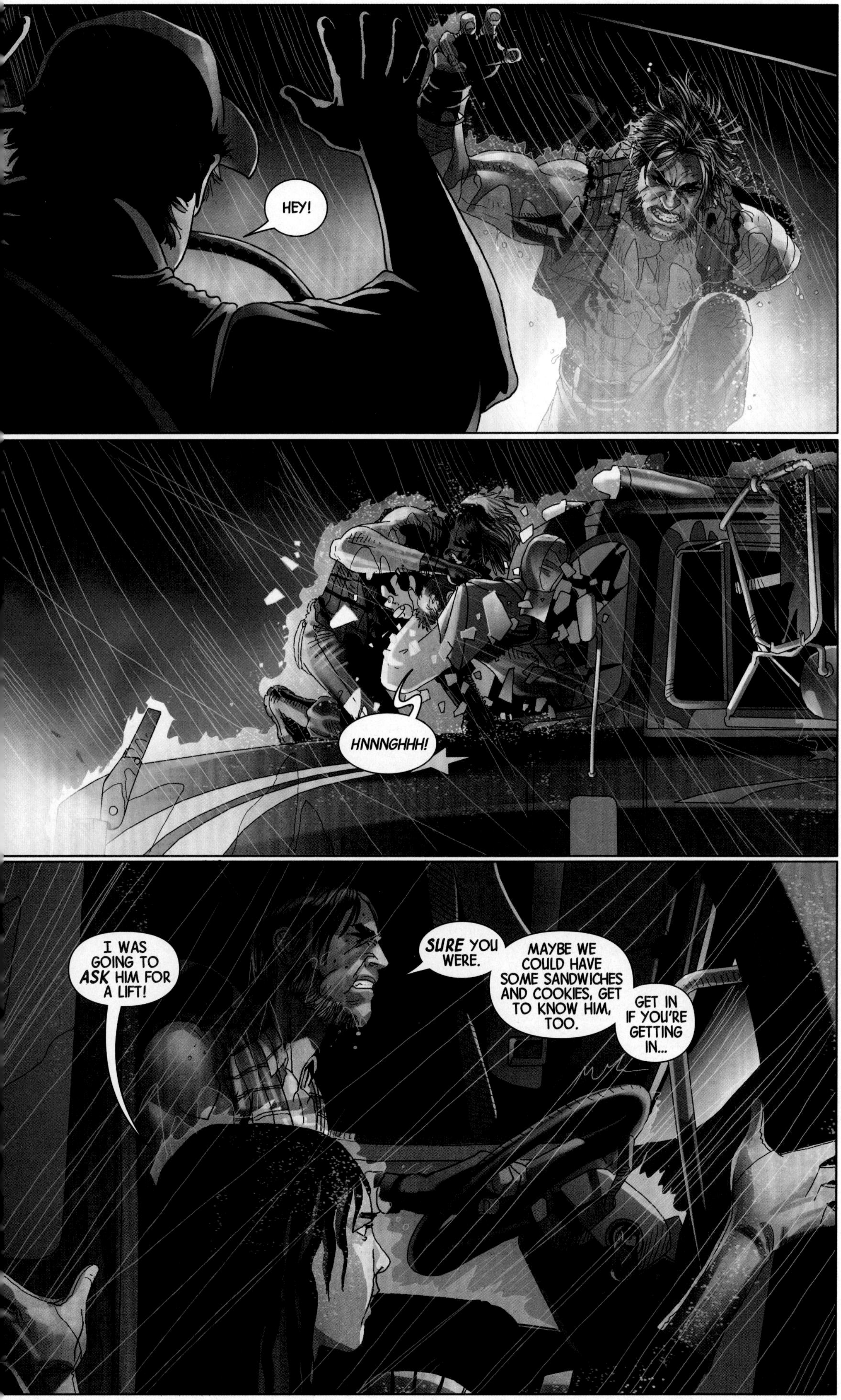
HEY!
HNNNGHHH!
I WAS GOING TO ASK HIM FOR A LIFT!
SURE YOU WERE.
MAYBE WE COULD HAVE SOME SANDWICHES AND COOKIES, GET TO KNOW HIM, TOO.
GET IN IF YOU'RE GETTING IN...

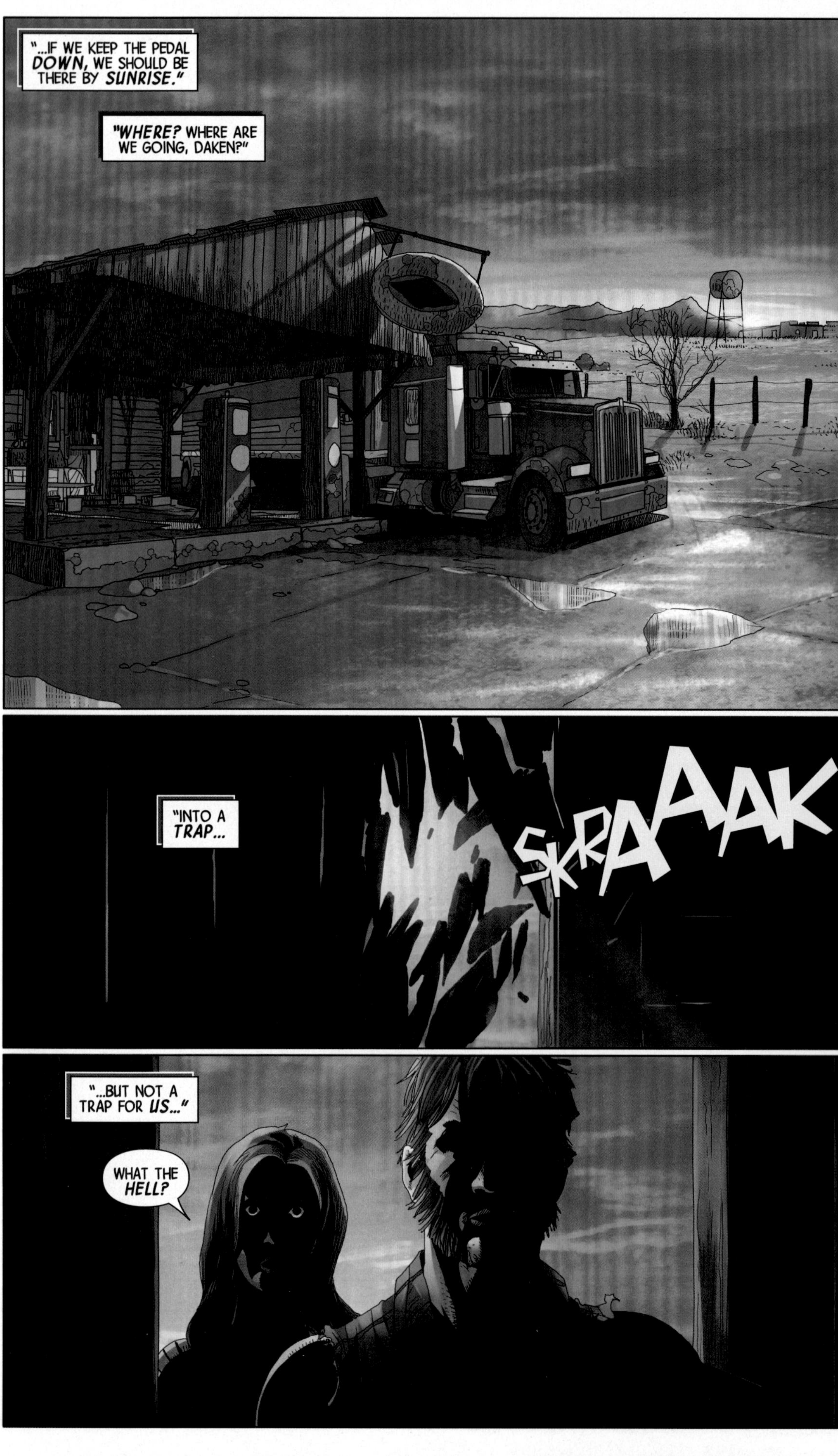
"...IF WE KEEP THE PEDAL DOWN, WE SHOULD BE THERE BY SUNRISE."
"WHERE? WHERE ARE WE GOING, DAKEN?"
"INTO A TRAP...
SKRAAAK
"...BUT NOT A TRAP FOR US..."
WHAT THE HELL?

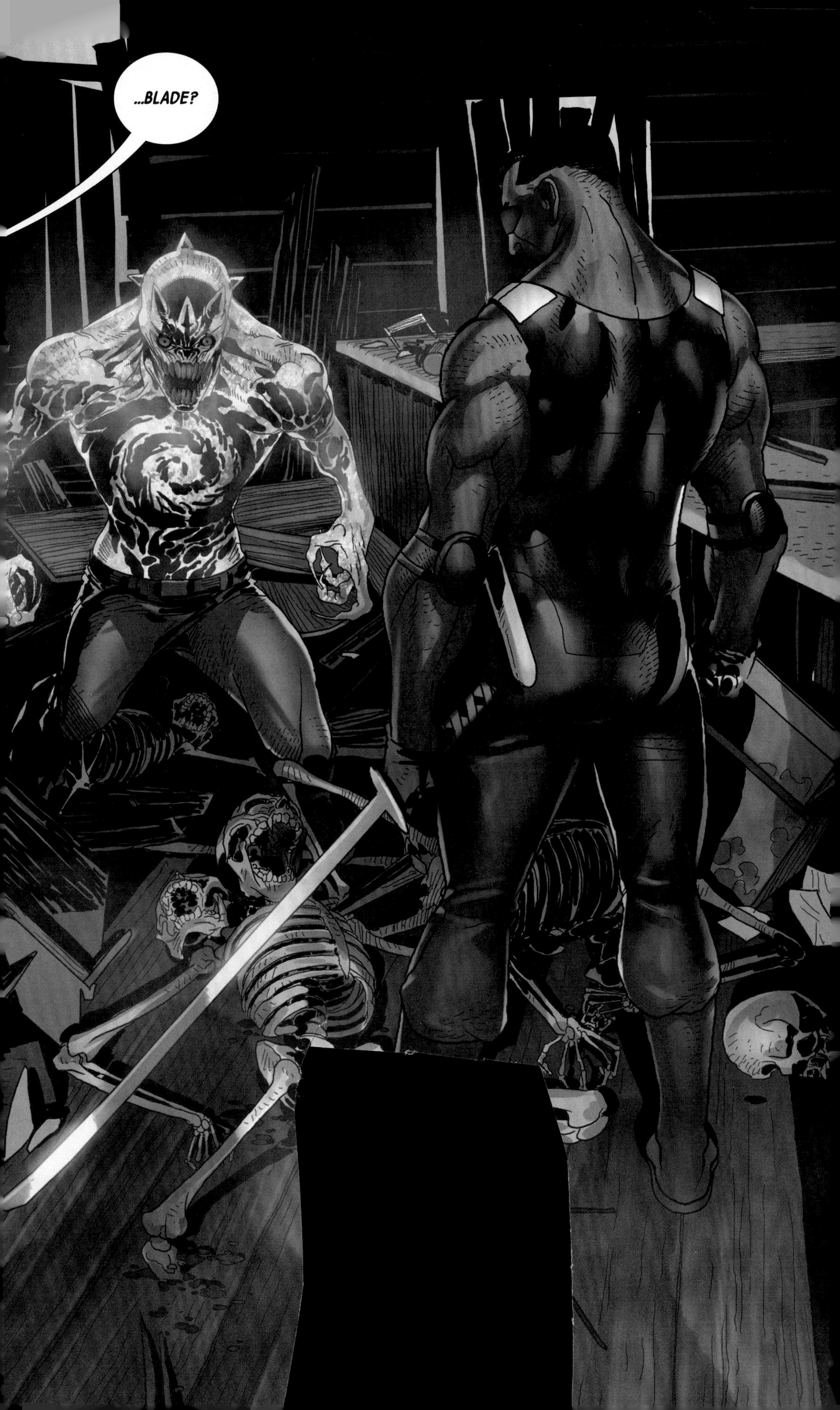
...BLADE?

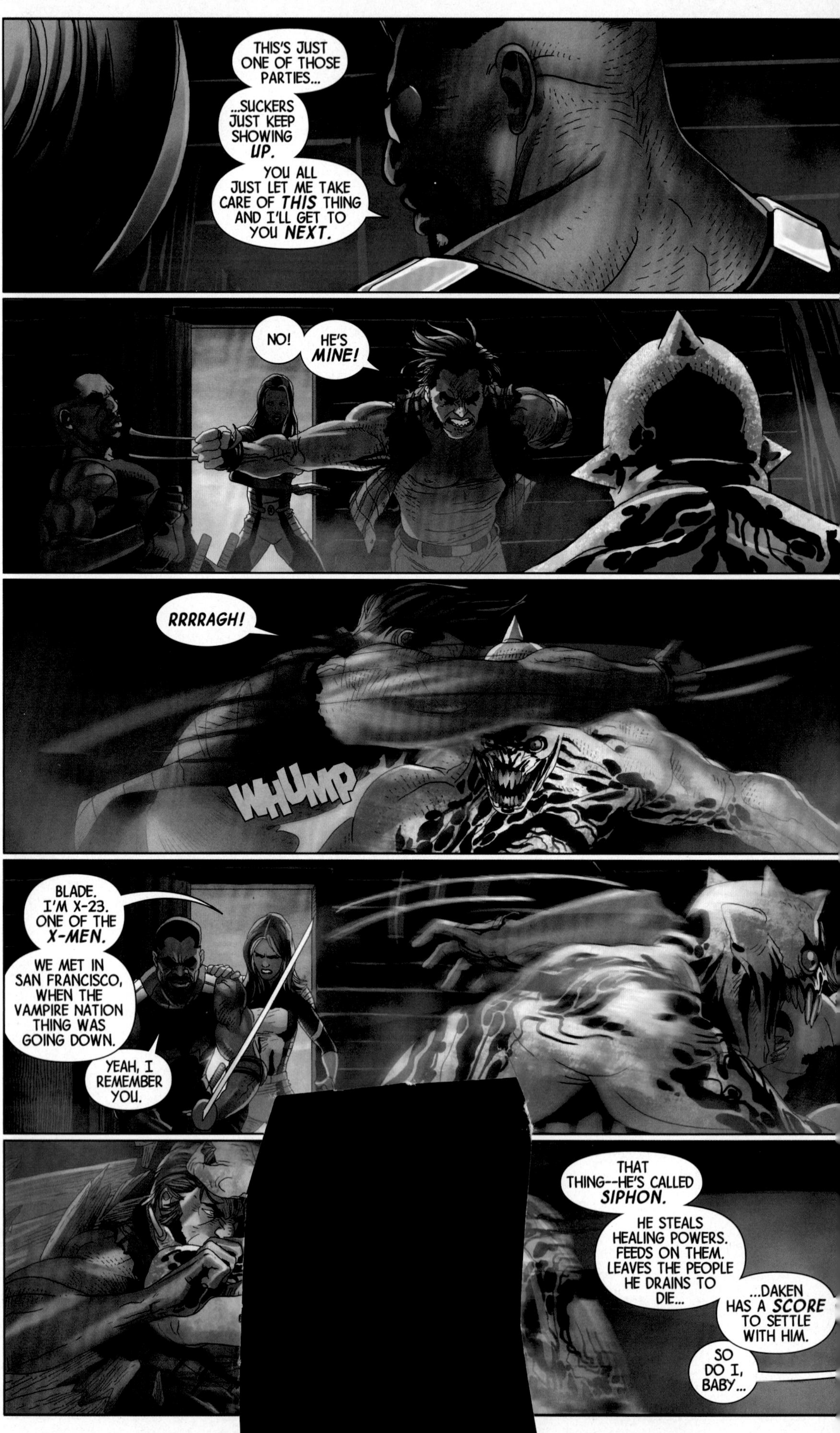
THIS'S JUST ONE OF THOSE PARTIES...
...SUCKERS JUST KEEP SHOWING UP.
YOU ALL JUST LET ME TAKE CARE OF THIS THING AND I'LL GET TO YOU NEXT.
NO!
HE'S MINE!
RRRRAGH!
WHUMP
BLADE. I'M X-23. ONE OF THE X-MEN.
WE MET IN SAN FRANCISCO, WHEN THE VAMPIRE NATION THING WAS GOING DOWN.
YEAH, I REMEMBER YOU.
THAT THING--HE'S CALLED SIPHON.
HE STEALS HEALING POWERS. FEEDS ON THEM. LEAVES THE PEOPLE HE DRAINS TO DIE...
...DAKEN HAS A SCORE TO SETTLE WITH HIM.
SO DO I, BABY...

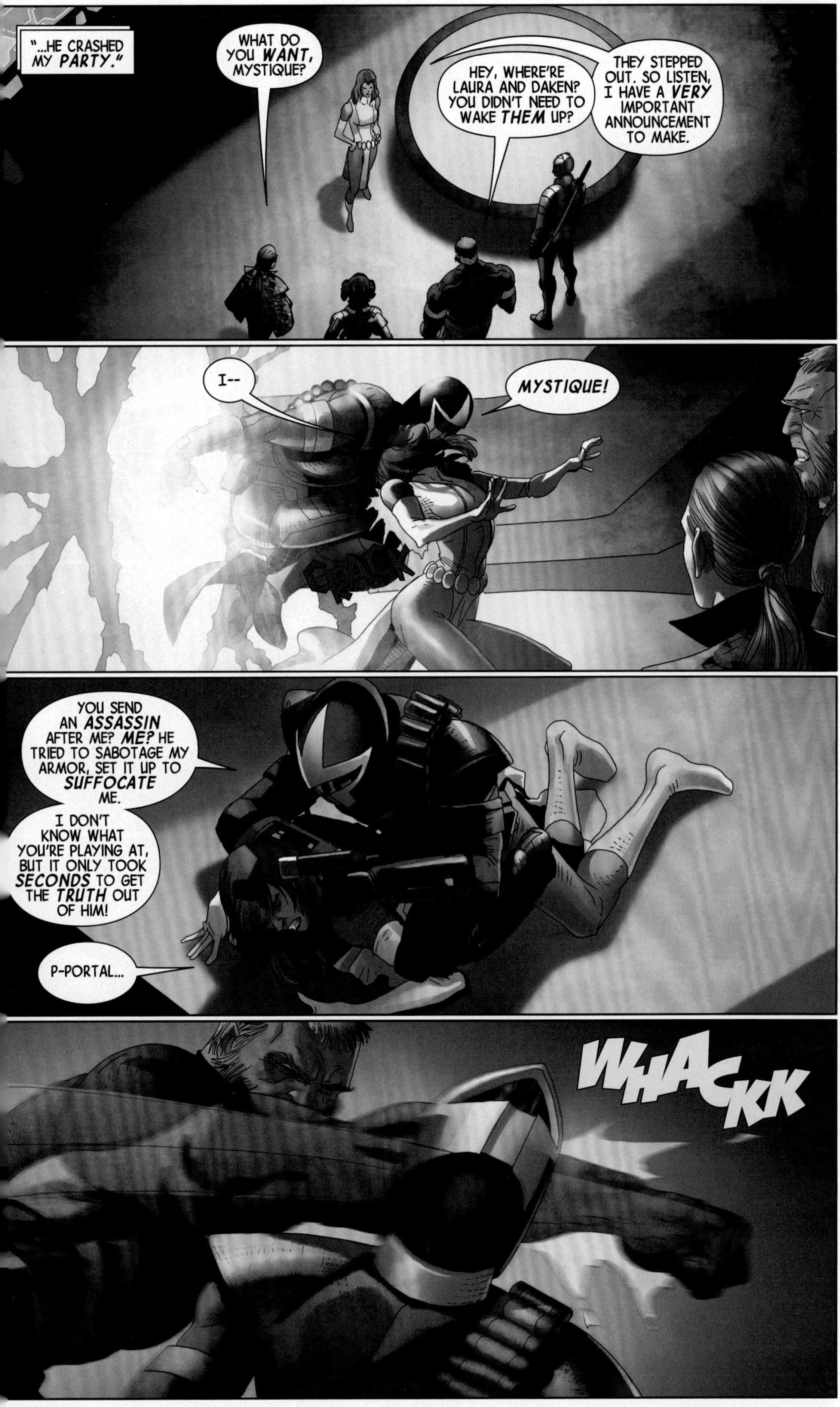
"...HE CRASHED MY PARTY."
WHAT DO YOU WANT, MYSTIQUE?
HEY, WHERE'RE LAURA AND DAKEN? YOU DIDN'T NEED TO WAKE THEM UP?
THEY STEPPED OUT. SO LISTEN, I HAVE A VERY IMPORTANT ANNOUNCEMENT TO MAKE.
I--
MYSTIQUE!
YOU SEND AN ASSASSIN AFTER ME? ME? HE TRIED TO SABOTAGE MY ARMOR, SET IT UP TO SUFFOCATE ME.
I DON'T KNOW WHAT YOU'RE PLAYING AT, BUT IT ONLY TOOK SECONDS TO GET THE TRUTH OUT OF HIM!
P-PORTAL...
WHACKK

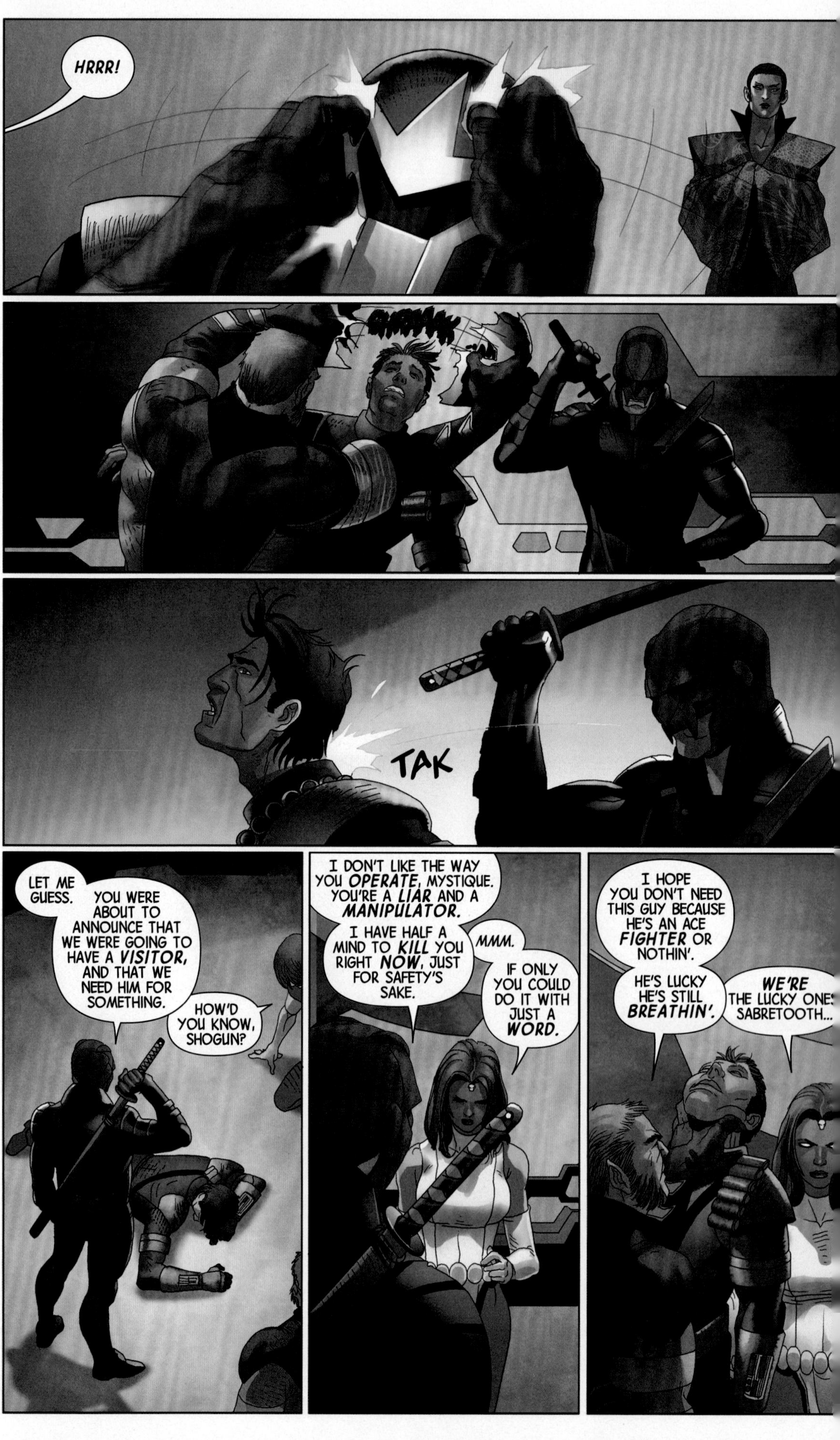
HRRR!
SHRAKK
TAK
LET ME GUESS.
YOU WERE ABOUT TO ANNOUNCE THAT WE WERE GOING TO HAVE A VISITOR, AND THAT WE NEED HIM FOR SOMETHING.
HOW'D YOU KNOW, SHOGUN?
I DON'T LIKE THE WAY YOU OPERATE, MYSTIQUE. YOU'RE A LIAR AND A MANIPULATOR.
I HAVE HALF A MIND TO KILL YOU RIGHT NOW, JUST FOR SAFETY'S SAKE.
MMM.
IF ONLY YOU COULD DO IT WITH JUST A WORD.
I HOPE YOU DON'T NEED THIS GUY BECAUSE HE'S AN ACE FIGHTER OR NOTHIN'.
HE'S LUCKY HE'S STILL BREATHIN'.
WE'RE THE LUCKY ONES, SABRETOOTH...

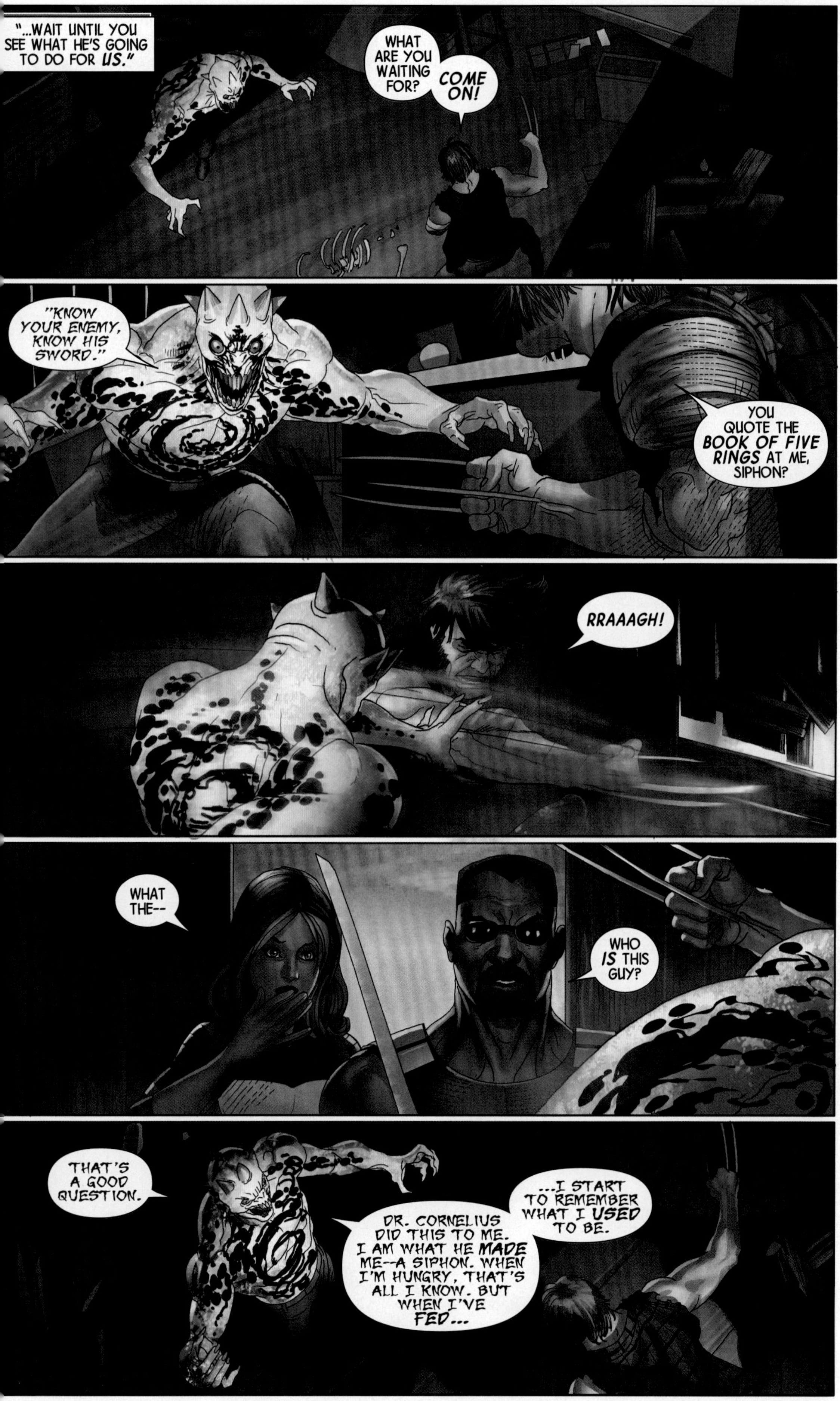
"...WAIT UNTIL YOU SEE WHAT HE'S GOING TO DO FOR US."
WHAT ARE YOU WAITING FOR?
COME ON!
"KNOW YOUR ENEMY, KNOW HIS SWORD."
YOU QUOTE THE BOOK OF FIVE RINGS AT ME, SIPHON?
RRAAAGH!
WHAT THE--
WHO IS THIS GUY?
THAT'S A GOOD QUESTION.
DR. CORNELIUS DID THIS TO ME. I AM WHAT HE MADE ME--A SIPHON. WHEN I'M HUNGRY, THAT'S ALL I KNOW. BUT WHEN I'VE FED...
...I START TO REMEMBER WHAT I USED TO BE.

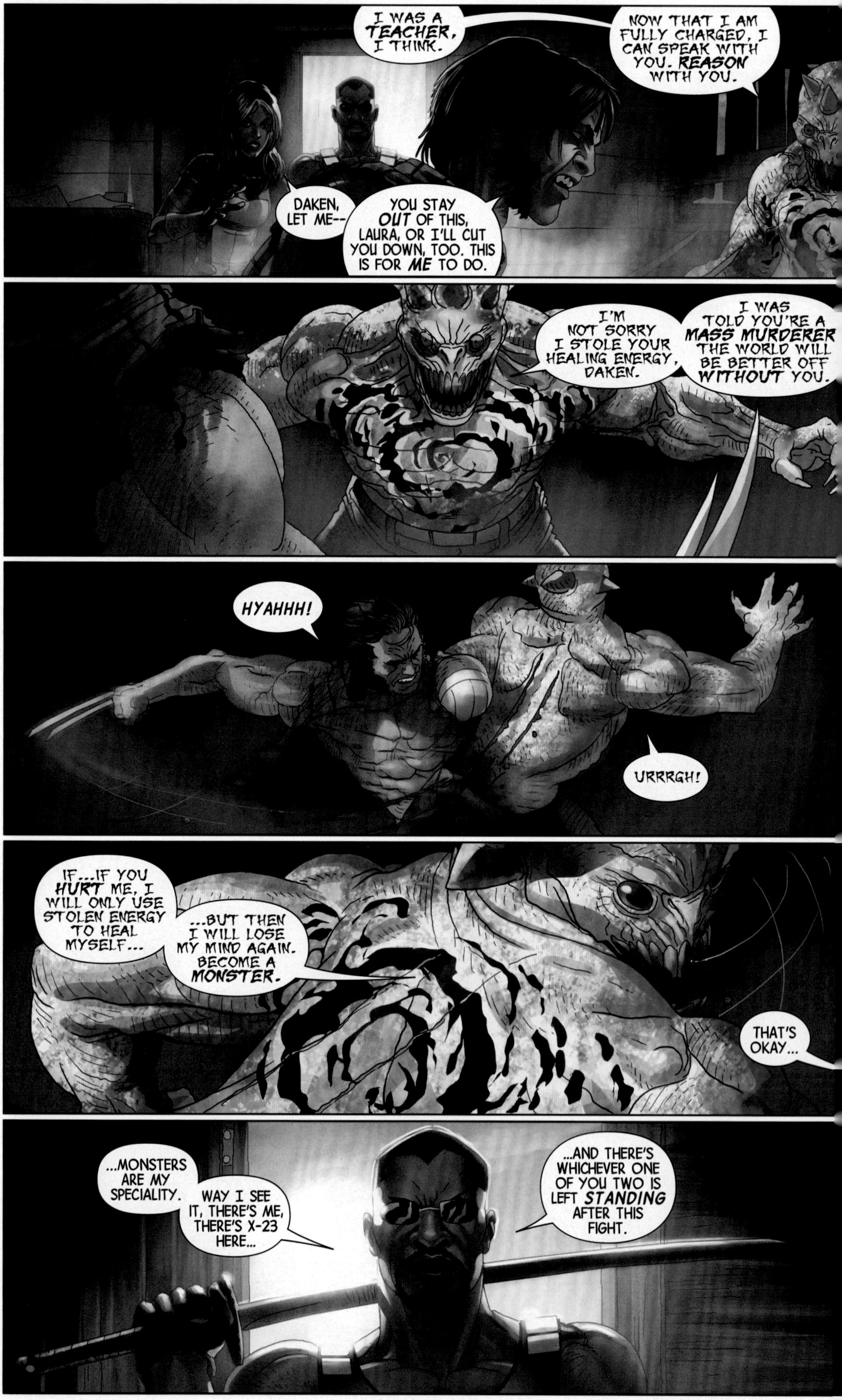

I WAS A TEACHER, I THINK.
NOW THAT I AM FULLY CHARGED, I CAN SPEAK WITH YOU. REASON WITH YOU.
DAKEN, LET ME--
YOU STAY OUT OF THIS, LAURA, OR I'LL CUT YOU DOWN, TOO. THIS IS FOR ME TO DO.
I'M NOT SORRY I STOLE YOUR HEALING ENERGY, DAKEN.
I WAS TOLD YOU'RE A MASS MURDERER. THE WORLD WILL BE BETTER OFF WITHOUT YOU.
HYAHHH!
URRRGH!
IF...IF YOU HURT ME, I WILL ONLY USE STOLEN ENERGY TO HEAL MYSELF...
...BUT THEN I WILL LOSE MY MIND AGAIN. BECOME A MONSTER.
THAT'S OKAY...
...MONSTERS ARE MY SPECIALITY.
WAY I SEE IT, THERE'S ME, THERE'S X-23 HERE...
...AND THERE'S WHICHEVER ONE OF YOU TWO IS LEFT STANDING AFTER THIS FIGHT.

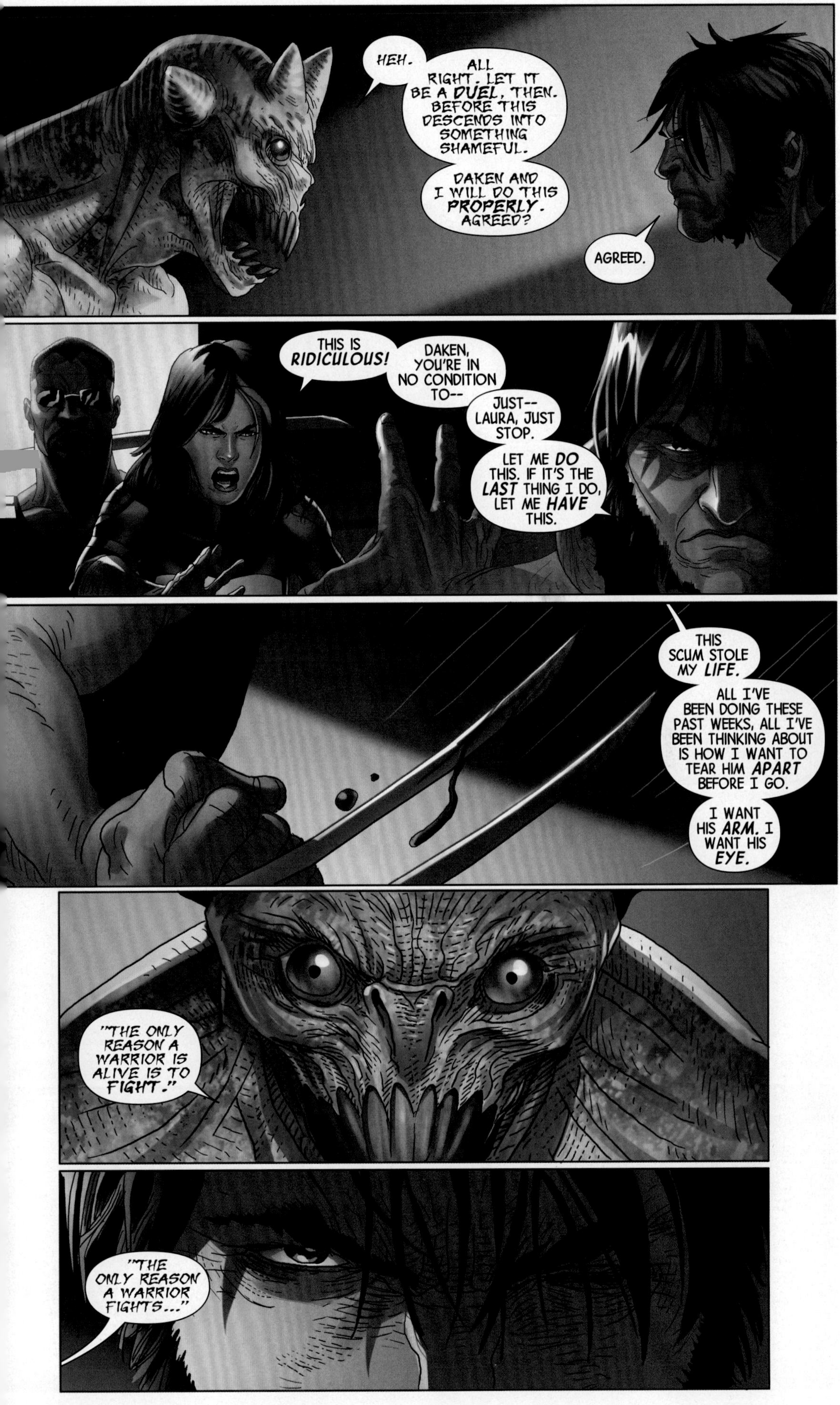
HEH.
ALL RIGHT. LET IT BE A DUEL, THEN. BEFORE THIS DESCENDS INTO SOMETHING SHAMEFUL.
DAKEN AND I WILL DO THIS PROPERLY. AGREED?
AGREED.
THIS IS RIDICULOUS!
DAKEN, YOU'RE IN NO CONDITION TO--
JUST-- LAURA, JUST STOP.
LET ME DO THIS. IF IT'S THE LAST THING I DO, LET ME HAVE THIS.
THIS SCUM STOLE MY LIFE.
ALL I'VE BEEN DOING THESE PAST WEEKS, ALL I'VE BEEN THINKING ABOUT IS HOW I WANT TO TEAR HIM APART BEFORE I GO.
I WANT HIS ARM. I WANT HIS EYE.
"THE ONLY REASON A WARRIOR IS ALIVE IS TO FIGHT."
"THE ONLY REASON A WARRIOR FIGHTS..."

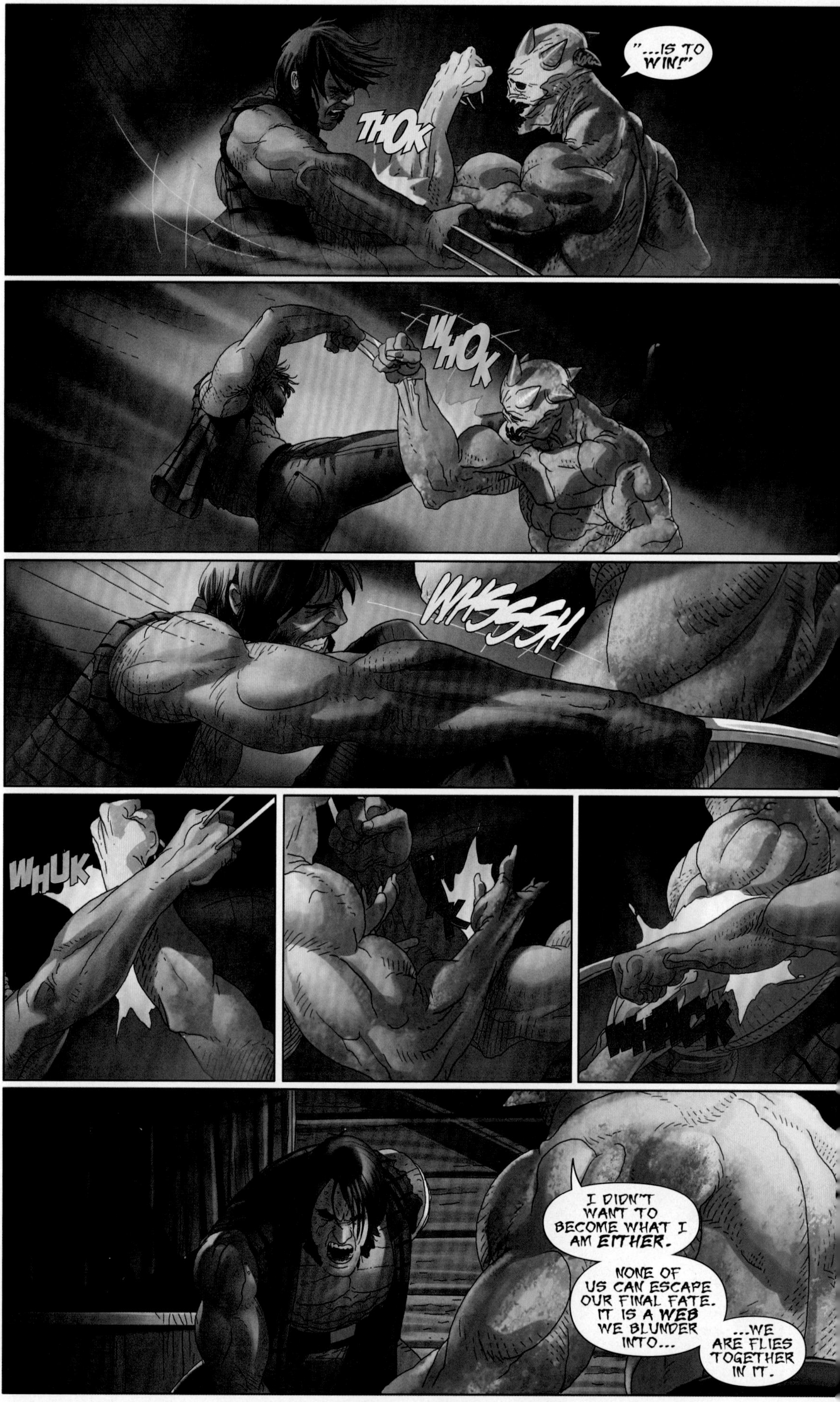
"...IS TO WIN!"
THOK
WHOK
WHSSSH
WHUK
WHACK
I DIDN'T WANT TO BECOME WHAT I AM EITHER.
NONE OF US CAN ESCAPE OUR FINAL FATE. IT IS A WEB WE BLUNDER INTO...
...WE ARE FLIES TOGETHER IN IT.

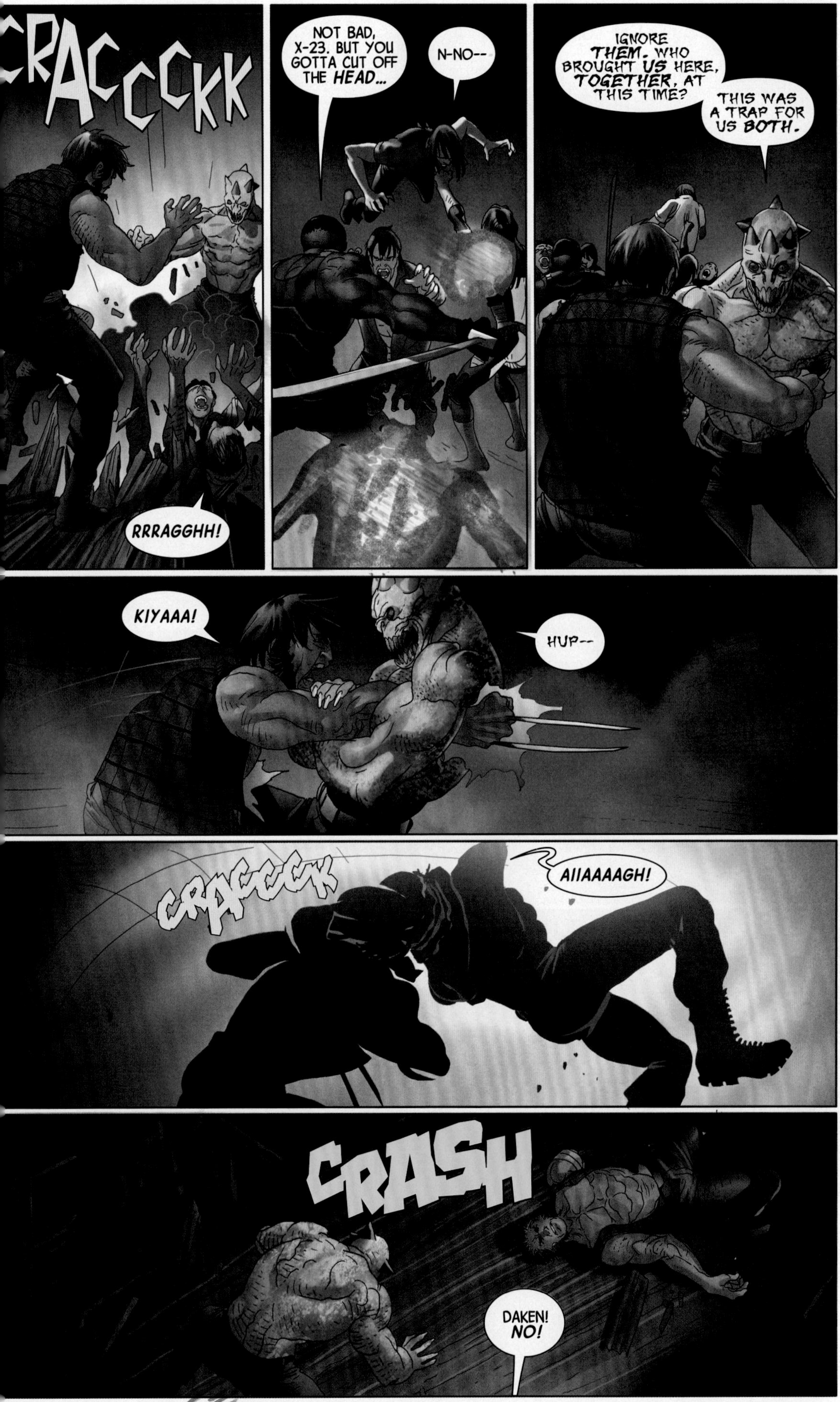
CRACCCKK
RRRAGGHH!
NOT BAD, X-23. BUT YOU GOTTA CUT OFF THE HEAD...
N-NO--
IGNORE THEM. WHO BROUGHT US HERE, TOGETHER, AT THIS TIME?
THIS WAS A TRAP FOR US BOTH.
KIYAAA!
HUP--
CRACCCK
AIIAAAAGH!
CRASH
DAKEN! NO!

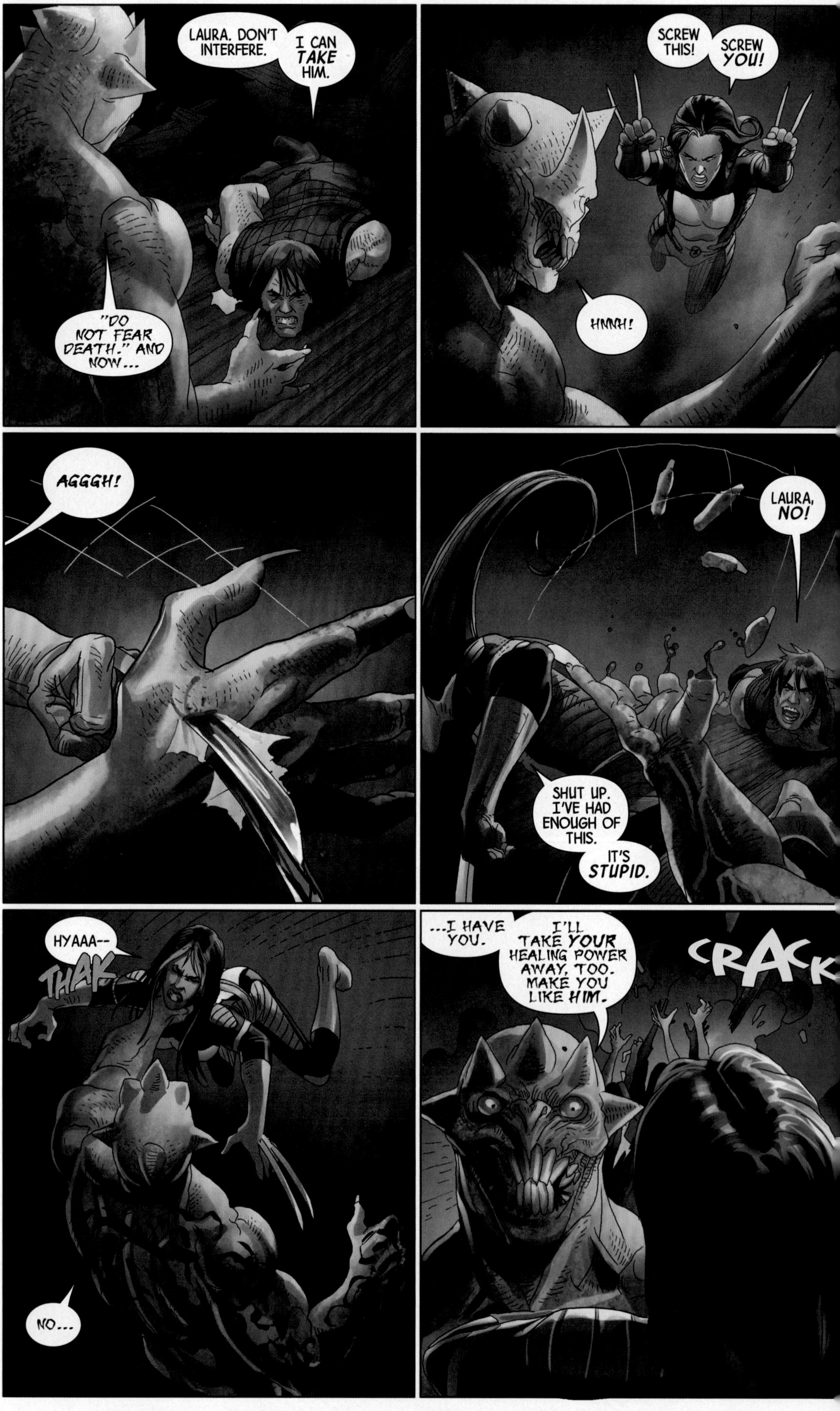

LAURA. DON'T INTERFERE.
I CAN TAKE HIM.
"DO NOT FEAR DEATH." AND NOW...
SCREW THIS!
SCREW YOU!
HNNH!
AGGGH!
LAURA, NO!
SHUT UP. I'VE HAD ENOUGH OF THIS.
IT'S STUPID.
HYAAA--
THAK
NO...
...I HAVE YOU.
I'LL TAKE YOUR HEALING POWER AWAY, TOO. MAKE YOU LIKE HIM.
CRACK

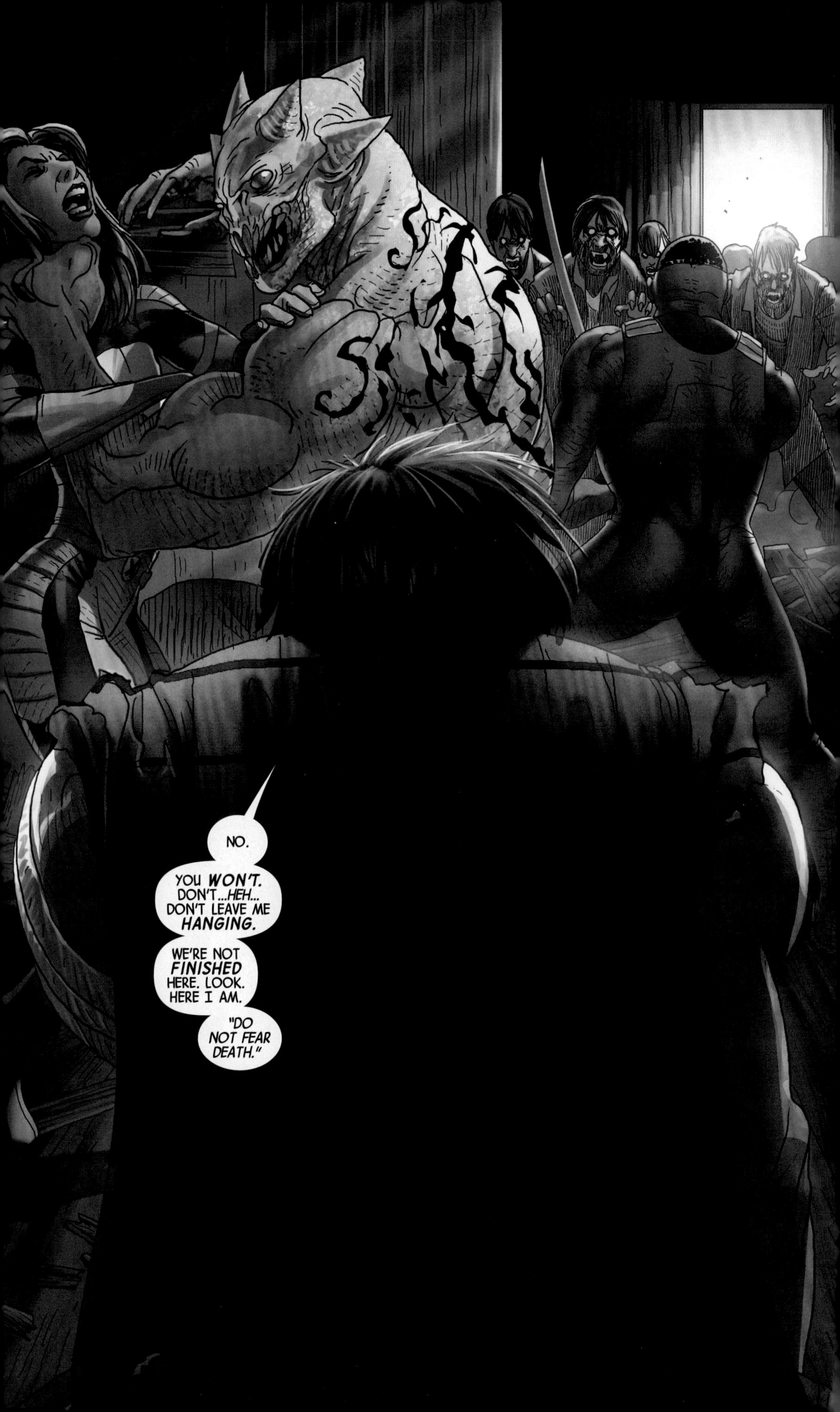
NO.
YOU WON'T. DON'T...HEH... DON'T LEAVE ME HANGING.
WE'RE NOT FINISHED HERE. LOOK. HERE I AM.
"DO NOT FEAR DEATH."

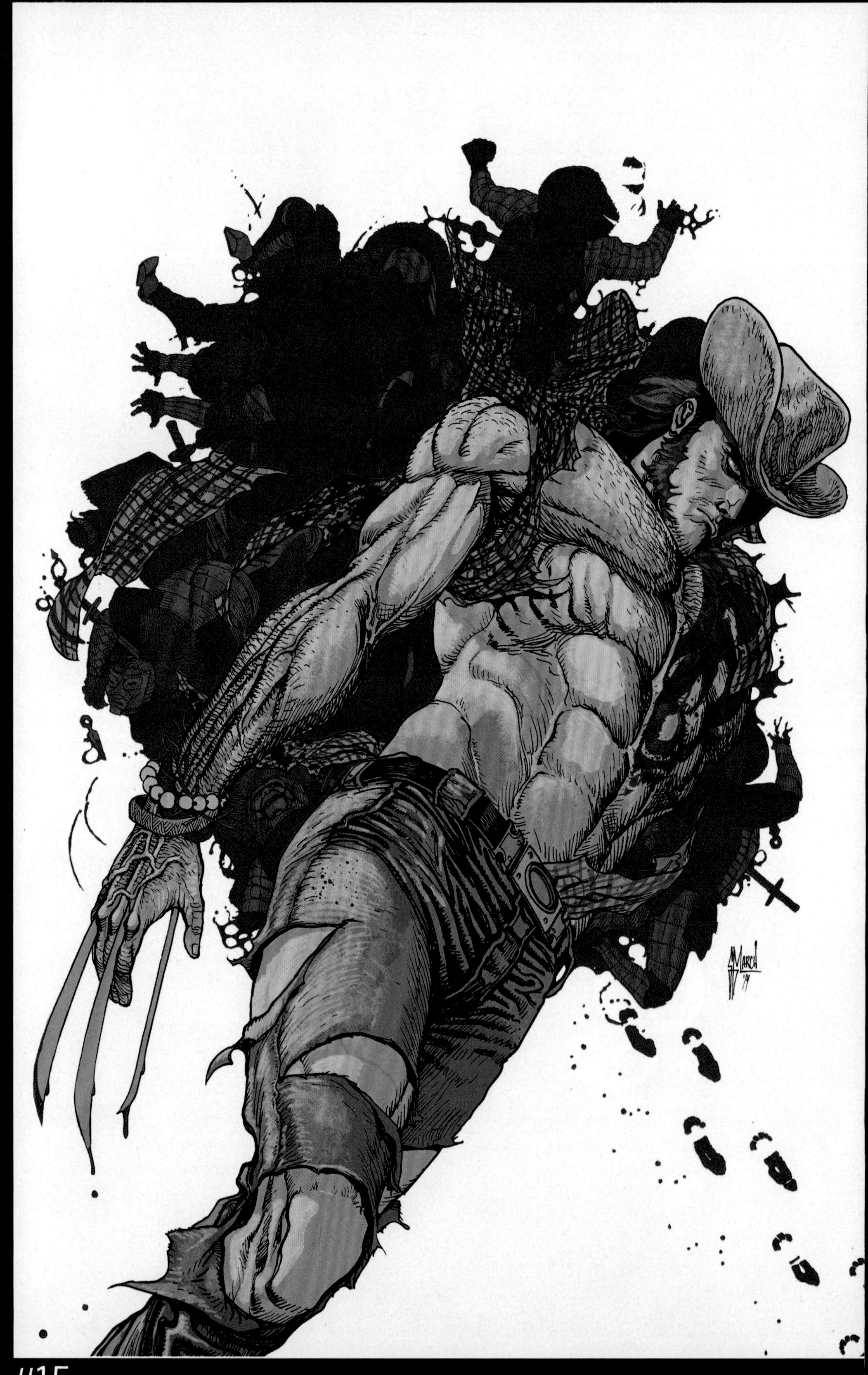

#15

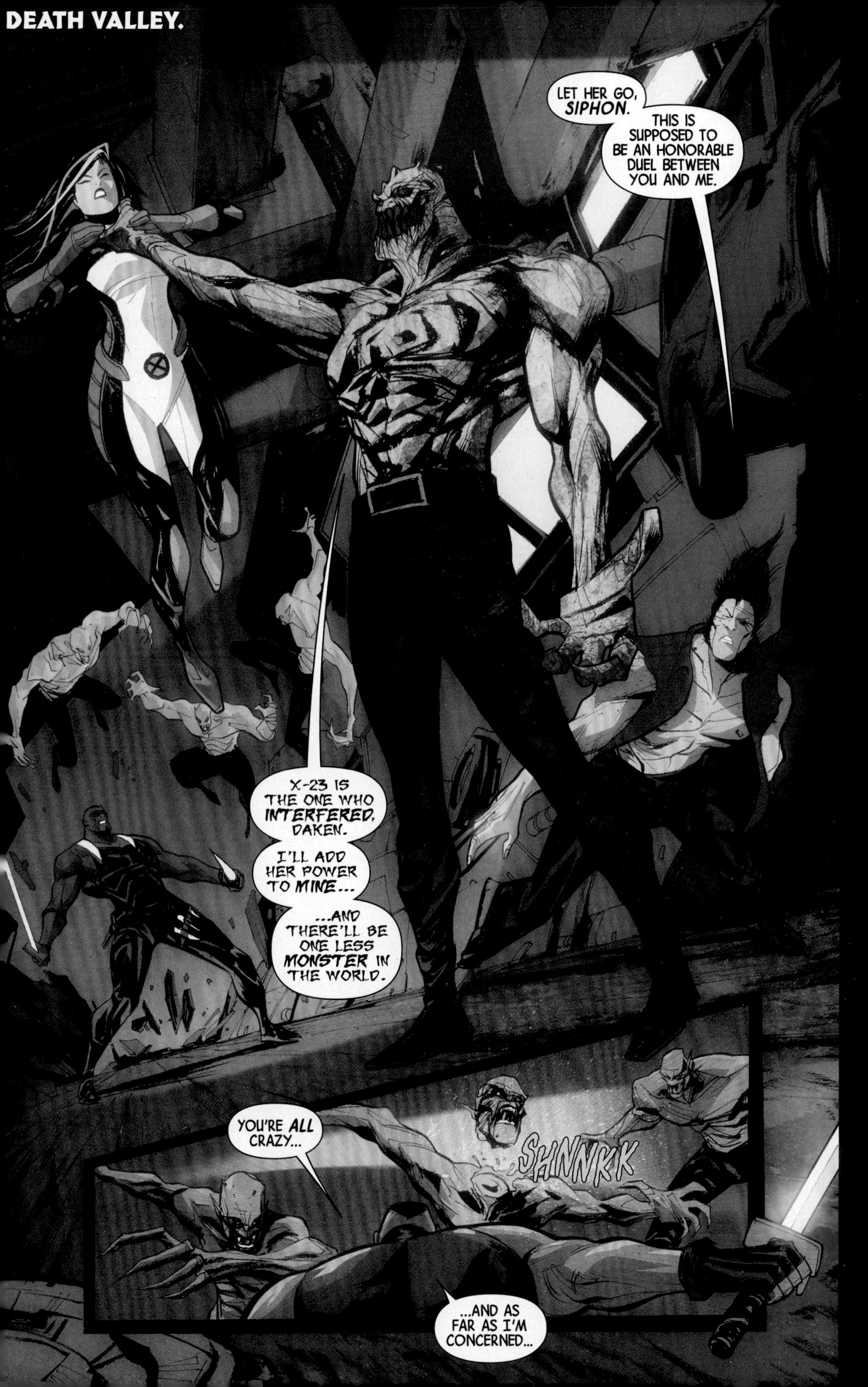
DEATH VALLEY.
LET HER GO, SIPHON.
THIS IS SUPPOSED TO BE AN HONORABLE DUEL BETWEEN YOU AND ME.
X-23 IS THE ONE WHO INTERFERED, DAKEN.
I'LL ADD HER POWER TO MINE...
...AND THERE'LL BE ONE LESS MONSTER IN THE WORLD.
YOU'RE ALL CRAZY...
SHNNKK
...AND AS FAR AS I'M CONCERNED...

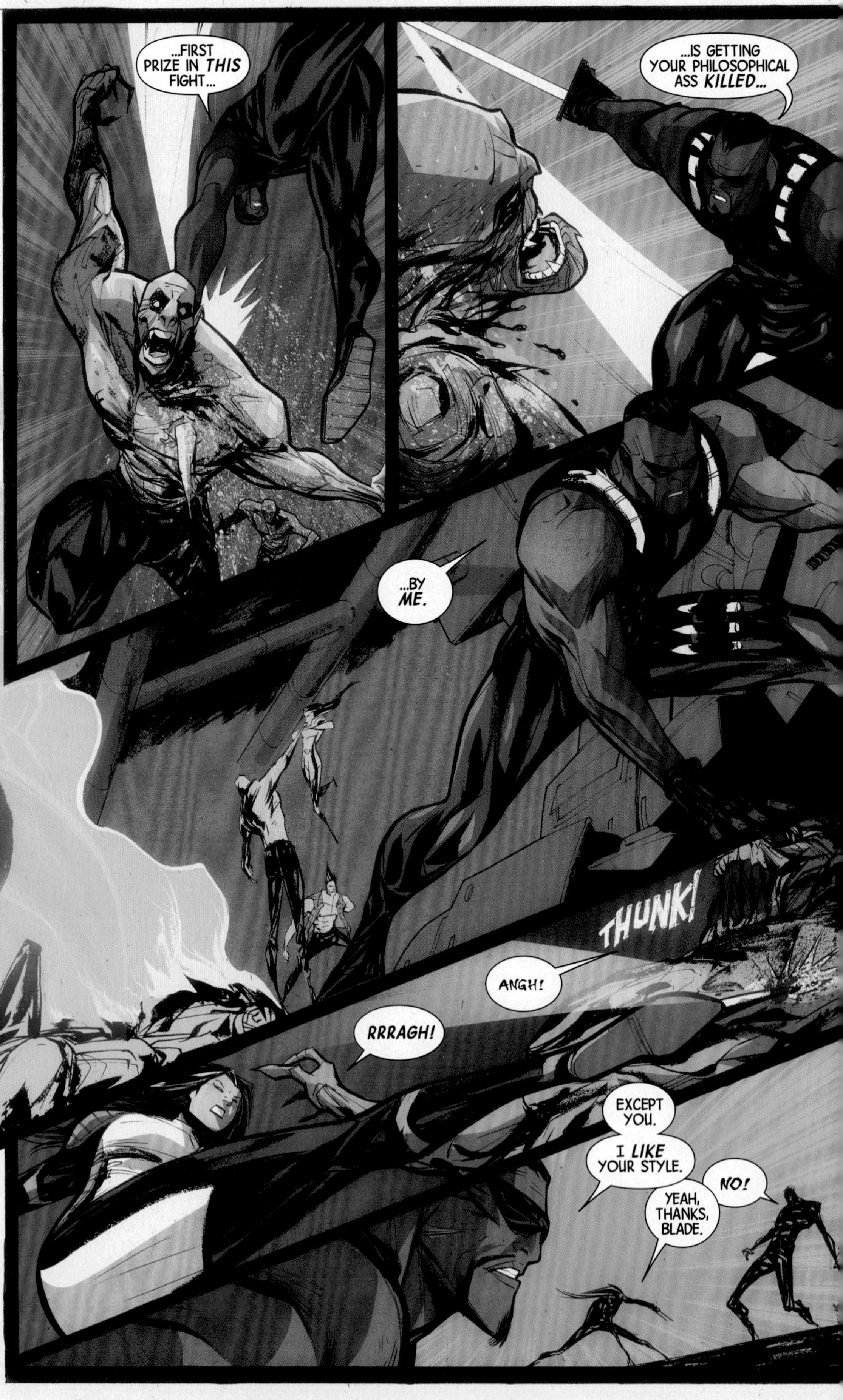
...FIRST PRIZE IN THIS FIGHT...
...IS GETTING YOUR PHILOSOPHICAL ASS KILLED...
...BY ME.
THUNK!
ANGH!
RRRAGH!
EXCEPT YOU.
I LIKE YOUR STYLE.
NO!
YEAH, THANKS, BLADE.

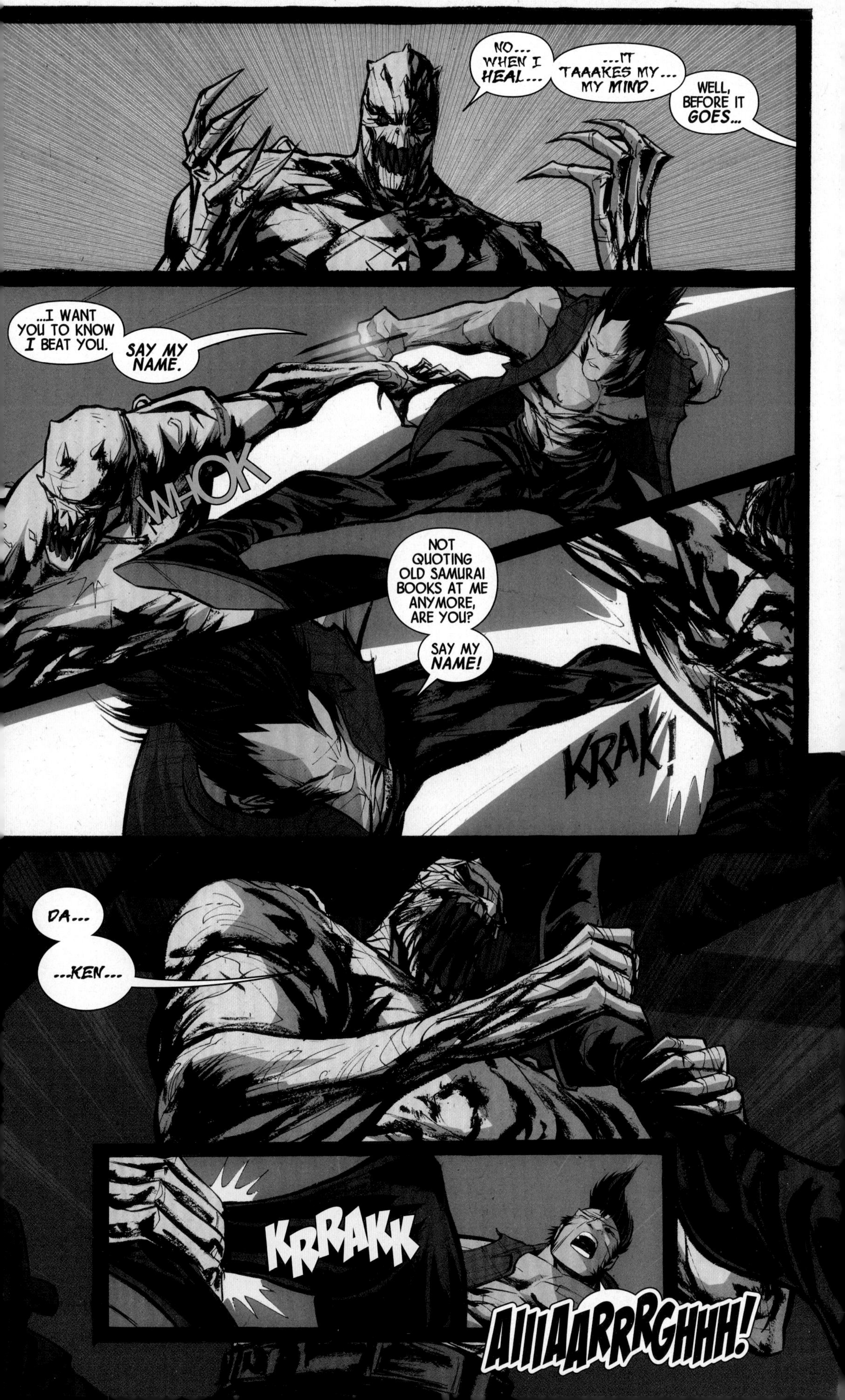
NO... WHEN I HEAL...
...IT TAAAKES MY... MY MIND.
WELL, BEFORE IT GOES...
...I WANT YOU TO KNOW I BEAT YOU.
SAY MY NAME.
WHOK
NOT QUOTING OLD SAMURAI BOOKS AT ME ANYMORE, ARE YOU?
SAY MY NAME!
KRAK!
DA...
...KEN...
KRRAKK
AIIIAARRRGHHH!

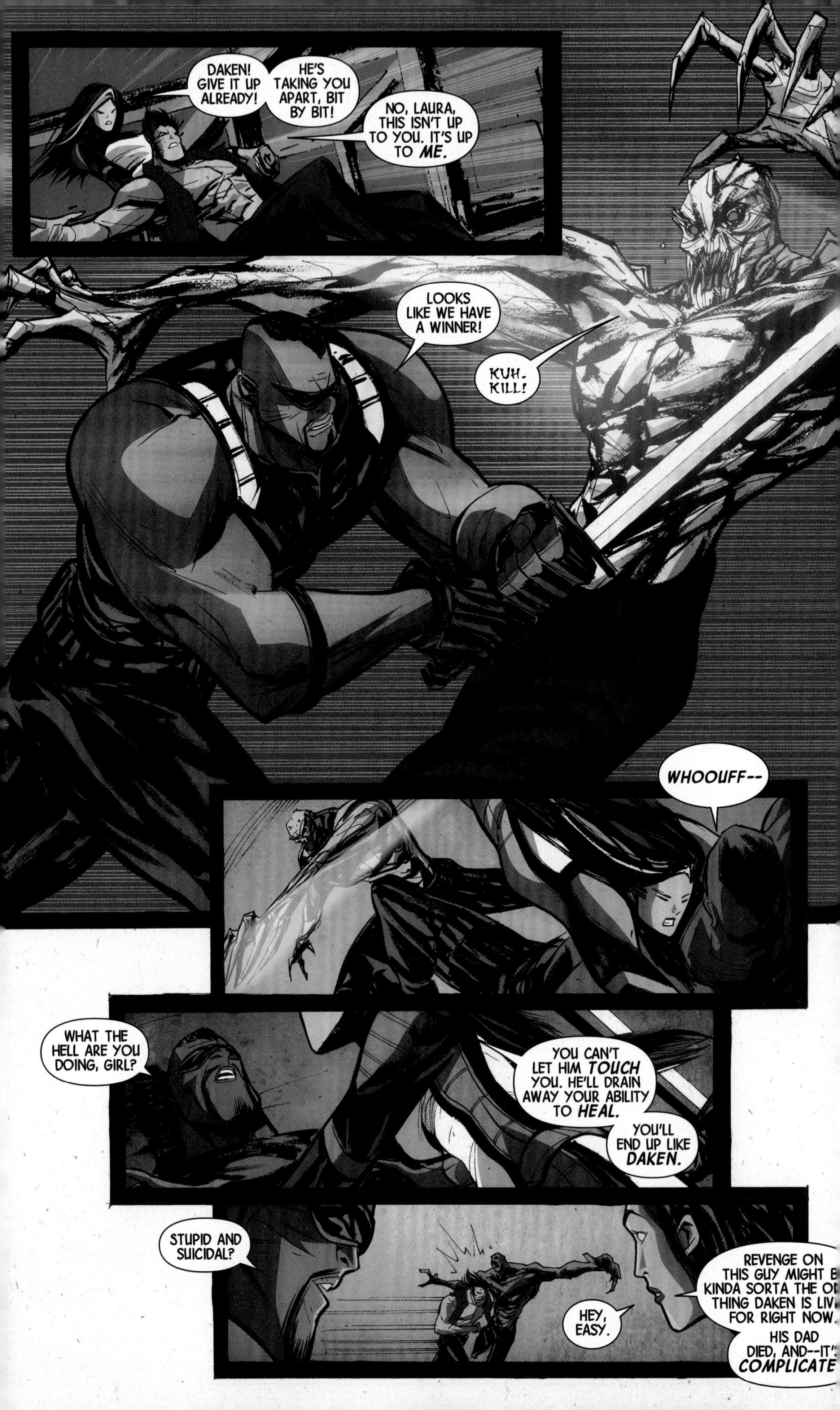
DAKEN! GIVE IT UP ALREADY!
HE'S TAKING YOU APART, BIT BY BIT!
NO, LAURA, THIS ISN'T UP TO YOU. IT'S UP TO ME.
LOOKS LIKE WE HAVE A WINNER!
KUH. KILL!
WHOOUFF--
WHAT THE HELL ARE YOU DOING, GIRL?
YOU CAN'T LET HIM TOUCH YOU. HE'LL DRAIN AWAY YOUR ABILITY TO HEAL.
YOU'LL END UP LIKE DAKEN.
STUPID AND SUICIDAL?
HEY, EASY.
REVENGE ON THIS GUY MIGHT B KINDA SORTA THE O THING DAKEN IS LIV FOR RIGHT NOW.
HIS DAD DIED, AND--IT' COMPLICATE

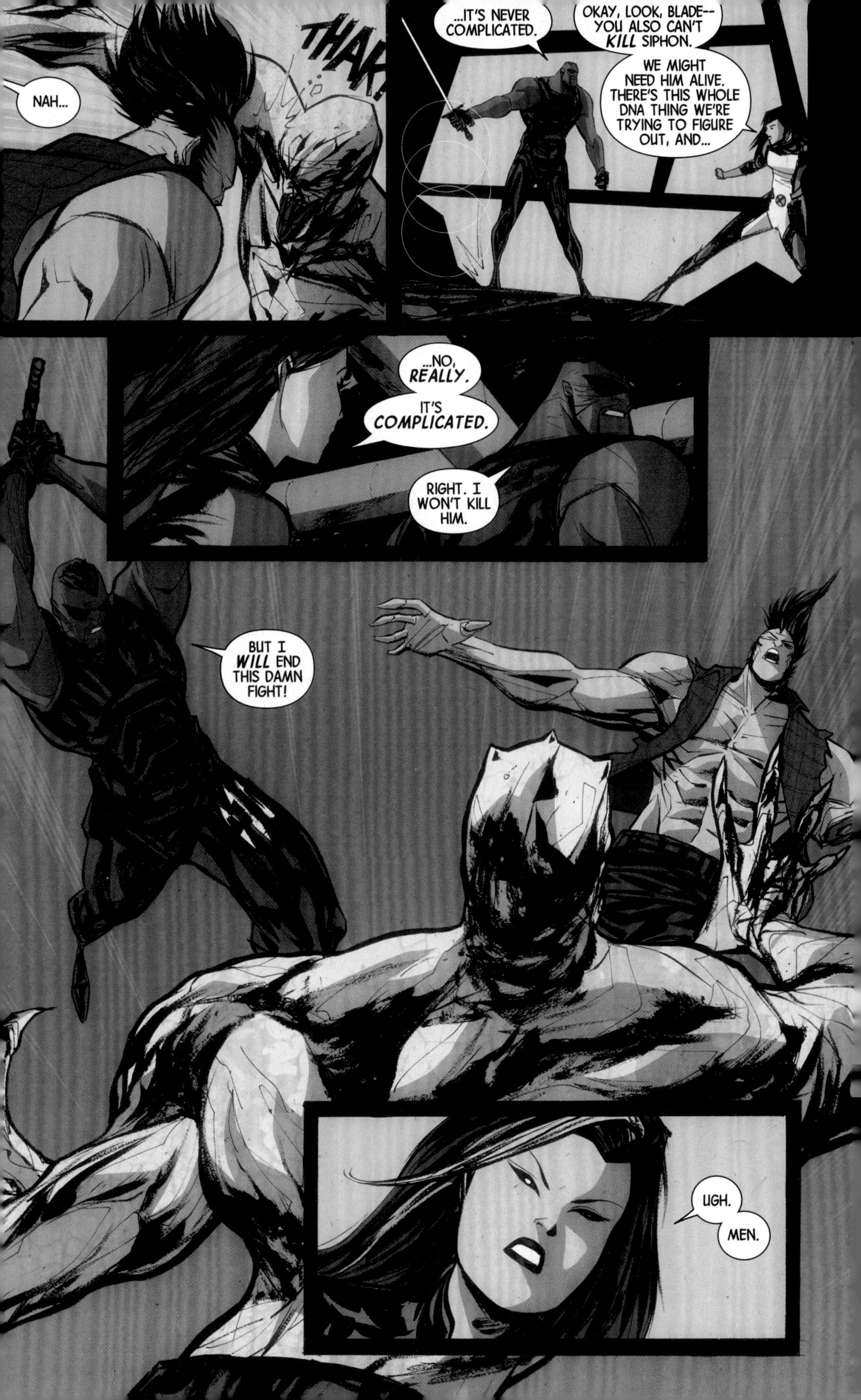

NAH...
THAK!
...IT'S NEVER COMPLICATED.
OKAY, LOOK, BLADE-- YOU ALSO CAN'T KILL SIPHON.
WE MIGHT NEED HIM ALIVE. THERE'S THIS WHOLE DNA THING WE'RE TRYING TO FIGURE OUT, AND...
...NO, REALLY.
IT'S COMPLICATED.
RIGHT. I WON'T KILL HIM.
BUT I WILL END THIS DAMN FIGHT!
UGH.
MEN.

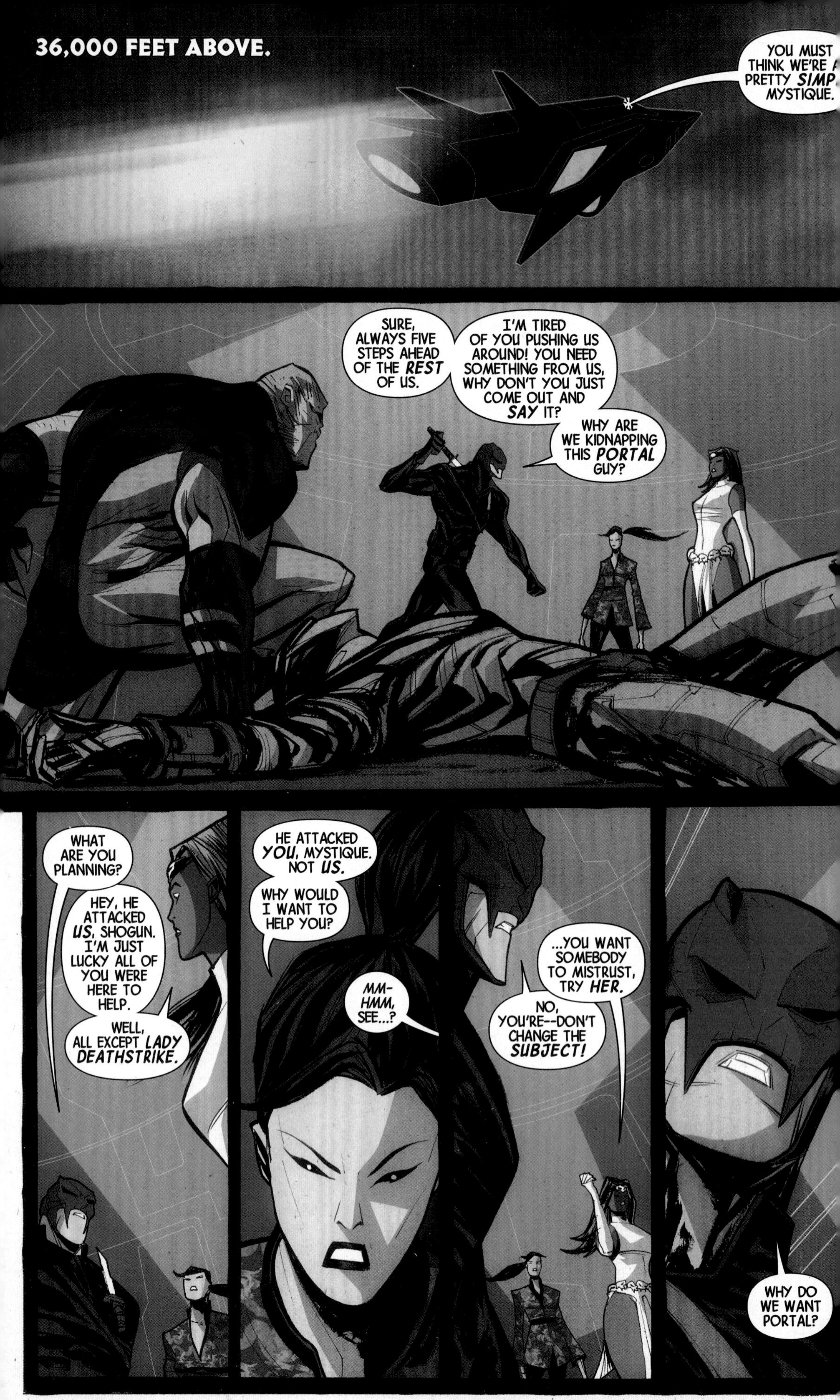

36,000 FEET ABOVE.
YOU MUST THINK WE'RE PRETTY SIMP MYSTIQUE.
SURE, ALWAYS FIVE STEPS AHEAD OF THE REST OF US.
I'M TIRED OF YOU PUSHING US AROUND! YOU NEED SOMETHING FROM US, WHY DON'T YOU JUST COME OUT AND SAY IT?
WHY ARE WE KIDNAPPING THIS PORTAL GUY?
WHAT ARE YOU PLANNING?
HEY, HE ATTACKED US, SHOGUN. I'M JUST LUCKY ALL OF YOU WERE HERE TO HELP.
WELL, ALL EXCEPT LADY DEATHSTRIKE.
HE ATTACKED YOU, MYSTIQUE. NOT US.
WHY WOULD I WANT TO HELP YOU?
MM-HMM, SEE...?
...YOU WANT SOMEBODY TO MISTRUST, TRY HER.
NO, YOU'RE--DON'T CHANGE THE SUBJECT!
WHY DO WE WANT PORTAL?

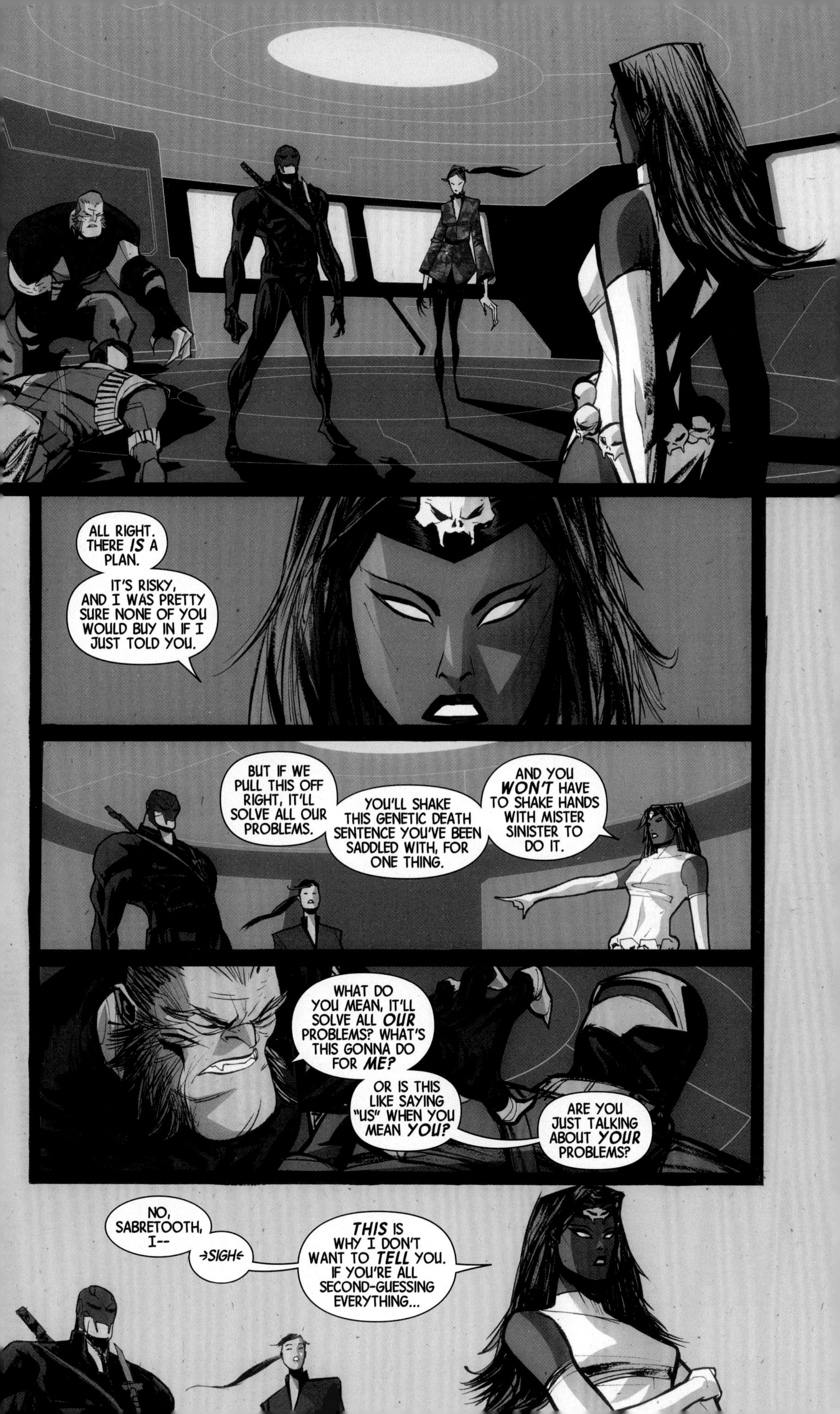
ALL RIGHT. THERE IS A PLAN.
IT'S RISKY, AND I WAS PRETTY SURE NONE OF YOU WOULD BUY IN IF I JUST TOLD YOU.
BUT IF WE PULL THIS OFF RIGHT, IT'LL SOLVE ALL OUR PROBLEMS.
YOU'LL SHAKE THIS GENETIC DEATH SENTENCE YOU'VE BEEN SADDLED WITH, FOR ONE THING.
AND YOU WON'T HAVE TO SHAKE HANDS WITH MISTER SINISTER TO DO IT.
WHAT DO YOU MEAN, IT'LL SOLVE ALL OUR PROBLEMS? WHAT'S THIS GONNA DO FOR ME?
OR IS THIS LIKE SAYING "US" WHEN YOU MEAN YOU?
ARE YOU JUST TALKING ABOUT YOUR PROBLEMS?
NO, SABRETOOTH, I--
→SIGH←
THIS IS WHY I DON'T WANT TO TELL YOU. IF YOU'RE ALL SECOND-GUESSING EVERYTHING...

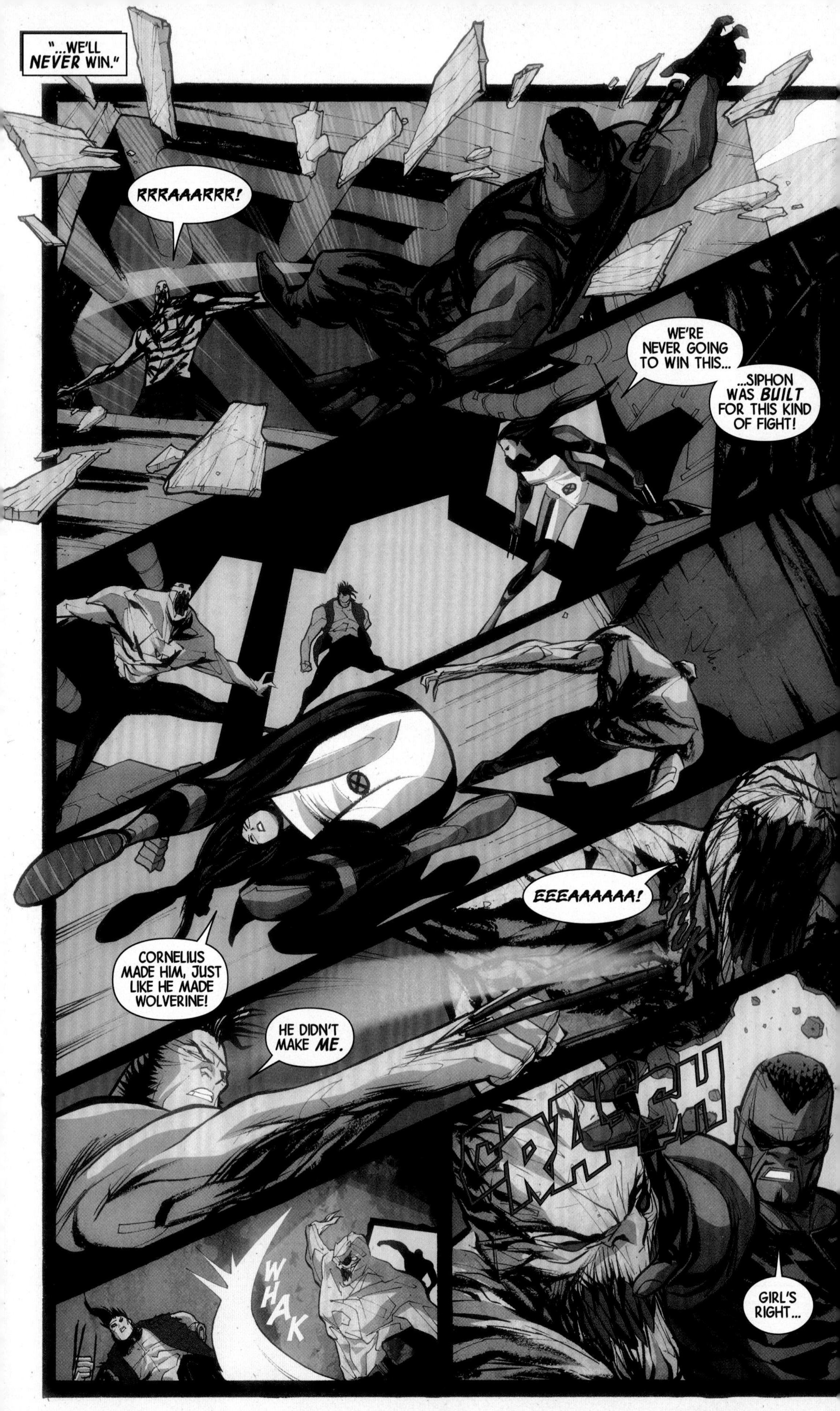

"...WE'LL NEVER WIN."
RRRAAARRR!
WE'RE NEVER GOING TO WIN THIS...
...SIPHON WAS BUILT FOR THIS KIND OF FIGHT!
EEEAAAAAA!
CORNELIUS MADE HIM, JUST LIKE HE MADE WOLVERINE!
HE DIDN'T MAKE ME.
WHAK
GIRL'S RIGHT...

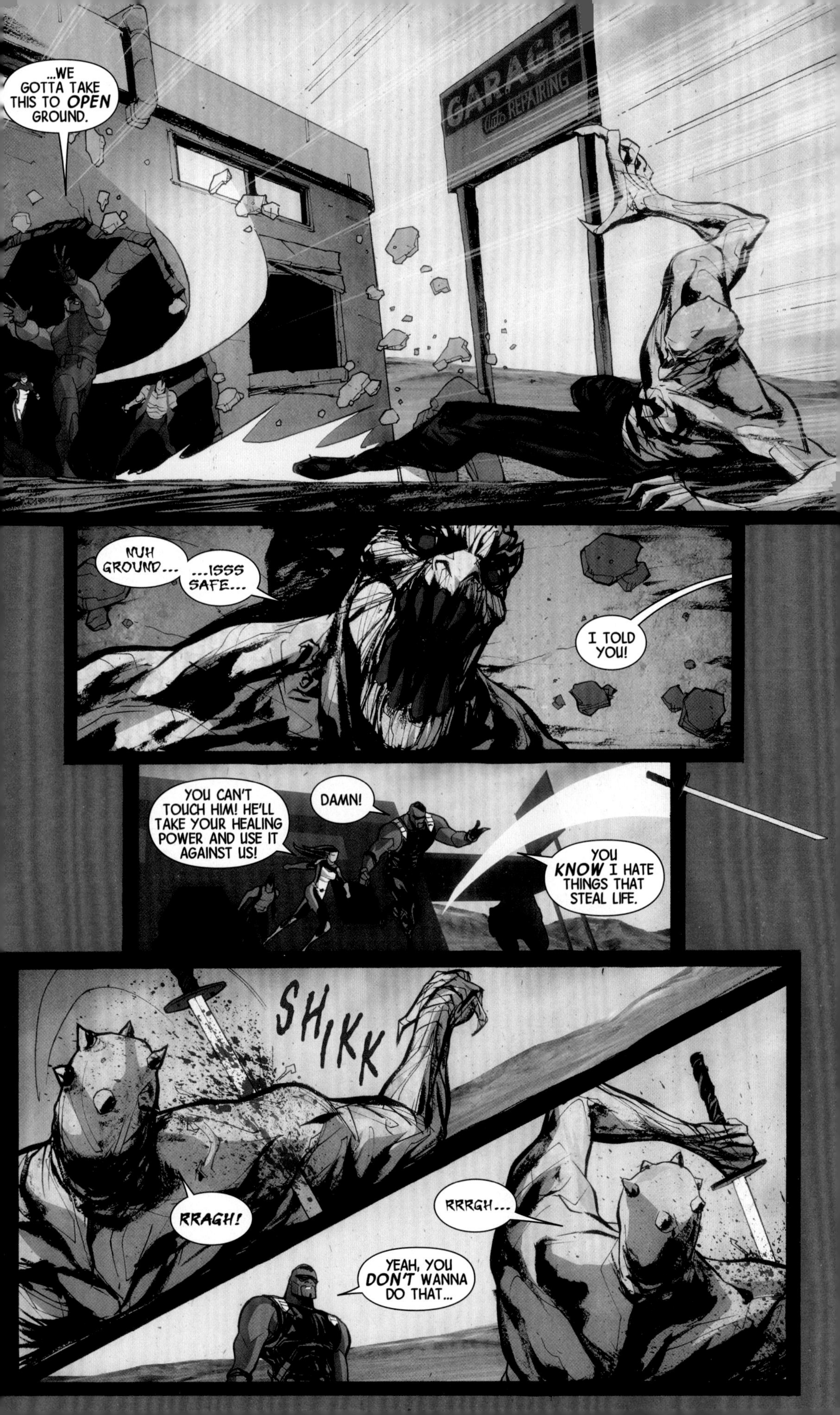
...WE GOTTA TAKE THIS TO OPEN GROUND.
GARAGE
Auto REPAIRING
NUH GROUND...
...ISSS SAFE...
I TOLD YOU!
YOU CAN'T TOUCH HIM! HE'LL TAKE YOUR HEALING POWER AND USE IT AGAINST US!
DAMN!
YOU KNOW I HATE THINGS THAT STEAL LIFE.
SHIKK
RRAGH!
RRRGH...
YEAH, YOU DON'T WANNA DO THAT...

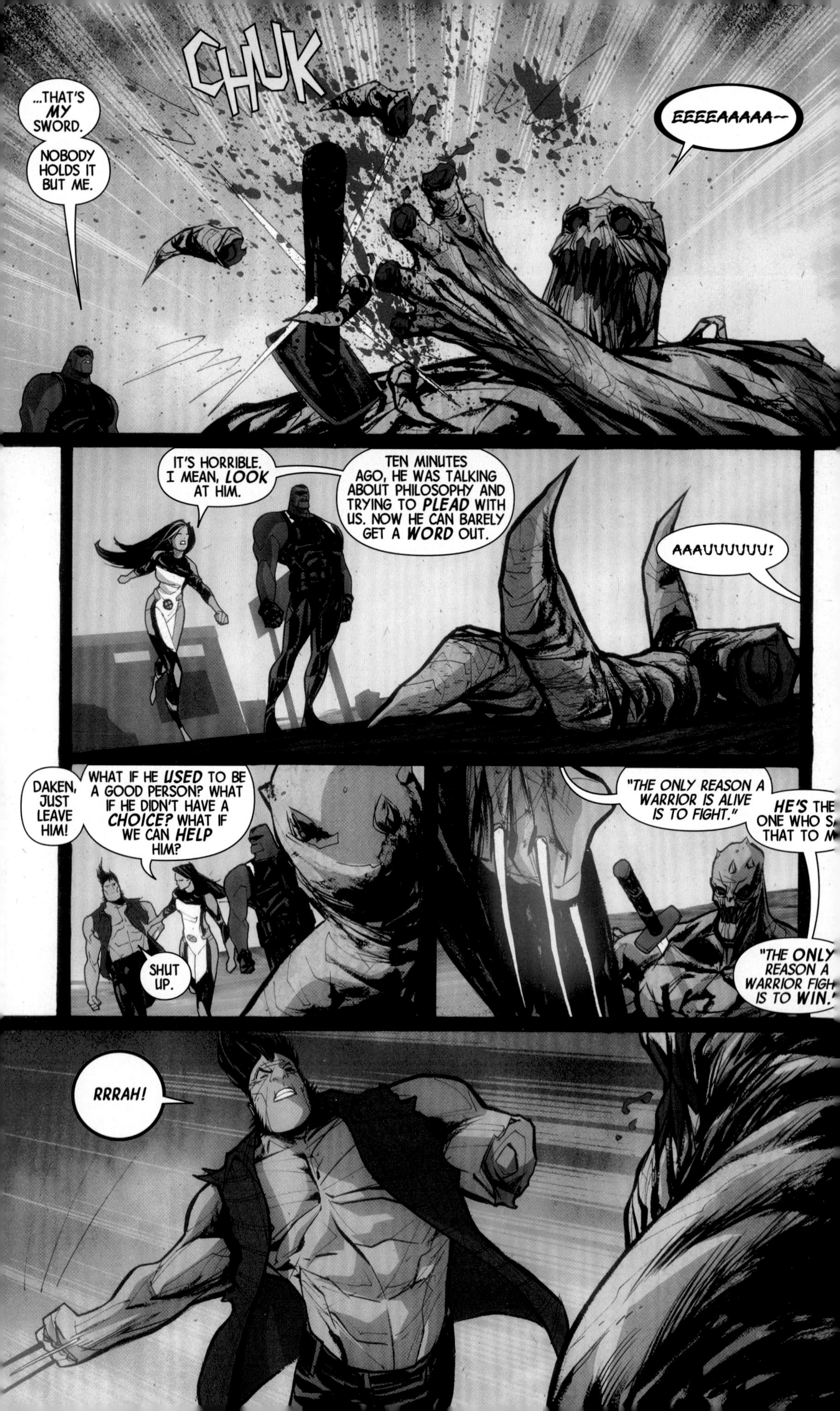
CHUK
...THAT'S MY SWORD.
NOBODY HOLDS IT BUT ME.
EEEEAAAAA--
IT'S HORRIBLE. I MEAN, LOOK AT HIM.
TEN MINUTES AGO, HE WAS TALKING ABOUT PHILOSOPHY AND TRYING TO PLEAD WITH US. NOW HE CAN BARELY GET A WORD OUT.
AAAUUUUUU!
DAKEN, JUST LEAVE HIM!
WHAT IF HE USED TO BE A GOOD PERSON? WHAT IF HE DIDN'T HAVE A CHOICE? WHAT IF WE CAN HELP HIM?
SHUT UP.
"THE ONLY REASON A WARRIOR IS ALIVE IS TO FIGHT."
RRRAH!

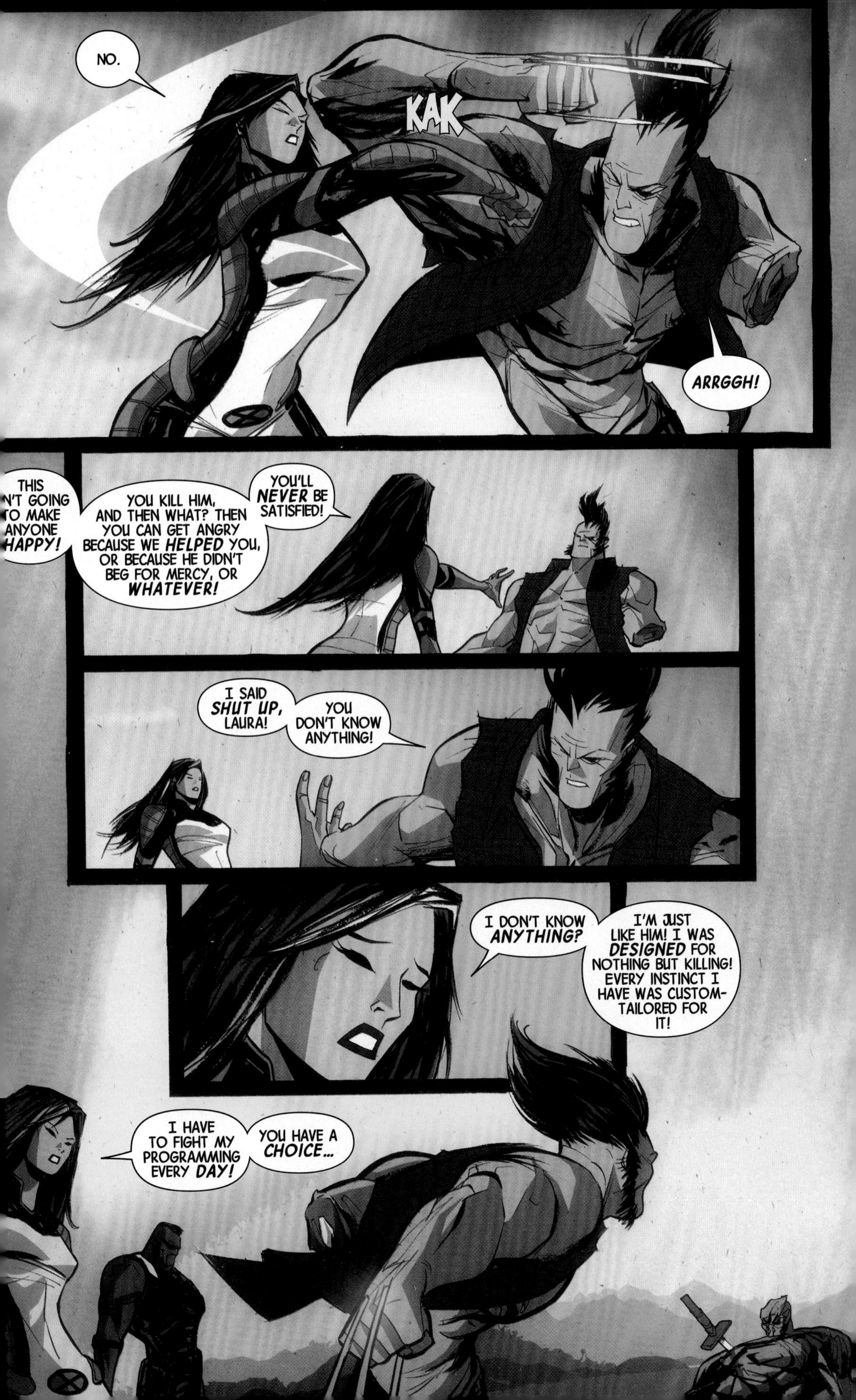
NO.
KAK
ARRGGH!
THIS N'T GOING TO MAKE ANYONE HAPPY!
YOU KILL HIM, AND THEN WHAT? THEN YOU CAN GET ANGRY BECAUSE WE HELPED YOU, OR BECAUSE HE DIDN'T BEG FOR MERCY, OR WHATEVER!
YOU'LL NEVER BE SATISFIED!
I SAID SHUT UP, LAURA!
YOU DON'T KNOW ANYTHING!
I DON'T KNOW ANYTHING?
I'M JUST LIKE HIM! I WAS DESIGNED FOR NOTHING BUT KILLING! EVERY INSTINCT I HAVE WAS CUSTOM-TAILORED FOR IT!
I HAVE TO FIGHT MY PROGRAMMING EVERY DAY!
YOU HAVE A CHOICE...

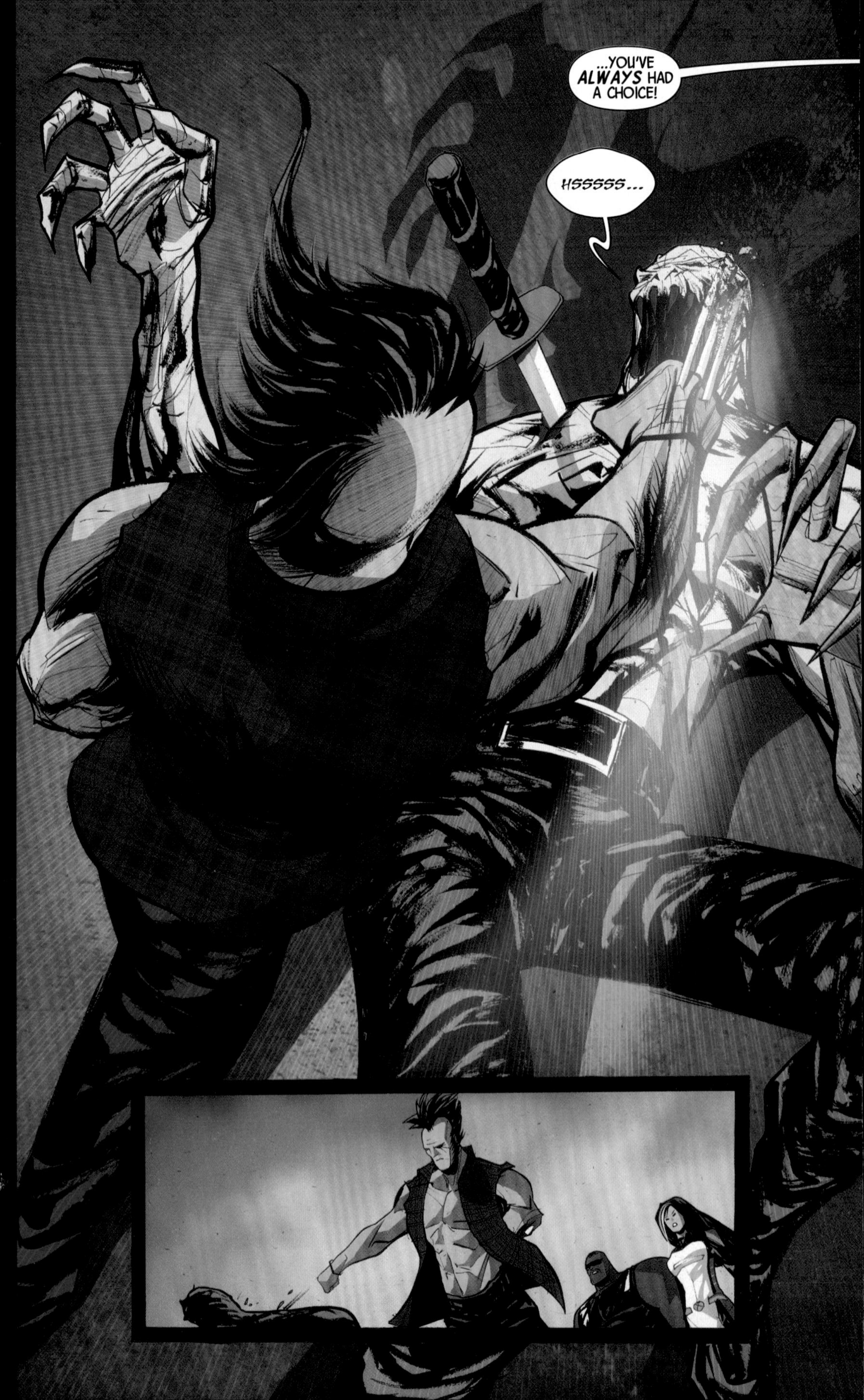
...YOU'VE ALWAYS HAD A CHOICE!
HSSSSS...

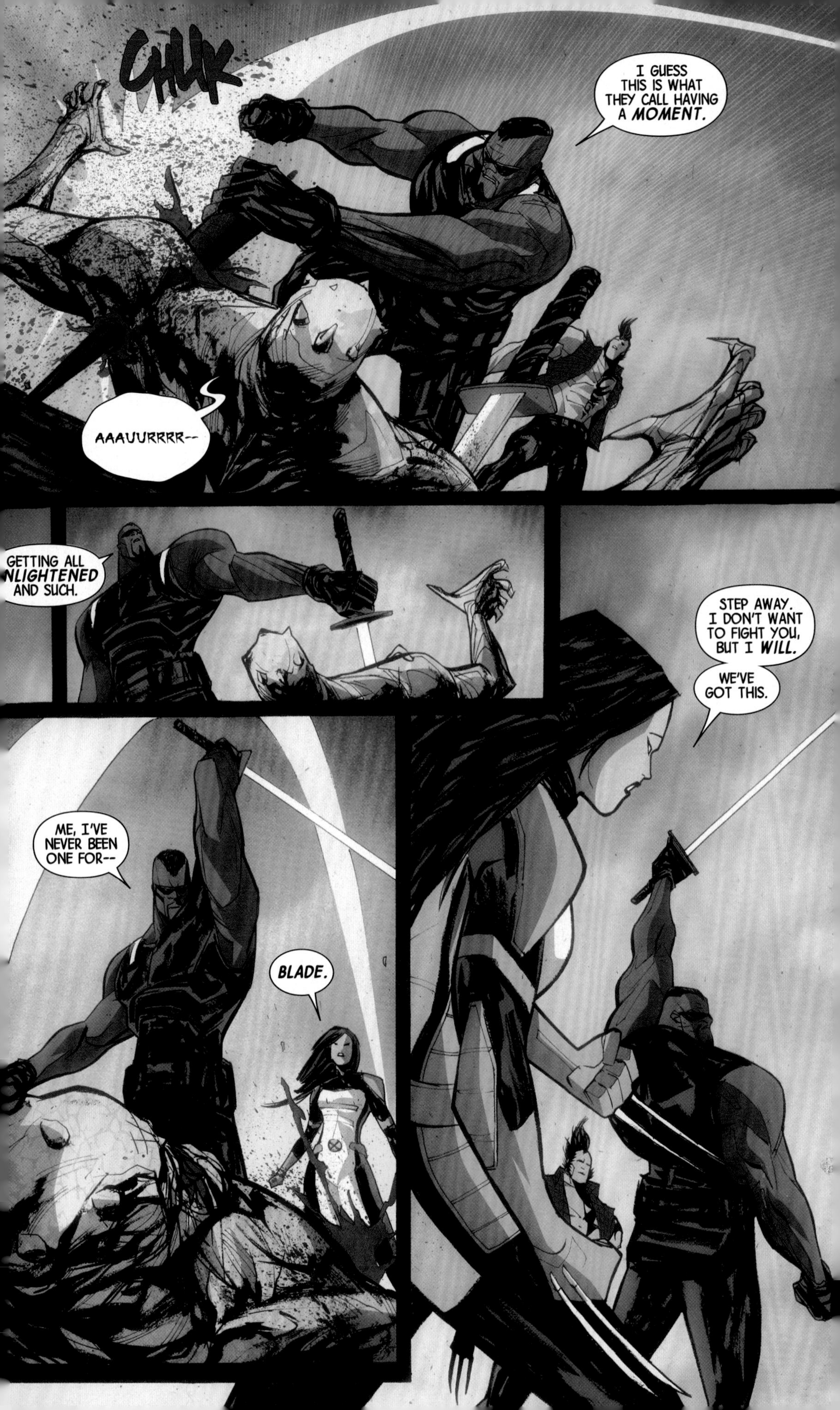
CHUK
I GUESS THIS IS WHAT THEY CALL HAVING A *MOMENT.*
AAAUURRRR--
GETTING ALL NLIGHTENED AND SUCH.
STEP AWAY. I DON'T WANT TO FIGHT YOU, BUT I *WILL.*
WE'VE GOT THIS.
ME, I'VE NEVER BEEN ONE FOR--
BLADE.

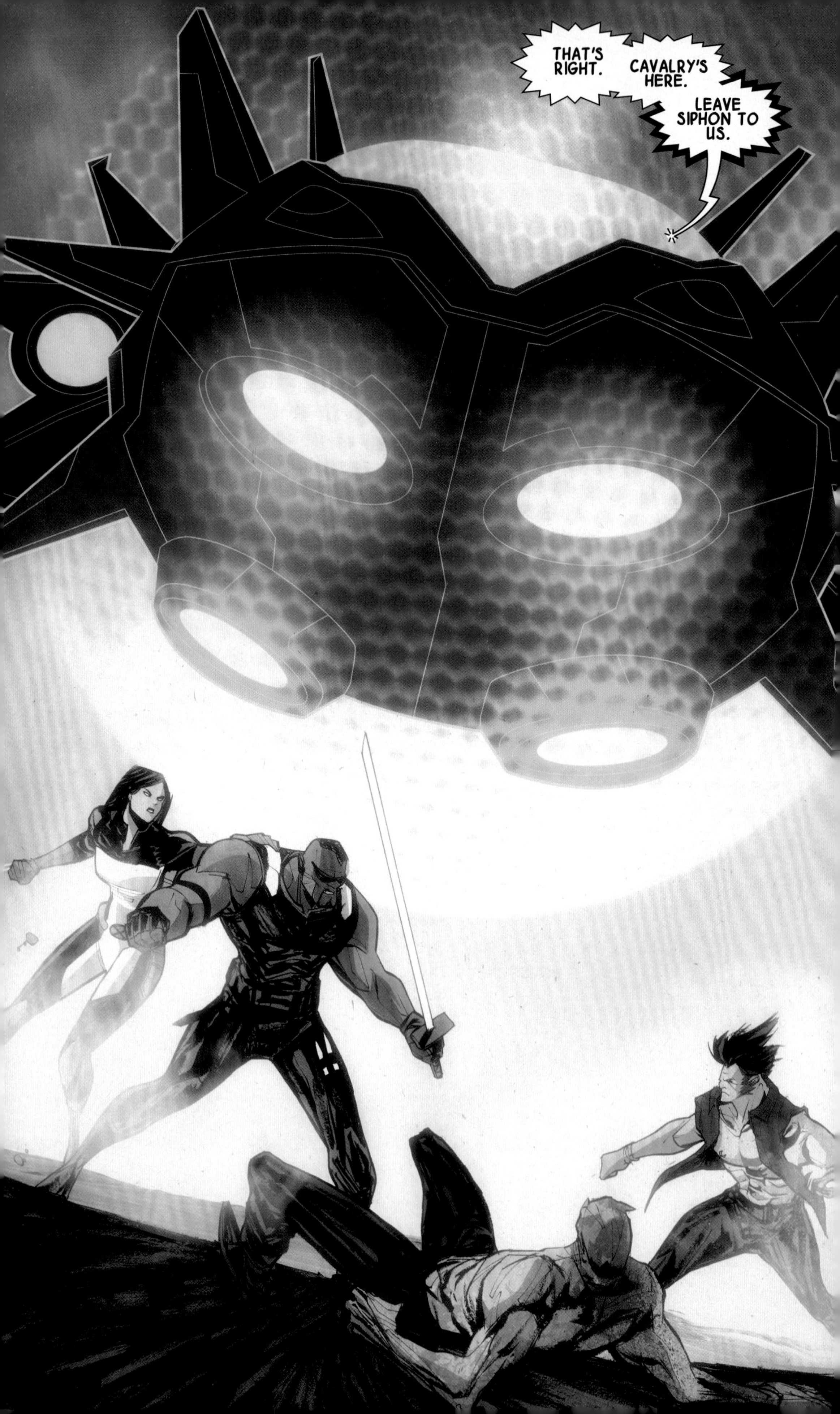
THAT'S RIGHT.
CAVALRY'S HERE.
LEAVE SIPHON TO US.

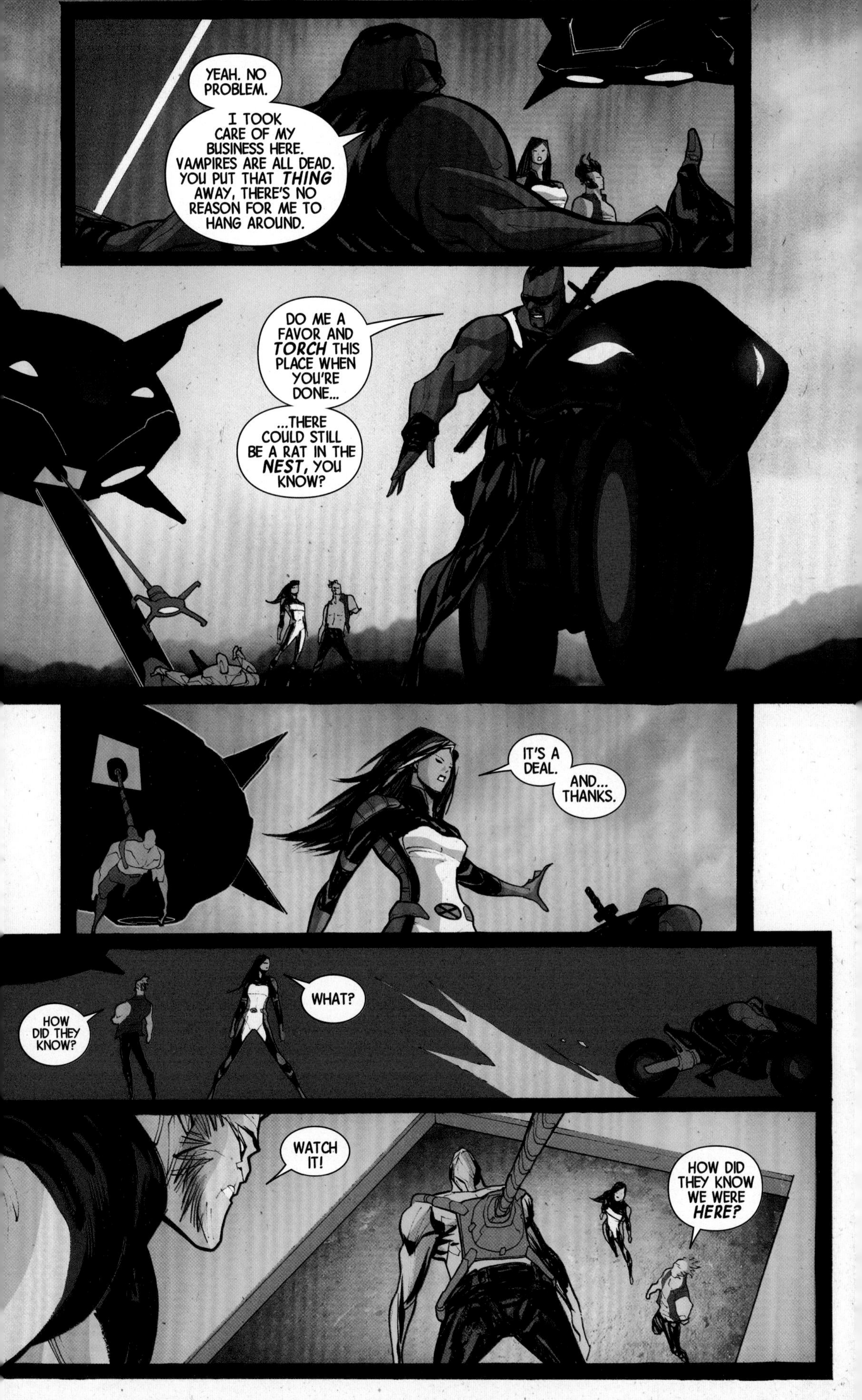
YEAH. NO PROBLEM.
I TOOK CARE OF MY BUSINESS HERE. VAMPIRES ARE ALL DEAD. YOU PUT THAT THING AWAY, THERE'S NO REASON FOR ME TO HANG AROUND.
DO ME A FAVOR AND TORCH THIS PLACE WHEN YOU'RE DONE...
...THERE COULD STILL BE A RAT IN THE NEST, YOU KNOW?
IT'S A DEAL.
AND... THANKS.
WHAT?
HOW DID THEY KNOW?
WATCH IT!
HOW DID THEY KNOW WE WERE HERE?

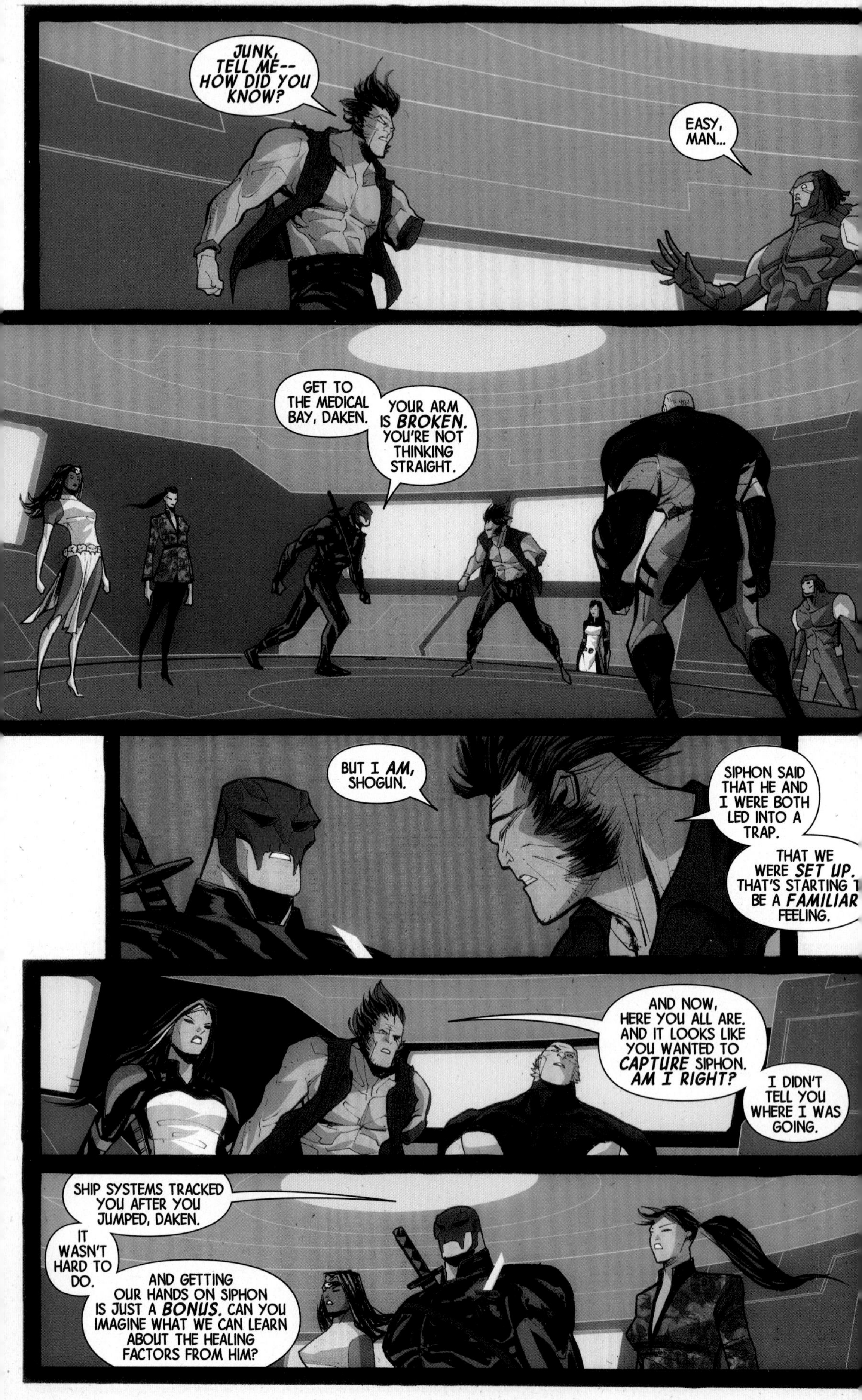
JUNK, TELL ME-- HOW DID YOU KNOW?
EASY, MAN...
GET TO THE MEDICAL BAY, DAKEN.
YOUR ARM IS BROKEN. YOU'RE NOT THINKING STRAIGHT.
BUT I AM, SHOGUN.
SIPHON SAID THAT HE AND I WERE BOTH LED INTO A TRAP.
THAT WE WERE SET UP. THAT'S STARTING T BE A FAMILIAR FEELING.
AND NOW, HERE YOU ALL ARE. AND IT LOOKS LIKE YOU WANTED TO CAPTURE SIPHON. AM I RIGHT?
I DIDN'T TELL YOU WHERE I WAS GOING.
SHIP SYSTEMS TRACKED YOU AFTER YOU JUMPED, DAKEN.
IT WASN'T HARD TO DO.
AND GETTING OUR HANDS ON SIPHON IS JUST A BONUS. CAN YOU IMAGINE WHAT WE CAN LEARN ABOUT THE HEALING FACTORS FROM HIM?

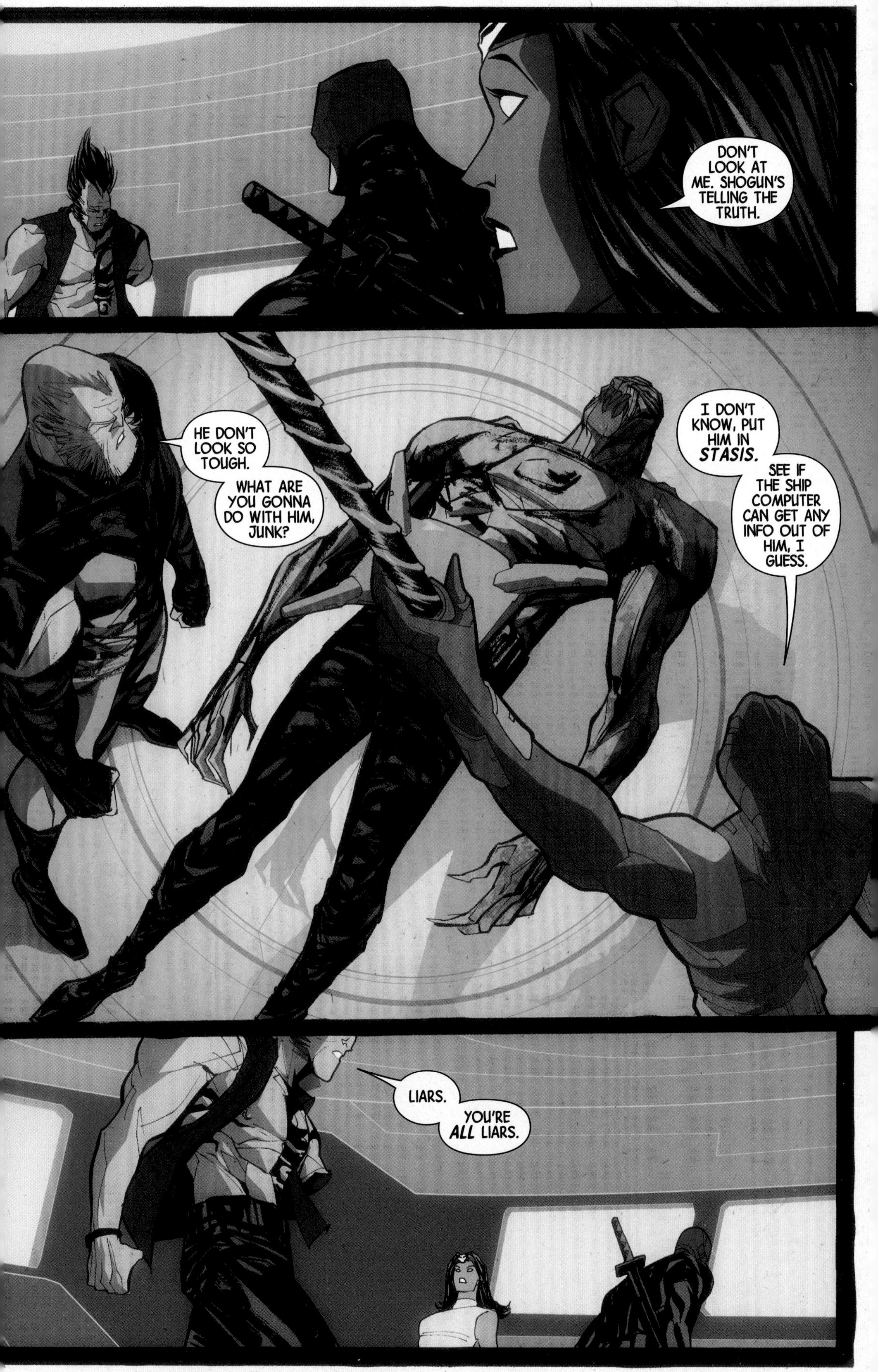
DON'T LOOK AT ME. SHOGUN'S TELLING THE TRUTH.
HE DON'T LOOK SO TOUGH.
WHAT ARE YOU GONNA DO WITH HIM, JUNK?
I DON'T KNOW, PUT HIM IN STASIS.
SEE IF THE SHIP COMPUTER CAN GET ANY INFO OUT OF HIM, I GUESS.
LIARS.
YOU'RE ALL LIARS.

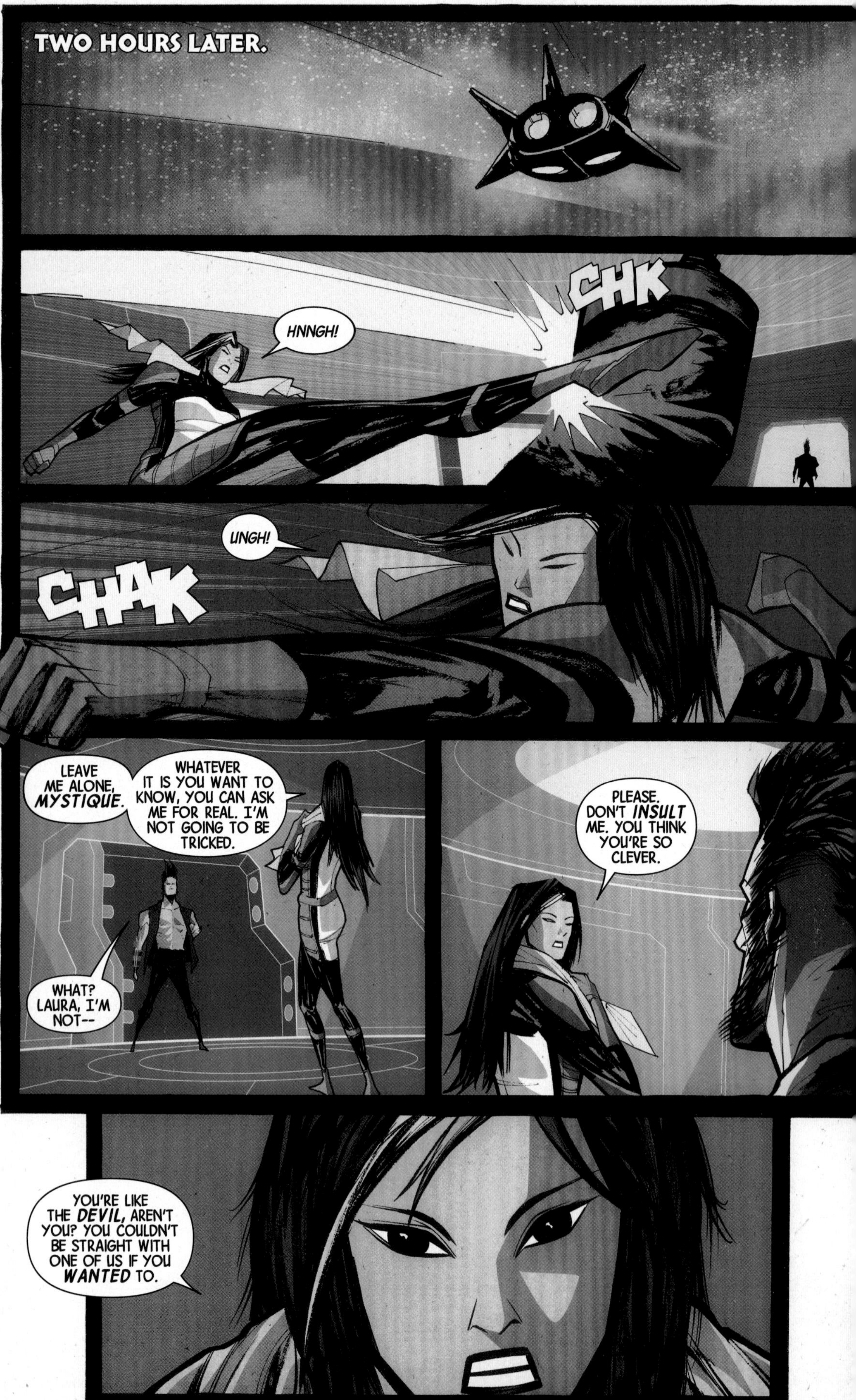
TWO HOURS LATER.
CHK
HNNGH!
UNGH!
CHAK
LEAVE ME ALONE, MYSTIQUE.
WHATEVER IT IS YOU WANT TO KNOW, YOU CAN ASK ME FOR REAL. I'M NOT GOING TO BE TRICKED.
WHAT? LAURA, I'M NOT--
PLEASE. DON'T INSULT ME. YOU THINK YOU'RE SO CLEVER.
YOU'RE LIKE THE DEVIL, AREN'T YOU? YOU COULDN'T BE STRAIGHT WITH ONE OF US IF YOU WANTED TO.

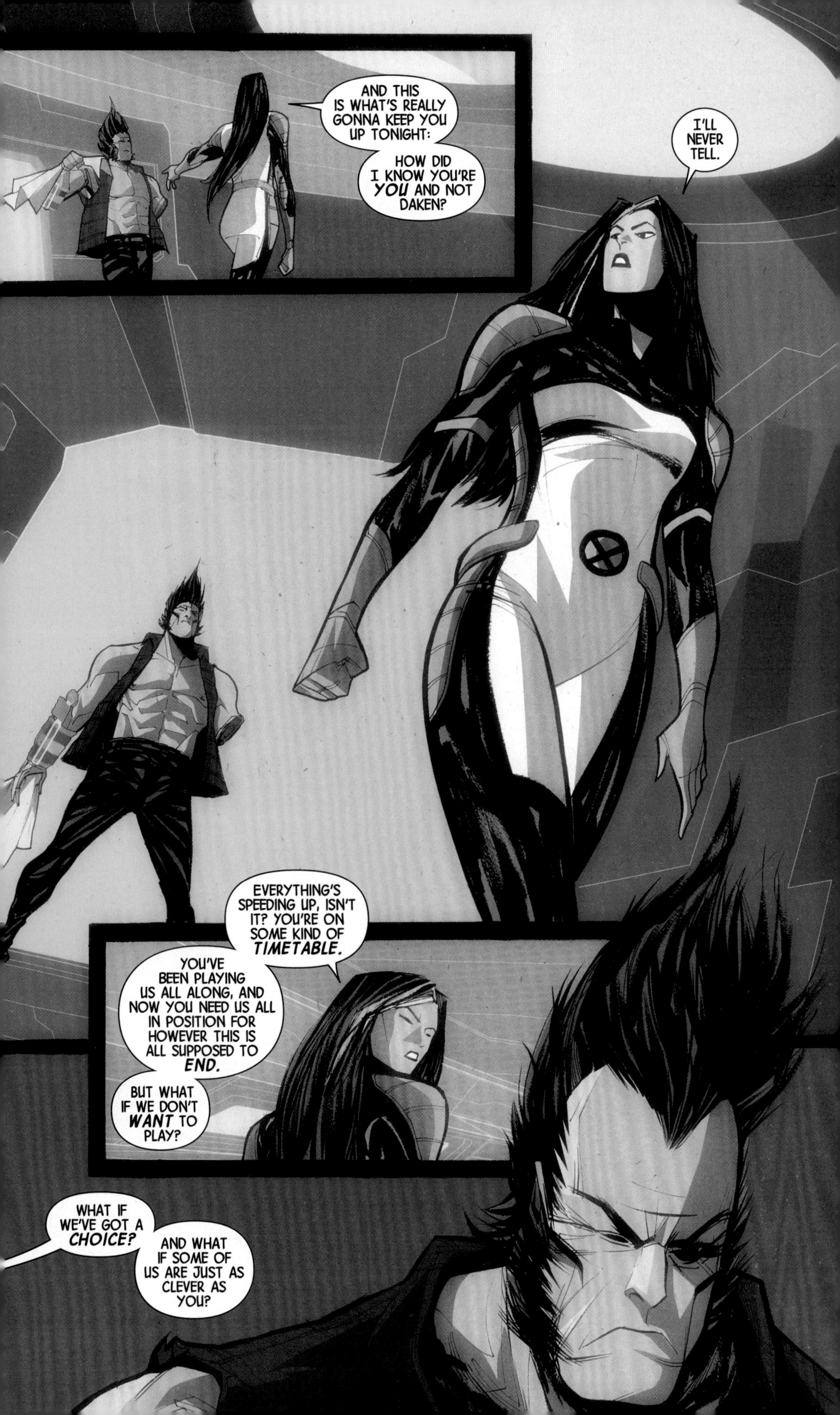
AND THIS IS WHAT'S REALLY GONNA KEEP YOU UP TONIGHT:
HOW DID I KNOW YOU'RE *YOU* AND NOT DAKEN?
I'LL NEVER TELL.
EVERYTHING'S SPEEDING UP, ISN'T IT? YOU'RE ON SOME KIND OF *TIMETABLE.*
YOU'VE BEEN PLAYING US ALL ALONG, AND NOW YOU NEED US ALL IN POSITION FOR HOWEVER THIS IS ALL SUPPOSED TO *END.*
BUT WHAT IF WE DON'T *WANT* TO PLAY?
WHAT IF WE'VE GOT A *CHOICE?*
AND WHAT IF SOME OF US ARE JUST AS CLEVER AS YOU?

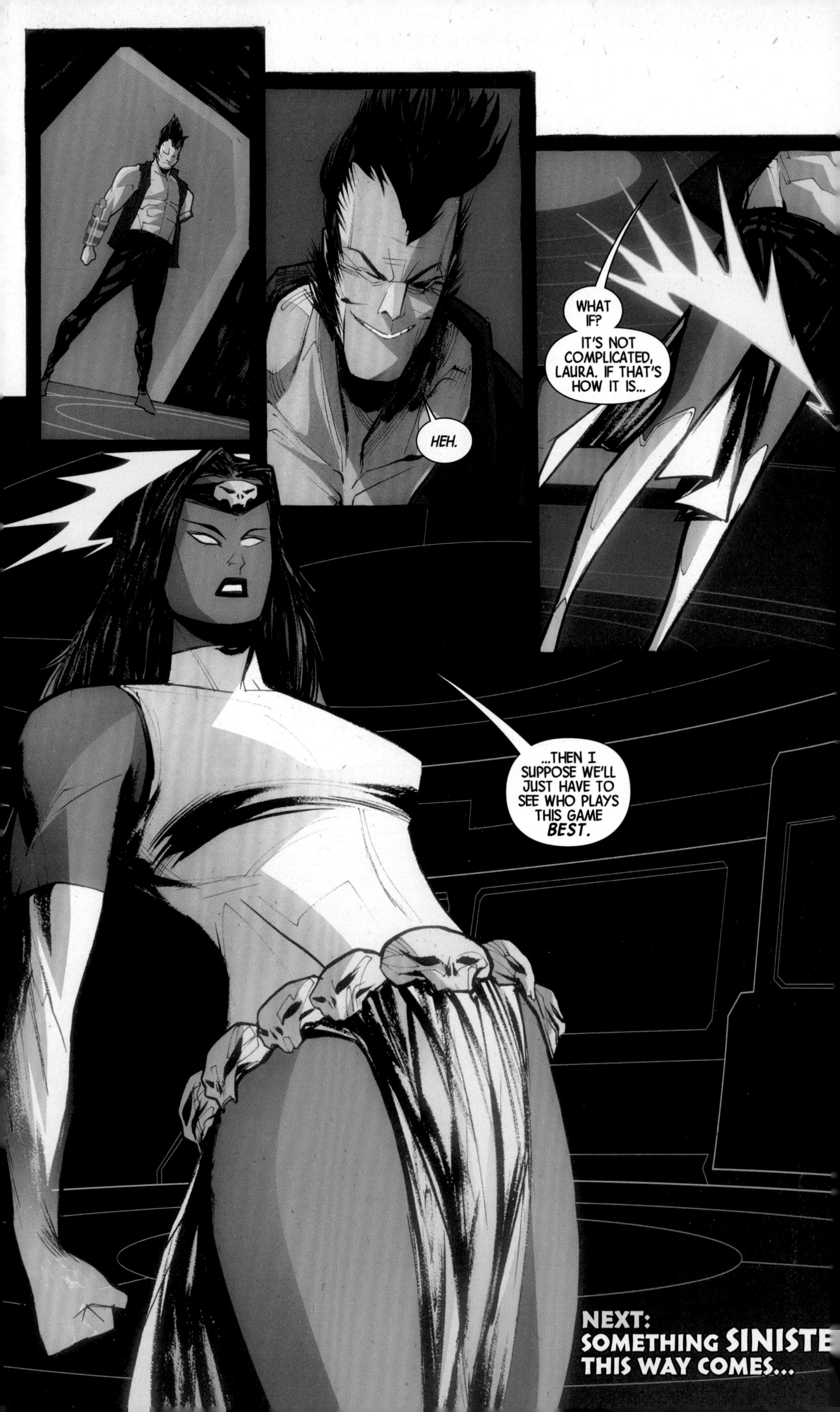
HEH.
WHAT IF?
IT'S NOT COMPLICATED, LAURA. IF THAT'S HOW IT IS...
...THEN I SUPPOSE WE'LL JUST HAVE TO SEE WHO PLAYS THIS GAME *BEST*.
NEXT:
SOMETHING SINISTE
THIS WAY COMES...

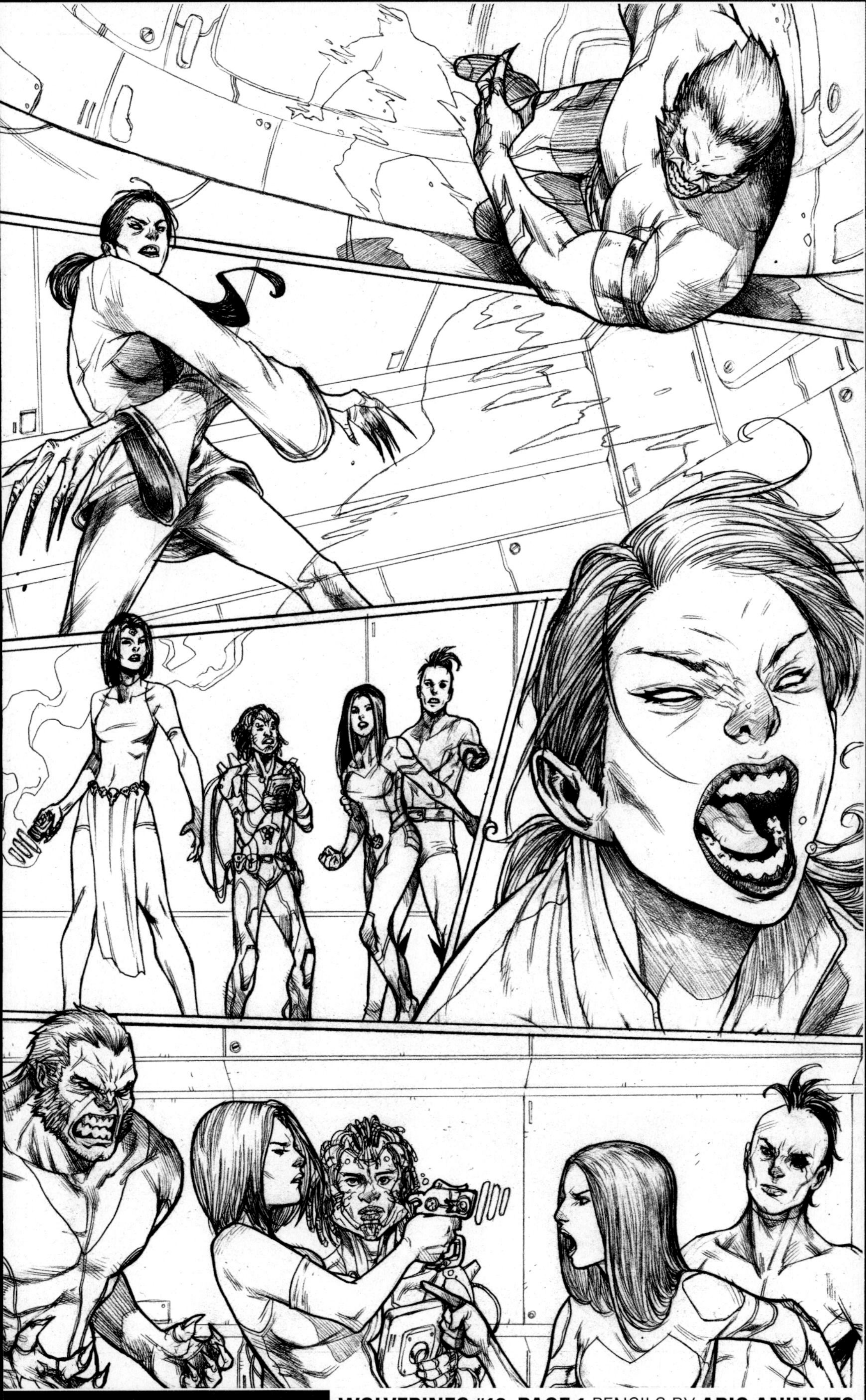

WOLVERINES #12, PAGE 1 PENCILS BY ARIO ANINDITO

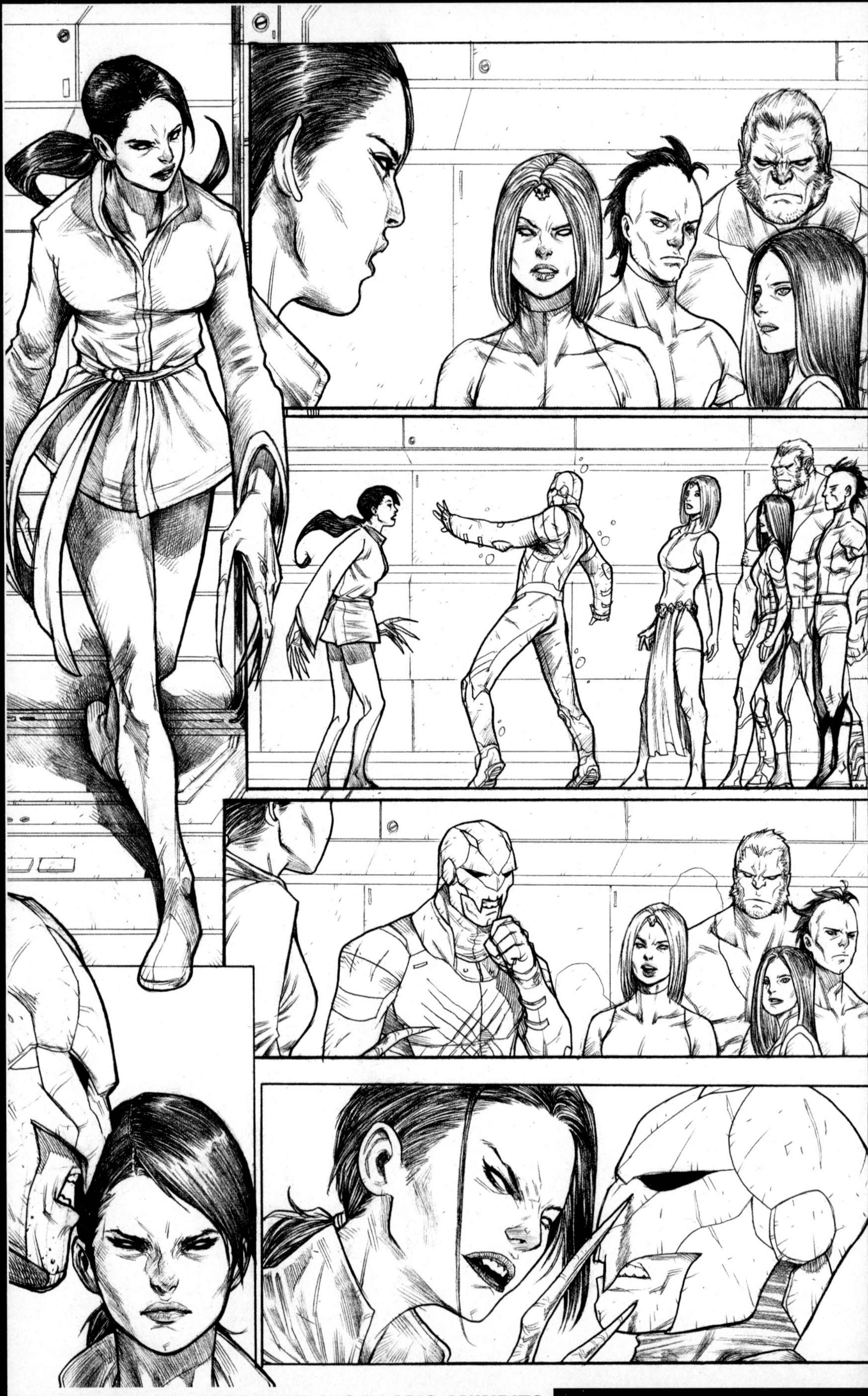

WOLVERINES #12, PAGE 15 PENCILS BY **ARIO ANINDITO**